Texans & Airships
I Have Known

by

Roy L. Fish

Panther  **Creek Press**
Spring, Texas

Published by Panther Creek Press
SAN 253-8520
116 Tree Crest
P.O. Box 130233 Panther Creek Station
Spring, Texas 77393-0233

Cover design by Adam Murphy
Houston, Texas

Manufactured in the United States of America
Printed and bound in Houston, Texas

1 2 3 4 5 6 7 8 9 10

Library of Congress Cataloguing in Publication Data

Fish, Roy Lee

Texans & Airships I Have Known

1. Texana   2. History, Texas

ISBN 0-9771797-0-2

For my grandchildren, Tamisha and Eric Denby,
and Karl, Kassidy and Larry Kridner.

Introduction

Individuals are threads in the fabric of society; their contributions are myriad and varied. We must know their work and shades of character to understand life outside our personal spheres. Artists, authors, poets and musicians enrich our lives. Barbers, beauticians and shoe shiners boost our self-esteem. Educators are of course invaluable. Among authors formerly or currently associated with Stephen F. Austin State University are Profs Bob H. Johnson, Francis Abernethey, Alfred S. Shivers, Archie McDonald and Karle Wilson Baker who received an honorary Litt D. from FSMU. Ardath Mayhar and Joe R. Lansdale invite you into their libraries. Preparing the way for the university—and, in fact, the substance of Nacogdoches and Texas—were Stephen F. Austin, Thomas Rusk, Gail Borden, Jr., Robert Potter and, of course, Sam Houston. Even Jack, the humble pony without a tail that carried Houston to Texas, contributed significantly to history.

John Tucker, 80, spins tales about old San Antonio, and a bacon poultice for supper. You'll meet Clarence Sasser of Rosharon, a medical aide in Vietnam, the first Texas Negro to earn the Medal of Honor.

Extraordinary airmen: Englishman Mike Allen of Nacogdoches, a bomber crewman in the RAF with an "old" Yankee pilot; Adlai T. Mast, Jr. of Nacogdoches, Yankee pilot in the RAF; David Lee "Tex" Hill, Flying Tiger legend of San Antonio; Wiley Post, record-setting aviator and space pioneer; Houstonian Tom Henry with the record number of combat hours for a fighter pilot in the Pacific Theater. Tom first became a celebrant while a cadet in San Antonio by getting arrested for the unauthorized use of a horse-drawn milk wagon. Thermon J. Hassell and seven-year old Carl T. Simons survived the attack on Pearl Harbor.

You will ride with naked Adah Menken on "The Wild Horse of Tartary," and (briefly and horrified) in Gail Borden's amphibious wagon, the Terraqueous Machine. You will pilot the Ezekiel Airship from a pasture in Pittsburg, Texas, the year before the Wright Brothers flew. Sam Houston shares nine barrels of liquor and invites you to ride to Texas. Belle Starr plays her piano for you. Robert Potter and Garland Roark take you sailing with the Texas Navy. Clarence Sasser binds your wounds. Max Lucado will share his pulpit and numerous books with you.

Several subjects in *Texans and Aitships* weren't Texans, but should have been; to them the author arbitrarily grants posthumous honorary citizenship in the great Lone Star State.

You will meet all of those Texans and more here. If I have done my job well, you will know them as I know them, including Sam Houston's friend and pony—Anna Raguet and tailless Jack, respectively, of course!

–Roy L. Fish. San Antonio, Texas, August 24, 2002

Acknowledgments

Numerous people and establishments contributed in various ways to this book. Among them are Wanda Bolinger, Curator, Polk County Museum, Livingston, Texas; Murphy Memorial Library, Livingston, Texas; Polk County Enterprise; Librarians at the Cody Branch of the San Antonio Public Library; Samantha Robb, Maysville, Oklahoma, Library; the Louisiana Division of Archives, Baton Rouge; Linda Reynolds, Assistant Director, East Texas Research Center, Stephen F. Austin State University, Nacogdoches, Texas; Darlene Mott, Librarian/Reading Room Supervisor, Sam Houston Regional Library and Research Center, Liberty, Texas; Gene Milford; Margie Cheek; Cary Clack, *San Antonio Express-News* columnist; and *San Antonio Express-News* reporter Sig Christenson.

Contributors, whose stories are greatly appreciated, include Ardath Mayhar, Marylois Dunn, Joe R. Lansdale, L. K. Feaster, Michael Allen, Adlai T. Mast, Tim James, Bob Murphey, Dr. Alfred S. Shivers, Dr. Archie P. McDonald, Gene Milford, John Tucker, Thermon J. Hassell, Carl T. Simons, Charlotte Baker Montgomery, Wayne Davis, Sharon Roark Zillmer, Tom Henry, Julia Mercedes Castilla, and Max Lucado.

Last, special thanks go to Guida Jackson, who for more than three decades has offered help and encouragement to this brick-layer-turned-writer and who many times saw merit in my work that I wasn't able to see.

Table of Contents

1
Belle Starr was no bandit queen
(Nor even a bandit)

Probably no character of the American West has been more mythologized, romanticized, idolized, demonized and ostracized than Belle Starr. Dime novelists of the nineteenth century portrayed her variously as a beautiful outlaw queen, a prostitute, a female Jesse James, a Robin Hood, a manipulator of judges, jailers and foolish geezers, an expert with firearms from the age of ten and petticoat terror of the plains; if she wore a petticoat, that would be the only fact in that portrayal.

Riding sidesaddle, she was an equestrian of such skill that no Yankee could catch her. She could fire two Colt .45s with deadly accuracy as her horse cleared a rail fence. Woe to blue coats who tried to stop her spying for her lover, guerrilla chief William Clarke Quantrill. Nor did the sheriff of Dallas dare to interfere with her hell-raising. She raced her horse up and down Main Street, shooting out windows and knobs off of wood scroll work. Then she refreshed herself in saloons before going home and taking a nap, confident that no law dog's shadow would darken her threshold.

Between drunken revelry and sex orgies, she led the Youngers and Jameses in robbing banks, stages, stores, carpet-baggers, stealing horses and cattle, murdering indiscriminately, and creating widows and orphans, while sharing the spoils with widows and orphans. Some write that she gave birth to an illegitimate daughter. One writer committed a journalistic cardinal sin by including a counterfeit diary! Current tabloids read like Scripture compared with such shameful and bogus publications. Nor has Hollywood sought authenticity. Noted biographer Glenn Shirley contends that some twentieth-century Belle biographers are little more credible than the original hacks. In contrast to lazy biographers, who create drama and events where there is none, Glenn Shirley produces documented sources, including photos.

The so-called beautiful outlaw queen was neither. The famous photo made by Rhoeder's Gallery in Fort Smith in May, 1886, should disabuse even the most rabid romantic of any notion of pulchritude. (That pistol was a studio prop.) If the black-haired and black-eyed woman in her velvet dress had been the size of her black mare, Venus, and on all fours beside the animal instead of sidesaddle, one might have difficulty distinguishing between them--even if Belle's face were parallel to the mare's posterior; and it is questionable whether the mare had more stable mates. Some biographers falsely claim that Belle never married.

Glenn Shirley's *Belle Starr and her Times: The Literature, The Facts, and The Legends* includes copies of Belle's marriage licenses to Jim Reed and Sam Starr. Whether she married Bruce Younger is questionable, and it is certain that she did not marry Jim July (Billy) Starr. More about these later.

Biographer Carl W. Breihan in *The Bandit Belle* cites records. He wrote that Myra Belle Shirley was born in the community of Medoc, about ten miles from Carthage, Missouri, February 5, 1848–the date on her gravestone and with which most writers agree, though the monument gives her birthplace as Carthage. Parents were John and Elizabeth Hatfield Shirley.

John was prominent in the Democratic party and strongly pro-slavery, though he owned only two. The scholarly John owned an impressive library and was commonly called "Judge." Elizabeth was descended from the Hatfields of the infamous Hatfield-McCoy feud on the West Virginia-Kentucky border. The Shirleys sold their prosperous farm of some 800 acres and moved into Carthage. They owned the Carthage Hotel, adjoining livery stable and blacksmith shop on the north side of the square. John helped to organize the Carthage Female Academy, which offered an education equal to the eighth grade--impressive for the time. Belle graduated there, then attended a private school in the Masonic Hall.

Several years prior to the Shirleys moving into Carthage, a new trail west had been established from Fort Smith through Indian Territory to the west coast. Many miners en route to Fort Smith and the minefields stayed in the Carthage Hotel. Young Belle played the parlor piano for guests. Some allowed that her playing was with less finesse than her mother's skill as a cook. During the 1920s, a former schoolmate of Belle's recalled that the Shirley family was of good repute.

Belle had five brothers and a sister. John A. M. "Bud," six years older than Belle, taught her to ride and handle firearms.

Before the Civil War, border conflicts blossomed between anti-slavery forces in Kansas (Redlegs) and the pro-slavers (Jayhawkers) of Missouri. In radical departure from using traditional armbands for identification, the innovative Redlegs wore sheepskin dyed red around their lower legs, thus their name.

Some of the most vicious outlaws ever to disgrace the earth raided back and forth across the border. William Clarke Quantrill, Charles Jennings, George Todd and the bloodiest of the bloody--"Bloody" Bill Anderson--didn't let Civil War politics or rules of war impede their robbing, burning, raping and murdering indiscriminately. Perfectly innocent farmers, tradesmen and servants were murdered simply because they were present. The bushwhackers laid waste to both states. They murdered prisoners, especially Union soldiers, often carving them and taking scalps while they lived. Belle's father admired Quantrill and his guerillas, and approved of Bud's involvement. Confederate Major General Sterling Price, twice governor of Missouri, found Bloody Bill Anderson's guerrillas horrid but employed them in his last ill-fated drive to regain Missouri. The author's great, great uncle, William Fish, received a hand wound riding with Price in this desperate campaign.

As did many successionist, Belle's eldest brother, Preston, moved with his wife and two children to Texas; they settled near Dallas.

War came to Carthage–numerous times. Bud was reportedly a spy for Quantrill. The oft-repeated tale of Major Eno capturing Belle on a spying foray and holding her captive in Judge Ritchie's home while troops went to Carthage to capture Bud is apparently pure hokum. Glenn Shirley writes that Major Eno's meticulously-kept diary makes no mention of such an event.

John Allison "Bud" Shirley was killed by Federal militiamen near Sarcoxie, Missouri, in 1864. He was twenty-one. Bud's five-year-old brother, Cravens, was renamed John Allison in honor of his fallen brother.

Union troops twice razed Carthage. Major buildings, even brick ones, were destroyed. Only a few shanties and chimneys remained among the ashes. Prior to the latest outrage, John Shirley moved his family to Texas in two covered wagons.

The Shirleys discovered that Dallas consisted of two thousand residents–many of whom were, unlike themselves, rowdy refugees–refuse of Confederate defeat, who further wasted themselves in numerous dance halls and bordellos. The Shirleys established a horse ranch at Scyene, which was less than a dozen miles southeast of Dallas. There is a Scyene sign on Dallas's East Loop 610, but the old community has long been swallowed by the metropolis.

James Reed hailed from a large and prosperous farming family near Rich Hill, Missouri; they favored the Southern cause, but didn't take up arms. Jayhawkers ravaged the area of Rich Hill to the extent that the Reeds relocated to Carthage in 1861; that is where Jim and Belle met; he was fifteen, she thirteen. Jim's quiet and religious propensities bent the knee to the callousness of war and, at seventeen, he joined Quantrill's bushwhackers.

Contrary to reckless publications, Belle never met Quantrill. Notable Quantrill lovers were Anna Walker and Kate Clarke. Blue Springs merchant and physician Riley Slaughter divorced nymphomaniac Anna. Kate was taken by force–more or less–and became willing mistress. Both women followed the axiom for success by doing what one knows and enjoys, for they established bawdyhouses after the war. Anna inherited money from her father and, ironically, set up shop in Baxter Springs, Kansas, scene of one of Quantrill's massacres. With money from Quantrill, Kate invested in a St. Louis bordello. There's no report of their return on investment, but the whole of Missouri lay between the brothels. Surely both former Redlegs and Jayhawkers were welcome.

As the war drew to a close, the Reeds moved back to Rich Hill, where Solomon soon died; his widow, Susan, and children moved near relatives in the vicinity of McKinney, Texas. They were again in touch with the Shirleys.

It is uncertain whether Jim Reed served with regular Confederates after Quantrill's band disintegrated. At war's end, Jim rode to Texas; he and Belle were married in Collin County, Texas, October 30, 1866. They lived and worked on the Shirley farm. The following year, Jim sold bridles and saddles for a Dallas manufacturer. As did many young men of the time, he nursed an ambition to own a ranch; he never realized his goal. Late in 1867, the Reeds returned to Missouri.

Following the war, the James and Younger brothers were credited with numerous robberies. The James gang robbed the Clay County Savings Association in Liberty, Missouri, on February 13, 1866. George Wymore, a student at William Jewel College, was killed by a stray bullet. Jim Reed was thought to have participated in some of the James's capers, including the robbery in Lexington, Missouri, on October 30, 1866, the date on which Jim and Belle got their marriage license in Texas.

The James-Younger gang exchanged the gold coins for more common currency in San Antonio. On their return to Missouri, they stopped at the Shirley farm to rest and recuperate; that was in July, 1866, several months before Belle and Jim married. Some biographers charge that during the gang's layover, Cole impregnated Belle; Cole stoutly denied that, and stated in his autobiography, 1903, that he next saw Belle at her in-laws in Missouri in 1868. Belle was about three months from giving birth. Pearl was named Rosie Lee Reed at birth, but nicknamed Pearl, for she was, naturally, considered a gem.

An elderly lady recalled her youth, attending church with Myra Belle and infant Pearl. Belle rode sidesaddle with Pearl tucked safely in her arms. Mrs. Younger suffered from hardship pressed upon her and family, and the harsh climate of Missouri. Federal militia forced her to burn her home; afterward, she and children lived in a small cabin. Cole and brothers took her to Texas in the fall of 1868.

Jim Reed had ample opportunity for success, given his rearing in an honest and prosperous family; however, horse racing and gambling in Fort Smith was preferable to perspiring in a field while using a mule's posterior for a compass. He often stayed in Indian Territory at Tom Starr's with Frank James and Cole Younger present. He got involved in a deadly and complicated feud over the ownership of a horse. Jim's brother, Scott, was mistakenly killed by one faction. Jim and brother Solomon, Jr. killed two of the opposition. Jim fled on horseback to California. Belle and Pearl followed.

The Youngers were respectable in Dallas. Cole worked cattle for several years. Jim Younger was a deputy sheriff in Dallas County, 1870-71. Jim and Bob sang in their church choir. John clerked in a Dallas store; however, according to Cole's autobiography, John ran with young, reckless fellows and tilted a bottle now and then. John shot the pipe from a fellow's mouth, which brought Sheriff (Colonel) Charles Nichols and John McMahon to arrest John. Nichols knew John in Missouri, and trusted him to finish eating and come along peacefully. Instead, John and a friend, Thompson McDaniels from Missouri fired on McMahon and Nichols. McMahon died instantly, Nichols later. Nichols wounded John in an arm. Cole said McDaniels killed the sheriff, John shooting McMahon. Only weeks after the event, Belle gave birth to a son in California on February 22, 1871.

The boy was named James Edwin for his father and Belle's slain brother–Edwin Benton, a horse thief killed in 1868 at age nineteen. About a month after "Eddie's" birth, federal authorities investigated Jim for possessing counterfeit money. They also learned he was wanted for murder in Arkansas. Jim fled to Texas on horseback. Belle and children followed, probably by stagecoach.

More robberies were chalked up to the Jameses and Youngers. Cole wrote in his autobiography that he was never involved in any robbery other than the disastrous attempt on the First National Bank in Northfield, Minnesota, on September 7, 1876.

Once Jim and Belle Reed were back in Texas, her family helped them to settle in Bosque County. Cole said he furnished them calves from his stock. But Jim's outlaw tendencies again boiled to the surface. In 1873, Jim and brother Sol teamed in robbery and murdered two men. Solomon fled to Missouri, never to be arrested. Jim and Myra went to Indian Territory and hid at Tom Starr's place, leaving Pearl and Eddie with Myra's parents in Scyene. Belle, disapproving of crime, returned alone to Texas and lived with her parents.

Mrs. Younger returned to Missouri and died of consumption.

Watt Grayson, former member of the Creek Supreme Court, and eventually chief justice of the Muskogee Nation (Creek), was robbed in

November, 1873. They put a rope around his neck and hoisted him, trying to learn the place of his wealth. He was semi-conscious when they threatened to hang his wife. He gave up his money. Of the several robbers, a teen-age witness identified one as Belle in a man's clothing. Other witnesses emphatically disagreed, saying that all of the robbers were obviously husky men; they were eventually identified, Jim Reed being one.

Though Belle disapproved of her husband's criminal activities, she disapproved more strongly his seducing young Rosa McComus of Dallas, who he took to San Antonio.

Jim and two accomplices robbed the Austin-San Antonio stage in April, 1874. Rosa was exonerated of any knowledge of the crime; she returned to Dallas alone, Jim's promise to marry her gone to the Territory with him.

Jim and company continued their outrages. A posse surrounded the home of one Starr (probably Tom), but the gang got away. Reed hid at the home of a friend several miles from Paris, Texas. John Morris, especially deputized to get Reed, caught up with him there. Morris proposed that they kill a man in Arkansas for his money. On the way, they stopped for dinner at a farmhouse. Morris tried to arrest Jim. Jim, still at the table, grabbed a gun then, using the table for a shield, ran toward the door. Morris repeatedly fired through the table, killing the outlaw (August 6, 1874). Since two of the South Texas stage robbers were at large, Morris collected only a fraction of the eleven thousand offered for the trio.

A congressional act of 1834 provided that an Indian robbed by a white man was entitled to be reimbursed from the federal treasury for money not recovered. Watt Grayson applied under the provision.

Myra Belle Reed's sworn testimony late in 1874, relates that her husband, W. D. Wilder and Marion Dickons told her of their plan to rob Watt Grayson. Several days later, the trio divided about $30,000 in gold and fifteen hundred to eighteen hundred in currency in Belle's presence. However, Belle had no money; Jim had died leaving her destitute. As was often the case, Jim had probably gambled away the spoils.

Dallas had been rife with crime for years, but law officers were lauded as efficient. The two Dallas newspapers published crime statistics early in 1874. Belle's name was absent. Obviously, the public hell-raising charged to her was false. Women who knew her said she was a modest rider and polite; therefore, one might wonder why, given her objection to crime, she didn't try to dissuade Jim from robbing Grayson. Considering his numerous crimes, she probably knew argument would be useless. Distances being great and travel slow–usually by horseback--maybe she didn't have time to warn authorities if she so desired. Perhaps she simply couldn't go against her husband. It seems that she could have been charged with foreknowledge of the crime. These are among mysteries that surely have challenged historians and lawyers ever since.

Almost exactly two years after Jim's death, and a long period of no contact with her in-laws, Belle's letter told them that Pearl was in school and dancing on stage, acquiring a local following. Some folk did not approve, perhaps because of her late father's stigma, but Belle wanted Pearl to learn to be independent. Myra mentioned that her father had recently died.

Myra faults Sol for not avenging Jim's death. She mentions that Jim's killer still lives in McKinney and Jim's old enemy, Pete Fisher–of the horse ownership feud--remains in Collin County. Therein, lies an additional facet of Belle's character. She well knew her husband's criminal career and that he was shot while resisting arrest; yet, she expected his brother to kill Deputy Morris. The very idea of letting an officer of the law live for defending himself and preventing escape! Perhaps she didn't consider that Sol stayed out of Texas because he was wanted for the two murders he and Jim committed in Bosque County. Belle states that she had Rondo, Jim's horse, for which she was offered two hundred dollars. She said she would gladly give Rondo to Sol had he avenged Jim's death. Her farm proved profitless, she said, and proposed to sell it. Myra complained of a headache and nerves so bad she could hardly write. Interestingly, she wrote the letter on stationery belonging to the Dallas County sheriff.

Pearl fainted on the stage late in autumn of 1876. A physician said her condition could have been fatal, and convinced her mother that she not return to dancing. It was this season when the Younger brothers–Cole, Jim, and Bob began serving life sentences for murder and attempted robbery at Northfield, Minnesota.

Due to unspecified trouble, Belle's brother, Cravens, left Texas. After John Shirley died, Eliza sold the farm and moved to Dallas. Eddie, five years of age, was sent to live with Grandma Reed at Rich Hill. Missouri.

Bruce Younger was a half-brother to Cole Younger's father; according to Belle's granddaughter, "Flossie," Bruce and Belle met in Coffeyville, Kansas, and married about 1878, but weren't together for long. They were seen in Galena, Kansas, about 1879. Galena was a lively mining town. Bruce was a small-time gambler. He and Belle haunted the gambling establishments. Former police judge, W. L. Lumbley–when a boy--saw Belle and Bruce about town. Both he and former county sheriff Evans spoke well of the couple.

Belle's former brother-in-law, Richard Reed, wrote in his "family narrative" that it was during Belle's marriage to Bruce Younger that Pearl was designated "Pearl Younger." Some biographers falsely claim that she was so named because Cole was her father.

As formerly mentioned, Belle accompanied Jim to Indian Territory following the South Texas stage robbery; therefore, she was acquainted with the Starr clan. She and Bruce lived among the prolific Starr families for some time. One of old Tom Starr's sons was the dashing Samuel. After Bruce removed from the scene, Belle and Sam married on June 5, 1880. Their ages are given as Sam, 23, Belle, 27. Glenn Shirley writes that Belle, taking advantage of a woman's right, finished her marriage vows five years shy of her actual age–and a last name that would forever shade her with infamy.

By marrying a Cherokee, Belle became a member of the Cherokee Nation. Sam chose an allotment west of Briartown, near Youngers' Bend. Tom named the crook in the Canadian River for the brothers who often visited. Tom and numerous others of the Starr clan lived all about. A cabin existed to which the couple added a room; they made numerous other improvements. Belle loved gardening. Pearl came to Youngers' Bend and was renamed again. She became Pearl Starr. She was not yet twelve years of age; one might wonder whether she suffered an identity crisis.

Years after settling at the Bend, Belle wrote a brief sketch of her life– more a philosophical vent: She cared not for the company of women, she wrote, having found them disgusting. Low white trash moving into the Nation were accorded the same credit. Her nephew, Henry Starr, only six years of age, would eventually express virtually her exact sentiments about trashy whites infesting the Nation. Belle merely wished to live out her life in peace and quiet with Sam and Pearl on the Bend. None of Belle's male acquaintances knew her location, nor did she wish it; however, even before they came, notoriety seeped up from Texas, and her home was soon reviled as a haven for outlaws. She soon found herself a prime target of gossip mongers. Ignorance, she said, was the main culprit.

Jesse James stayed for a while with Belle and Sam. Only after Jesse left did Belle tell Sam his identity.

Jesse and Frank escaped after the botched robbery attempt at Northfield, and resumed criminal careers–pulling some jobs with the Ford brothers, Charles and Bob. Jesse and family lived in a rented house in St. Joseph, Missouri. Jesse made Bob a present of a pistol on April 2, 1882. The ingrate shot Jesse through the head with it the next day in Jesse's home. Bob had made a devil's deal with Governor Crittendon for the reward.

Glenn Shirley wrote that Jesse's visit to the Bend resulted in a lot of published lies. Word was that Belle built accommodations for outlaws, arranged for stolen horses to be driven to Texas, and for horses stolen in Texas to be driven through Youngers' Bend. Robbers Cave was a popular hideout for Civil War deserters, rustlers and guerrillas, and reputedly a Starr favorite dodge. The location is now a game preserve of more than eight thousand acres with an excellent view of Lake Carlton near Wilburton. There are a great many furnished cabins and campsites.

Truth is Myra Belle Shirley Reed Starr was not charged with any crime until she was thirty-four years of age. She never had money or charm to influence any official. In modern vernacular, we might say she got many "bum raps." Belle's peaceful life on the Canadian River lasted almost exactly two years–a measly respite from years of turmoil. In July, 1882, Belle and Sam were charged with stealing two horses. Deputy Marks' widow said in an interview in 1937, that Belle fought like a wildcat when her husband arrested her in September, 1882. He relieved her of two derringers and a pistol. She later grabbed a guard's pistol and fired at him. Belle dropped tools and silverware and various other items as the prison wagon rolled toward Fort Smith. He finally had to restrain her as he had the men. If true, Belle's first arrest was memorable, and might have become the basis for her hell-raising reputation.

Perhaps Deputy Marks took advantage of Belle's bogus reputation to build his own in his wife's eyes: Her fearless husband disarmed the infamous outlaw queen, the genius behind the Youngers and Jameses! Wouldn't that be a fine tale to spread about! It might even get a man elected sheriff!

A Mr. Childs was to be a witness for the Starrs, but he--apparently the culprit–fled to Texas. Sam's father and Uncle James Starr, Junior, made bond.

The trial began in March, 1883. According to a Fort Smith newspaper, Belle's notorious reputation filled the courtroom with the curious. John West, Indian policeman and neighbor of the Starrs, swore to Belle and Sam's guilt. Belle became furious when prosecutor William H. H. Clayton befuddled ignorant Sam with legal verbiage, then insulted his lack of education. In March, Sam was sentenced to one year and his wife to two six month terms in the Detroit House of Corrections, with the possibility of release in nine months.

Belle wrote to Pearl, urging her to be strong, and the family would soon be together again. Eddie would join them, she wrote. Pearl chose to live with friend, Mrs. McLaughlin. in her hotel in Parsons, Kansas.

Belle began prison life by making chairs, but soon got cushy assignments, tutoring the warden's children and performing menial chores. .

Tom Starr kept a caretaker on his son's place during their nine months in prison. Though Belle blamed John West for her conviction, she remained true to her benevolent reputation among those who knew her. When John's wife gave birth to a son, Belle stayed in their home for several days. Nevertheless, her detractors accused her of resuming outlaw ways. She was said to peddle whiskey in Catoosa–cattle trail terminus and railhead hell hole, haunt saloons in Fort Smith and to race Venus on the boardwalks–Dallas rumors resurrected and embellished. Citizens of Dallas and Fort Smith recalled that Belle rode with decorum. The ignoramuses of which Myra wrote–early-day rednecks--allowed her no rest. Youngers' Bend was an enormous intellectual vacuum.

Glenn Shirley notes in *Belle Starr and her Times* that, in 1937-38, the Oklahoma Historical Society bound in a collection of interviews titled *Indian-Pioneer History* totaling about 60,000 words, that approximately 100 elderly people either knew Belle or those close to her, and no one mentioned a single escapade laid to her by myth mongers and hack writers. Nor had Fort Smith police ever arrested her. The Fort Smith newspaper describing the packed courtroom notwithstanding, it seems that If Belle were truly the "Queen of Outlaws," newspapers all over the Territory would have scrambled to herald her trip to prison, but scarcely anyone noticed–or cared. And this in a time when huge crowds dropped industry of import to witness the hanging of little-known outlaws. Belle and Sam went quietly to prison and returned in the same manner.

Biographers differ as to whether Belle had a piano at the Bend. A freighter supposedly delivered one in 1884, the journey requiring several days from Fort Smith. A doctor making a house call in 1888, claimed to have seen the instrument. Having learned to play while a young girl, it follows that Belle probably owned one. Music would reduce monotony in the silent country. 1884: Eddie, thirteen, had recently left the Reeds to live with Grandmother Shirley in Dallas. The Reeds and Starrs enjoyed visiting with one another. But the year brought dark shadows upon Youngers' Bend as had 1882.

John Middleton of Arkansas was a petty thief who, when released after a year sentence, graduated to robbery and murder–even credited with torching the courthouse at Waldron, Arkansas. He and Sam Starr were acquainted. Fugitive Middleton came to Youngers' Bend. He needed help to escape the Territory. Belle and Pearl witnessed John buying a sorry mule, which turned out to be stolen. Pearl lent her saddle to Middleton, who drowned while crossing the Poteau River. The saddle on the surviving mule was identified as Pearl's; thus, another horse-stealing charge was heaped onto Belle. The actual thief said he witnessed

Middleton buy the animal from a stranger, thus getting Belle free of the charge.

Perhaps the life that satisfied Belle's desire to live the remainder of her life in peace with her garden, books and piano, bored her husband. Gardens and flowers do not generate the cash available in stagecoaches, stores and mail hacks–cash for gambling and revelry in low establishments. Sam soon found Cherokee policeman John West on his trail for various crimes, one of which was robbing three farming brothers. A teenaged girl believed Belle to be one of the villains.

Belle went to Fort Smith for a hearing before the commissioner. In the anteroom she spied the reporter who had published an outrageous account of an interview with her. She thoroughly lashed him with her riding crop before calmly entering. No witness could identify any of the trio of robbers. The girl' 's former statement implicating Belle was pure piffle. Belle walked free.

Frank West, brother of John, killed Belle's favorite mount, Venus, and wounded Sam. Sam escaped to recuperate at a brother's home. Belle convinced him to surrender to Fort Smith authorities, for that court was more lenient than the Indian court. Bonded out, Sam and Belle attended the Seventh Annual Fair of Western Arkansas at the Sebastion County Fairgrounds. This in October, 1886.

There were mock military battles and other wild west exhibits. Belle entered to demonstrate her equestrian skills, which must have been impressive. The Carthage, Missouri "Light Guard Band" took home several hundred dollars in prize money and an account of the hometown celebrity's fast riding and trick shooting.

The month after the Fair, Tom Starr was sentenced for two whiskey violations, the total terms being eighteen months imprisonment in the Federal Penitentiary at Menard, Illinois.

Sam's bitterness increased. He particularly hated John and Frank West. Belle suggested they lighten up and attend a Christmas dance at the Surratt home about a week before the holiday. Sam, Belle, Eddie and Pearl attended. Then Frank West came. Sam upbraided him for killing Belle's mare. They drew and killed one another. The ball that went through Sam's body wounded a young boy's jaw.

Sam's death drastically altered Belle's status. She was no longer a member of the Cherokee Nation. A Cherokee's allotment entitled him to the use of his chosen land, but no deed was given. Should one surrender the allotment, he was entitled to compensation for improvements; thus, Belle's situation was established. The Nation would pay her for improvements and sell them to the next resident or she could marry another Cherokee and remain. A convenient compromise presented itself in the form of another Starr–One Billy Starr, known as Jim July.

Jim was not a full-blood Cherokee. The young and handsome lad could easily choose among attractive women; he had an air of polish acquired in Indian schools. He could pow-wow with virtually all of the Five Civilized tribes in their own language. His relation-ship to the Starr clan is uncertain, but was more or less accorded the status of Tom's son. Jim was also noted for his talent for relieving others of their not-so-surplus horse flesh–a common trait in the extended family. Jim and Belle jelled. Though Venus was dead, the mare's remains probably weren't much uglier than her former mistress; however, the lucrative opportunity was attractive, and Jim grabbed it. He moved in with Belle; they noised about that they had a common law marriage, which was given full legal status under both Cherokee and Federal law; thus, through the simple act of Jim hopping into Belle's bed, she remained secure on the allotment, and he gained it all–the land, cabin, piano, smokehouse, corrals, milk cow, Belle and her corn patch and bed plus two step-children.

Belle was thirty-nine. Jim was twenty-four. Pearl was nineteen. Eddie was near seventeen. Eddie hadn't been around Sam, his first step-father, much; we don't know his attitude toward him, but he didn't like his second stepfather. Perhaps his resentment prodded him to commit minor violations, for which his mother sometimes applied the quirt. The youth was inclined to cling to the dark side as had his late stepfather and his current one.

Belle objected to Pearl's desire to marry a local fellow, for she had always determined that Pearl marry money. Life with legitimate and adequate money would certainly spare the girl the sordid and skimpy livelihood that tarnished cash had afforded her mother. Myra Belle sent her daughter to stay with friends in Arkansas. Belle faked letters from Pearl to the man, saying that Pearl had married. Consequently, the suitor married. Upon learning the truth, both Pearl and the man were furious. They met secretly. Belle became enraged upon learning that Pearl was pregnant, and demanded the father's identity. Pearl refused to tell; she also refused her mother's insistence that she have an abortion. Consequently, Pearl went to live with Grandmother Reed at Rich Hill, Missouri. Pearl went with Grandma to Siloam Springs, Arkansas. Flossie was born there in April, 1887. Flossie Hutton eventually *wrote in Belle Starr's Daughter* that her father was a neighbor at Youngers' Bend–a mixed blood Cherokee named Bob.

To Myra Belle's disappointment, Eddie ran about with a relative of his stepfather, one Mose Perryman. The couple ended up with a horse that turned out to be stolen. Eddie and Mose camped. While Eddie slept, Mose shot him, the ball entering close to his nose and exiting at an ear.

Mose left the stolen animal and went to a house. He explained that a stranger had attacked Eddie and him during the night. Miraculously, Eddie was found alive, then taken to that house. Though seriously wounded, he could talk and charged Mose with shooting him. The Investigation favored Ed; he said that unknown to him, Mose had stolen the horse.

Belle sent money to a relative in Missouri, urging her to pass it on to Pearl, so that she could come if she wanted to see her brother alive.

The Perrymans and Jim July persuaded Eddie to drop the charge of attempted murder, in exchange for their help on the theft charge. Their help proved non-existent. Eddie was indicted. He maintained that Mose was the thief and applied for witnesses who could prove that Mose gave him the stolen horse in lieu of a debt of twenty-five dollars. Authorities, including Judge Parker, sensed that Eddie was truthful. Released without bond, he returned to Youngers' Bend. Relations between Eddie, his mother and stepfather worsened. Pearl had come, leaving Flossie behind, as Belle had requested. Pearl and Eddie had always been close. She stayed to try to promote better relations between her brother and their mother. Belle still wanted Flossie put up for adoption.

The International Indian Fair at Muskogee was in September, 1888.

Author Glenn Shirley notes in *Belle Starr and her Times*, the "Vinita Indian Chieftan," Oct. 4, 1888, that Pearl and another lady competed in a riding contest, Pearl riding bareback. The Indians who were to stage a wild exhibit failed to show up, so Belle filled in. There's no mention whether Pearl won or of Belle's performance.

In latter 1888, Belle, Pearl and Jim July attended numerous dances. Jim didn't dance, merely chaperoned. Mother and daughter had developed a good relationship; that is until Belle learned that Flossie was with Aunt Mamie Reed in Wichita Kansas. Myra became adamant that Pearl give up Flossie. Pearl still refused. Myra Belle faked a letter from Pearl authorizing Mamie to put Flossie in an orphanage. Should Mamie refuse, Belle threatened to have Flossie stolen by Gypsies. Flossie wrote that roving Gypsies were mean and to be avoided. Flossie also wrote that she learned thirty-five years later the location of the orphanage. The paper Belle forged was dated Nov. 19, 1888. (*Belle Starr and Her Times*).

Though Jim July Starr had legitimately gained the right to enjoy the allotment and improvements made by the sweat of his predecessor, he was no more inclined to be satisfied than had Sam. About a month after Belle's granddaughter was born, John West took Jim July in hand for stealing a horse. And this after Belle publicized that outlaws were not welcome to her place! Actually, thievery had noticeably decreased after her declaration; in appreciation for that, a Mr. Owen, Indian agent at

Muskogee, wrote Myra a complimentary letter, which he also had published in newspapers of Indian Territory. Belle scorned her husband in public and walked away. Friends bonded him out.

Indian Territory had much rich land and few men to cultivate it. A bill signed in 1867, authorized Indians to bring in white tenant farmers. Twenty years later, there were twice as many whites as Indians in the Territory.

In 1888, Myra Belle contracted with Edgar Watson to farm part of her land. Mrs. Watson told Belle that her husband had fled a murder charge in Florida. Belle knew she could lose her land if a rogue was found there. She offered Watson a refund and asked him to move. He refused. Pearl overheard their argument. Finally, Myra hinted that Florida authorities might be interested in his whereabouts. January, 1889, the Watsons moved across the river to a Jackson Rowe cabin.

February 2, Bill (Jim July) set out for Fort Smith to answer the horse-stealing charge. Belle rode with him. They spent the night with a friend east of Whitefield. Next morning, Jim continued toward Fort Smith; Belle headed for home. She stopped at a store shortly before noon. She told the proprietor that she feared for her life.

Tenant farmers commonly gathered at the Jackson Rowe home on Sundays. Several families were there, including Belle's nemesis, Edgar Watson, when she arrived about four o'clock. Eddie had been staying there, but had just crossed the river to visit a friend. Watson left upon Belle's arrival. She visited briefly, then rode on.

The trail led around Watson's cabin and to the river crossing. From the fence corner came a shotgun blast that tore into Belle's back and neck. She landed in mud and puddles. The killer rushed closer and fired a load of smaller shot into her left shoulder and face.

A young boy, returning from a visit in the Cherokee country, found the ferry unavailable; he swam his horse to the south bank. A horse with sidesaddle raced past him and swam to the north bank. He found Belle about half a mile from the river. He rode back to the river and met Pearl. Pearl had come when her mother's horse arrived. Pearl went alone to her mother and found her barely alive.

Several people heard the blasts. Belle's body was loaded into a wagon and put upon a bed at Alf and Martha White's.

Someone telegraphed Jim July at Fort Smith.

Eddie learned of his mother's murder when he returned the following morning. He and others traced the tracks from the fence corner toward Watson's cabin. Watson's hired man said Watson was with him when the fatal shots were fired.

Belle was buried in her yard without song or ceremony. The pistol that Cole Younger reportedly gave her was placed in her hand. As soon as she was buried, Jim July arrested Edgar Watson at the muzzle of his Winchester. Next morning, Jim July, Eddie and Jackson Rowe escorted Watson to Fort Smith and convinced authorities to hold him.

While in custody, Watson told deputy Hutchins that Jim July borrowed his shotgun and killed Belle. The markings on shells fired by Watson's gun matched those of the ones used to kill her. Hutchins said July told a neighbor on the morning of the murder, that he was going to kill Belle. Of course, it strains credibility that Jim would create two witnesses–Watson and Hutchins! To believe Watson and Hutchins, one must believe that, after Jim and Belle spent the night with a friend east of Whitefield, he doubled back, following her, told a neighbor of his intention to murder, borrowed Watson's gun, killed Belle, then returned the gun and rode to Fort Smith! Against all common sense, Judge Parker believed that the heresy and Watson's tale would convict July! Perhaps this irrationality was a prelude to the judge's eventual removal. July was astonished that he had become the accused. He jumped bond on the theft charge and ran with outlaws.

At Watson's hearing, his attorney said the evidence was circumstantial. Watson was discharged and immediately fled to Florida.

Speculation ran rampant. Everybody and his cousin had a theory, if not "facts": Belle killed John Middleton for money taken in a certain robbery–a crime that never happened. Middleton killed Belle to avenge his brother. Eddie killed his mother because she beat him. Jim July doubled back and killed his wife, because she scolded him in public and refused to bond him out. Decades later, people swore that so-and-so told him that so-and-so confessed to his late uncle, aunt, or great uncle. One of the most preposterous developments occurred during the 1930s when one Nana Devena confessed on her death bed that she killed Belle through mistaken identity!

Eddie had a solid alibi, and most other rumored suspects, excepting Watson, were ruled out by logic.

Hutchins and another deputy shot Jim July and killed his horse near Ardmore. July's main bondsman withdrew his offer of reward, because the fugitive, before being shot, notified him that he would surrender. Deputy Heck Thomas brought July to the prison hospital. July said the deputies ambushed him and ought to be charged with murder if he died– and he did, in January, 1890.

In July, 1889, Eddie was convicted on two counts; one for receiving stolen goods–riding equipment from the stolen horse he said Mose Perryman gave him to cancel a debt--and theft of the horse. He was sentenced to five years and two years.

Pearl married Will Harrison, brother of her good friend, Mabel, but soon deserted him. He divorced her.

Pearl settled into a crib in a bawdy house in Van Buren, Arkansas, to earn money to try to get her beloved brother released. Her chosen profession proved lucrative enough that she soon hired two prominent attorneys. The lawyers obtained a presidential pardon for their client in 1893.

Pearl continued plying her trade; she opened her own brothel–the Green Pea--in Fort Smith's sleazy district.

During Pearl's time, few opportunities existed for women in the professions–it was a man's world. Men chewed tobacco, smoked and loitered unmolested on streets. If a woman as much as paused on a street, she had better be waiting for a streetcar; if not–and especially if an inch of ankle was exposed--she was inviting a proposition and arrest. And woe to her if a cigar corrupted her lips. Snuff was about the only vice allowed as respectable for women, and that pretty well confined within walls. Unless a female became an "Outlaw Queen," she could keep house (domestic), diaper children and stir perpetually steaming pots on woodburning stoves. Given such prospects, Pearl opted for self-employment and instant cash.

Eddie was very disappointed in his sister. He returned to Cherokee country and was soon charged with a whiskey violation, which was dismissed for lack of evidence. Though there were many reputable members of the family, the stream of Starr outlaws that flowed into Commissioner Wheeler's court through the years must have given him occasion to pause.

The nineteenth century witnessed numerous outlaws and lawmen changing sides. Sheriff Henry Plummer in Montana was hanged for his gang's outrages. Of the five Dalton brothers, Bob, Grattan, Emmett and Frank had served as U. S. deputy marshals; Bill studied law; however, Frank was the only one to die on the right side of the badge, killed by a whiskey runner while serving the Federal Court at Fort Smith. Emmett survived the aborted robbery in Coffeyville, Kansas, that took Bob and Grat's lives and became a respectable film maker and businessman in Los Angeles. As formerly mentioned, Jim Younger was also a Dallas County deputy.

Probably few were surprised that Eddie Reed was deputized a U. S. Marshal for the Western District of Arkansas, and hired as a train guard on the Katy's run between Wagoner and McAlester. This was from late 1894 to early 1895, when Bill Cook's gang tallied a high score of robberies. Crawford Goldsby, known as Cherokee Bill, was a Cook henchman who would become especially infamous and prominent in the

Starr saga. However, Ed never encountered Cook and company.

Ed was assigned to Wagoner, Indian Territory. He married Jennie Cochran, a Cherokee teacher of Claremore.

Among former law officers turned criminal were the Crittendon brothers, Zeke and Dick; in October, 1895, they rode wildly into Wagoner and, equally as wild, expended much ammunition at places of business.

A proprietor was slightly wounded. The city marshal chose to not interfere with the Crittendon sport, leaving one to wonder whether he got reelected–or whether he had the gall fo run for reelection. Someone summoned Deputy Marshal Edwin Reed.

According to the "Vinita Leader," Oct. 31 (*Belle Starr and Her Times*), Eddie dispatched both Crittendons when they resisted arrest. Again, Eddie appeared before the long-suffering Commissioner Wheeler; however, he must have been pleased to exonerate Deputy Reed for bravely upholding the law of the Western District of Arkansas. The Starr and Reed reputations had been redeemed to some degree. Eddie further burnished the Reed and Starr credit by reining in Cherokee prison escapee, Watt Wafford. Eddie and Jennifer enjoyed a more or less normal life, that of a teacher and a successful and reputable officer of the law.

This was indeed a high station for Eddie, his late mother and stepfather having served time for horse-stealing, and the stepfather having committed numerous crimes that didn't involve Belle. Also, Belle's third and fourth husbands–Bruce Younger and Jim July Starr--were notorious, July expiring from a deputy's bullet. Surely everyone in Wagoner knew Eddie's background; nevertheless, they respected him. He had purged Wagoner's streets of dangerous elements. One can safely assume that the ladies spoke kindly to Jennifer and the men tipped their hats to the school "ma'rm." We might think of that situation in the current term of "Main Street America."

Even so, switching from outlaw to law officer didn't rule out occasionally imbibing. If Eddie tilted the jug now and then, he was more fortunate than was his father-in-law. Mr. Cochran partook of rotten whiskey in the sinkhole run by Joe Gibbs and J. N. Clark, said establishment reputed to sell cigars, whiskey and promote gambling. The proprietors put the unconscious old man in the alley in order to make it look like he died from the harsh cold. But he survived. Eddie entered the dive to arrest Clark and Gibbs and they shot him dead ("Vinita Indian Chieftan" Thurs., Dec. 17, 1896. *Belle Starr and Her Times*). At least one writer threads a nefarious theme throughout the Reed-Starr saga, portraying Eddie as a habitual, alcoholic offender, who raised hell in a Wagoner saloon and was shot dead by the two bartenders, who were roundly thanked by the populace. Biographer Glenn Shirley's documentation refutes the canard.

Following Jim July's death and Edgar Watson's release, no further attempt was made to find Belle's slayer. Biographer Croy investigated Edgar Watson in Florida, and learned that his wife had told Belle the truth. Watson had butchered a brother-in-law before fleeing to Indian Territory. Upon returning to his home state, he embarked upon a killing spree that totaled thirteen men and one woman. Little wonder that practically all biographers are satisfied that he murdered Myra Belle. His tally of homicides probably exceeded the combined total chalked up by all of the killers in the Reed-Starr saga with the exception of Old Tom Starr, who reputed to have run up a score of more than fifty. Florida officers blasted Mr. Watson from this world.

Eddie's sister's reputation raced in the opposite direction from his. Pearl continued operating the Green Pea. She gave birth to Ruth in 1894. When Ruth was three years of age, Pearl married musician Arthur Erbach. Arthur and Pearl had a son in 1898. Father and son died of malaria. Arthur expired several weeks after his son was born; the baby lived less than one year.

Jennette Andrews resulted from Pearl's common-law arrangement with Dell Andrews, whose reputation was considerably less than stellar. Perhaps neither Ruth nor Jennette were gems in their mother's eyes as she was to Belle, for she assigned both to a convent in St. Louis. And perhaps Mr. Andrews found parenthood inconvenient to the pursuit of his career–horse-trading and gambling.

Rosie Lee "Pearl" Reed, Starr, Younger, Erbach, Andrews might have given the impetus for the invention of the revolving door, for morals and liquor violations had her hauled to jail so often for several years that the hinges on her cell door scarcely cooled between arrests. Fort Smith authorities–finally and fully exasperated–exiled her. None of her notorious relatives and in-laws was relegated to that level other than being shipped to federal prison. Movie producers might better have considered Pearl for their subject instead of her maligned mother.

July 6, 1925, Pearl died in an old hotel in Douglas, Arizona, on the border with Mexico. Daughters Jennette and Ruth buried her as "Rosie Reed" in the town's Calvary Cemetery. One can only envisage that she perished in despair, degradation and poverty in a dreary room superheated by the Arizona July sun. She died of stroke, and little wonder. Even prostitutes deserve better. Further, she was buried far from her mother and kinsmen in what had become the state of Oklahoma.

Pearl had, however, while prosperous in Fort Smith, had her mother's grave reconstructed and secured, for robbers had tarried but briefly in opening it and stealing the pistol from her hand. Some people in that area had surpassed the "redneck" stage and become ghouls. Pearl had slabs tilted together in a peak and an engraved marker cemented in place. It is engraved with images of a star, a bell, and Belle's mount, Venus.

BELLE STARR

Born in Carthage, Mo.

Feb. 5, 1848

DIED

Feb. 3, 1889

Shed not for her the bitter tear,

Nor give the heart to vain regret:

Tis but the casket that lies here,

The gem that filled it sparkles yet.

Paul Wellman's *Dynasty of Western Outlaws* links violators from William Clarke Quantrill to gangsters of the early twentieth century. Tom Starr was the patriarch of the Starr clan villains, as well as the most prolific killer; ironically, he was the only one to die of natural causes. Tom's son, Sam, Billy Jim July Starr, and grandson, Henry Starr (George's son), carried on the family tradition of living by the sweat of other's brows. Their most common mediums of exchange were illegal whiskey, the lariat and the bullet.

Myra Belle Starr's chief folly was choosing rotten husbands and company; that is ironic, because she publicly disapproved of crime. However, it seems contradictory that she let Jesse James hide at Youngers' Bend and, as noted earlier, she wanted her brother-in-law, Solomon Reed, to kill deputy John Morris for killing her outlaw husband, Jim Reed, and Pete Fisher, Jim's old enemy. Nevertheless, Belle's only conviction was for horse stealing, the evidence of which was shaky. Her sincere attempt to keep renegade Edgar Watson off of her property probably resulted in her murder. She neither rode with nor slept with Quantrill. She had no child by Coleman Younger. She had no illegitimate children. Nor did she rob with the James and Younger brothers, didn't elope with a jailer or charm judges into releasing criminals. Neighbor women spoke well of her decorum and benevolence.

To sum it mildly, Myra Belle Shirley Reed Starr's life was hectic. The Cherokee allotment she strove to keep is hers forever. May she rest in peace.

2
Henry was a Starr

Henry starred in more bank robberies than anyone in American history–surpassing the combined total of the Doolin-Dalton and James-Younger gangs--and boasted about it on his deathbed. He was also the first to use an automobile in a bank robbery. He preferred to perform in banks, but country stores and railways weren't beneath his dignity–especially in the beginning. His tour–including imprisonment–stretched from his birthplace near Fort Gibson in Indian Territory to Ohio, Colorado, Kansas, New Mexico, Arizona, Arkansas, Texas and Oklahoma.

Paul Wellman (*Dynasty of Western Outlaws*) credits Quantrill with being the root of that dynasty, but Tom Starr was an equal tendril. Tom, Henry's notorious grandfather, was the patriarch of the outlaw clan. Tom's father, James, had been prominent in governance of the Cherokees in Tennessee and Georgia, known as the Old Nation. James Starr, Stand Waitie and others signed the "Removal Treaty of 1835," an agreement to voluntarily give up their land and go west, rather than being forced by the federal government. The treaty was in violation of Cherokee law, subjecting the signers to the death penalty. The Starrs and other Cherokees removed to Western Arkansas. John Ross led the opposition.

The opposition imposed death. The Ross faction arrived in Arkansas and assassinated three signers. James Starr and Stand Waitie were warned and escaped the same fate intended for the same day. War was in effect; murders proliferated by both factions. Eventually, 32 John Ross men shot James dead and mortally wounded his crippled 14-year-old son, Buck, who died several weeks later. The mob relented killing the next three younger boys–the eldest not yet 12–only when their mother and grandmother hugged them to themselves. Tom told that he killed all of the 32 assassins, except the few who died natural deaths.

Blood from the John Ross and Old Settlers factions ran for 11 years, creating scores of widows and orphans, and poverty. President Jackson and Congress hammered out a treaty to settle the issue. One provision was that any member of the Cherokee Nation who had committed a crime was pardoned. The Removal Treaty of 1835 was ruled valid. When Ross balked, President Jackson gave him an ultimatum. Ross relented; he and Stand Waitie shook hands as the president watched. The date was August 14, 1846. Waitie would become a Confederate general of the Indian Brigade, and Tom would scout for him. John Ross and his "Pin" Indians overran the Cherokees in 1862. The Pin Indians were named for the crossed pins they wore on their shirts; they were anti-slavery and pro-Union, and gave General Waitie much trouble.

Tom settled near Briartown, Indian Territory, and named the nearby crook in the Canadian River "Youngers' Bend" for the brothers who frequently visited the area. Quantrill occasionally visited.

Tom Starr was a strong giant at several inches past six feet, with huge feet. After the war, he became active in thievery and peddling whiskey in the Nation. He had eight sons, one being Sam, who became the ill-fated husband of Belle. Another son was George "Hop," Henry's father. Unlike his late Uncle Sam Starr, who robbed a post office, a mail hack and wealthy farmers and ranchers, Henry became a banker–of sorts! His stock consisted of guns and a fast horse. No mask for this bold bandit!

Henry boasted of being a student the equal of the best in his class at the Fort Gibson Indian School. He wrote in *Thrilling Events* that he left school at the age of eleven when his father became ill. However, note number five of Chapter One in Glenn Shirley's, *Last of the Real Badmen*, Lewis R. Walker said in 1956 that he was a schoolmate of Henry's at the Cherokee Male Seminary at Tahlequah, and Henry was expelled for fighting. Henry, he said, was always spoiling for a fight, and did exactly that when another boy tried giving Henry a haircut, running the clippers across the middle of his head. Henry wrote that he was born four miles from Fort Gibson and rode a horse to school there. Walker's statement is inconsistent with Henry's autobiography. Tahlequah is approximately 20 miles from Fort Gibson, and Henry ceased his studies at age 11; therefore, it is impractical to assume that he rode 40 miles per day to the Seminary and back. Nor did Henry mention boarding in Tahlequah; besides, his family was too poor to pay room and board. Henry claims to have handled a team and raised a good crop of corn.

George Starr was one-half Cherokee; his wife, Mary Scott, was one-quarter Cherokee, three-fourths Scotch-Irish. Henry George was the youngest of three children. Sisters were Elizabeth, the older, and Addie.

Henry's father died in 1886. Henry was 13. Shortly thereafter, Mary married neighbor C. N. Walker. Henry describes his stepfather in very ugly terms, saying he wanted nothing but Mary's property, which he got. Further, Mary believed the lies Walker told her about her son. On one occasion, his mother told Walker and the hired hand to hold Henry while she whipped him. Henry's threat of death got him released, and he went to live with Elizabeth and her family.

Henry was riding for a ranch when his trouble with the law began. Charles Eaton charged him with stealing his horse. A mean deputy marshal arrested him in Nowata. En route to Fort Smith, Henry was chained at all times, even to his hotel bed.

In Fort Smith, an officer recommended a lawyer, who took all of Henry's money—$22, and a bill of sale for his horse and saddle. Henry described the shyster as typical of the leeches who thrived through the infamous Fort Smith court. He refused to dignify the lawyer by name. Eaton had earlier profusely thanked Henry for his good care of the horse which had strayed. Henry was dumbfounded at the turn of events.

Officers escorted Henry into the notorious Fort Smith jail–stinking, filthy and overpopulated with both lice and 200 inmates. The prisoners were allowed to be as loud and as rancorous as they wished.

An inmate tried to take advantage of Henry, proclaiming a kangaroo court in session. The sheriff went along with the charade. In lieu of a 50-cent fine for entering jail without permission of the prisoners, the fat one proposed to keep the gold ring on Henry's finger for security; that ring belonged to Henry's girl friend. The prisoner grabbed for the ring. Though in chains, Starr slugged both the "judge" and the sheriff. Inmates moved to assist their buddy, who was getting the worse of it, but a burly, full-blood Creek kept them at bay while Henry finished his opponent.

About the only traits that Henry held in common with other criminals were flinging an occasional curse and stealing. He abstained from coffee, tobacco and alcohol. Though of meager education, he developed a polished demeanor and read classics–elements that sharply distinguished him from practically all other criminalsand authorities.

Henry's cousin, Charlie Starr, failed to bond Henry out when the lying deputy obtained time to produce witnesses–none of which materialized. Faced with the reputable rancher, Charlie Starr, Eaton–the only witness–admitted that Henry had not stolen his horse. The commissioner made a show of castigating the deputy and Eaton, which Henry ridiculed as pure hypocrisy. The fact that Eaton wasn't jailed for perjury only deepened Henry's contempt for the court.

According to Henry, complainant Eaton, as witness for the prosecution, received $20 travel pay and one and one-half dollars per day pending trial. The deputy got $40 for mileage pay, $125 for jailing his prisoner, and 50 cents each for meals for himself and his prisoner, some of which Henry didn't get. Henry said he was jailed without a hearing in order for the deputy to receive the jailing fee. Henry didn't believe that judge Parker took graft, but allowed the practice. Cowboy Henry Starr had colorful terms for the corruption.

An acquaintance of Henry's asked him to carry a satchel for him. Two deputies stopped him and found whiskey in it; they arrested him for intent to sell whiskey to Indians. One of the arresting deputies testified that he doubted that the youth knew about the whiskey; nevertheless, he was fined one hundred dollars–a princely sum for a cowboy.

Though Henry had ridden several years for ranches and was of good repute with their owners, two scrapes with the injustice of the District Court persuaded him that if he were to be hauled in charged with theft, he would play the game to the hilt.

He was well-known in Nowata, where he was the fastest athlete in town. He recruited an unnamed associate and they robbed the Missouri-Pacific depot in Nowata of 400 dollars. In a manner which became typical of Henry's daring, he planned the robbery for a time when a bunch of deputies were camped within shouting distance. They easily escaped, but Henry was caught the next day. That was in July, 1892, when Henry was 19. A bond of 2,000 dollars was signed by E. E. Starr–treasurer of the Cherokee Nation; Ridge Paschal–Cherokee politician and lawyer; and Chief Harris. The bandit never intended going to trial, and he didn't.

Henry robbed with a random accomplice or two or more. They accumulated an impressive number of crimes. The railroad hired Floyd Wilson and an ex-soldier to find Henry. They tore down his sister's door when they went there looking for him. The next day, six witnesses saw them ambush Henry in front of the X U ranch, several miles from Nowata. Two bullets pierced his clothing. Henry fired four rounds into Wilson, killing him instantly. The other fellow feigned death. Henry said they had boasted they would kill him on sight; they hired out for the reward and their warrant was phony. Now that he had killed–something he claimed he never wanted to do–there was no turning back.

Stories grew more exaggerated as Henry's career flourished. Someone swore he had seen the bandit's bullet-pocked chest armor, which didn't exist. He did, however, possess uncharacteristic traits; he ran away with May, fled with another's wife, robbed without a mask, openly insulted and taunted lawmen and a governor. He attended shindigs while officers frantically searched for him–once having danced at a friend's home until the narrow hours, just before robbing the bank in Caney, Kansas; this was the first of numerous bank heists over the course of many years. The next day, they counted their take at a friend's home far removed from the scene of the crime. They were disappointed that the haul was just shy of $5,000! They learned the following day that the cashier had tossed $16,000 behind ledgers!

He was again bonded out.

In April,1893, ten years after Uncle Sam and Aunt Belle went to the federal prison in Detroit, Henry thrilled to lead the six most desperate bandits in the Indian Territory. They outfitted a wagon with full provisions. Expenses were high with food costing between $25 and $35 per day. They owned expensive weapons and fired many rounds for practice. Having friends throughout the Territory, they flaunted themselves everywhere. They were contemptuous of deputies and bragged they could whip any posse. Henry charged that some deputies who claimed to be tough and relentless actually did little more than haul in harmless boys; they didn't dare try to arrest genuine law-breakers. He couldn't recall any deputy killing an outlaw in a fair fight.

The gang decided to do something more exciting than robbing trains; in June, 1893, they robbed the bank in Bentonville, Arkansas and shot up the town for good measure. Several citizens and one bandit were badly wounded, but the gang escaped. For a week, Sheriff Jacob Yoes trained 20 deputies, the "Starr Militia," before foolishly threshing the brush for nothing. Nevertheless, the crime would hound Henry to his dying day.

Henry and May Morrison were taken in a covered wagon to Emporia. with gang member Kid Wilson as bodyguard. From Emporia, they traveled by train to Colorado Springs. They intended to tarry a day or two to rest and outfit May with a wardrobe before continuing to the west coast. However, Henry and Kid were surprised and captured. Starr said that he was betrayed for $500 by a man now dead (1914). May, only 17, was sent home. Again, Henry complained about petty theft by lawmen: Not only was he not allowed to have an attorney, he wasn't allowed to buy food with the money police took from him; however, he was allowed to pawn a valuable diamond for a paltry sum and a fake ticket. Deputy Brown of Denver and an Arkansas officer escorted Henry and Kid to Fort Smith. In stark contrast to officers of the Fort Smith Court, Deputy Brown merited Henry's respect.

Newspapers along the route to Fort Smith featured the infamous bandits on front pages, and included gross lies about May. Tales as to how Henry and May Morrison met rivaled those of merry old England and Gypsy bandits. The media reported that May hailed from a wealthy family in an eastern state. While robbing a train, Henry abducted her to his hideout, and she fell in love with the handsome, daring Cherokee. Unreadable trash appeared in a St. Louis newspaper. Reader reaction along the way outraged Henry. May and Henry had been sweethearts for several years. In her defense, he said they intended to marry on the west coast, as Indian Territory was, at the moment, hazardous to his freedom.

A large contingent of officers, including Sheriff Galbraith of Benton County, Arkansas, met the bandits at Monette, Missouri. In *Thrilling Events,* Starr wrote that he showed contempt for Sheriff Galbraith for haranguing him with stupid questions. In effect, Henry told him it was beneath his dignity to talk to a hillbilly officer. Starr and Wilson were delivered to Fort Smith. Reporters and the curious crowded the depot.

William H. H. Clayton, Col. William M. Cravens and Judge Thomas

Barnes defended Henry. Clayton and Barnes were former district attorneys for the Fort Smith court. Biographer Glenn Shirley has Clayton prosecuting Sam and Belle in March, 1883; this is inconsistent with the caption beneath Clayton's picture on page 164 of Shirley's book, which has Clayton out of office between 1875-1889.

Starr, Frank Cheney and Kid Wilson had robbed the train at Pryor Creek. Frank was on the run, but his brother, Alf, was convicted of that crime. Henry and Kid were convicted of more than a dozen counts of highway robbery, and Henry was convicted of murder. Henry chalked up Alf's conviction as another example of that court's injustice. According to Henry, numerous witnesses were with Alf elsewhere during the robbery, but Alf's attorney, Byers, refused to let Henry testify in Alf's behalf! The fifteen hundred dollars reward was divided between Byers, assistant prosecutor McDonough and the arresting officer, Heck Bruner. Henry condemned Judge Parker–again.

Starr praised his attorneys. Cravens and firm enjoyed more or less steady employment defending the Starr clan.

Henry claimed to have several witnesses that he killed Floyd Wilson in self defense. Judge Parker's abrasive comments and rulings resulted in what might have been a record of reversals–nine—from the US Supreme Court. Parker instructed the jury for almost three hours–perhaps another record. Incredibly, he told the jury that, given Henry's record, he had no right to claim self defense! The jury, scarcely out long enough to appear sincere, found Henry guilty of murder in the first degree.

Though convicted on fourteen counts of highway robbery and one of murder, Starr went on trial for his very first crime–the Nowata depot job. Though he was guilty, he was once again chafed by the legal system.

A detective swore that Henry confessed the crime to him. Henry viewed this case as proof of the prosecution's weakness in the murder trial, else why try a condemned man at extra expense?

Kid Wilson and Alf Cheney were each sentenced to twenty-four years, of which Alf served ten. Of course, Henry was sentenced to hang. Judge Parker harangued him for twenty minutes. Henry's attorney's got a hearing before the United States Supreme Court, which ruled that manslaughter was the maximum charge that could be considered. Henry was scheduled for a new trial in the fall of 1895.

July, 1895, Crawford Goldsby "Cherokee Bill," awaiting the rope, attempted to escape, using a smuggled pistol. Goldsby was a member of the infamous Bill Cook gang. Firing from his cell, Bill killed a guard. Henry offered to disarm Bill if the guards wouldn't shoot Bill. Starr calmly reasoned with the killer, returned with the weapon and gave it to a guard. If Henry's often outrage at the injustice of the Western District of Arkansas Federal Court at Fort Smith had been loud condemnation, the court's next action must have been explosive; the results destroyed Judge Parker's career. Still stinging from the U. S. Supreme Court's reversal, the assistant prosecutor and the judge connived to hang Starr–the high court be damned. Both Henry and Cherokee Bill were arraigned for attempting to escape and murdering the guard! The arraignment was in the presence of the jury which would preside over Henry's second trial for slaying Floyd Wilson! Jail personnel were incensed.

The Wilson case involved highly-irregular procedure, seating Starr while another case was tried. In less than thirty minutes, the jury handed down a verdict of first degree murder. One wonders whether this direct and flagrant violation of the Supreme Court's ruling is the only such event in this nation's history.

Starr said that Judge Parker–who sentenced approximately 130 to death, 88 of whom were executed–boasted that he wanted to hang one hundred. Judge Parker, he insisted, dominated jurors, at least half of whom were backwoods ignoramuses. Also contributing to the situation were professional jurymen and witnesses, who were sometimes brought from great distances and kept in Fort Smith for months at government expense. Sometimes only one or two witnesses out of many were called to testify; they freely spent their per diem in flop houses, saloons and whorehouses, one of which was the Green Pea, owned and operated by Henry's cousin by marriage–Pearl Reed Starr.

After the Supreme Court tossed Henry's second conviction, Parker challenged Chief Justice White in a newspaper, charging White of being ignorant of the law! White accused his honor with arrogantly misusing power. Congress braked Judge Parker's rampant abuse.

Judge Isaac Parker, appointed by President Grant, presided over the vast Indian Territory for nearly 30 years, was relegated to issues of internal revenue. Their benefactor and source of per diem and expenses dethroned, the court leeches crept away. Parker told critics that he was only God's instrument. He died within a year of being demoted. At that time, 13 inmates were under sentence of death–enough to fill Judge Parker's self-imposed quota of 100 plus a bonus of one. Four were acquitted and the rest received reduced sentences. Further reforms confirmed and corrected the corruption of Parker's administration.

Former Congressman John R. Rogers assumed the bench warmed for so long by Parker. Rogers, Senator Vest of Missouri and Fort Smith businessmen correctly saw that the city and court needed a clean image if the city was to enjoy a good reputation and prosperity. On the senate floor, Vest described the Fort Smith court and jail as a disgrace to civilized society. Parker's court–and it *was* his personified–was finally recognized as a macabre monument to both lawlessness and Parker's inverted interpretation of justice. The gallows and jail walls that had for so long been one of the showplaces of the town were removed in January, 1898. Judge Rogers sentenced Henry to three years for manslaughter and a few years for each of four robberies, totaling 13 years. Henry compared this with the 24 years each that Judge Parker gave to Kid Wilson and Alf Cheney for only one robbery. And Cheney wasn't even guilty. Judge Rogers encouraged Henry to conduct himself well and he would, in time, recommend a complete pardon. In Jan., 1898, after four and one-half years in Parker's Federal Hotel, Henry left for prison in Columbus, Ohio.

Henry knew many people in Fort Smith and appreciated their kindness. He often contributed to the newspaper, the "Elevator." Despite the jail's notoriety, Henry made good use of his time there. He read numerous books and garnered education that he thought might help him earn an honest living. His philosophy was that only a fool would behave contrary to prison rules–philosophy that his Uncle Sam Starr seemed to have rejected. Henry was a star inmate both at Fort Smith and in Ohio.

For some unexplained reason, Henry's sentence forbade hard labor. In addition, Warden E. G. "Coggin" (*Thrilling Events*); ("Coffin" in *The Last of the Real Badmen*) granted him privileges. He learned several skills. Henry's mother tried many times to secure for him a pardon. Finally, she appeared before the Cherokee National Council at Tahlequah, through the services of perennial Starr attorney, Col. Wm. Cravens. The Council drew up an eloquent resolution requesting the president to pardon Henry. His mother took the resolution and numerous affidavits and testimonials to President Theodore Roosevelt, who, being an outdoorsman and admirer of courage, was sufficiently impressed by Henry's disarming Cherokee Bill. The chief executive ordered Henry's sentence commuted to end on January 16, 1903. Starr had served more than ten years. But Arkansas officials had not forgotten Henry.

Upon his release, they called upon the Cherokee Nation to extradite him for the Bentonville bank robbery in June, 1893. The Nation refused, for Arkansas didn't honor their requisitions.

In 1902 Rep. Walter Eaton and a photographer traveled about taking pictures that Eaton hoped would promote the townsite he proposed for Porum. They saw Ollie Griffin milking a cow and asked her to pose. The photo, captioned "The Cherokee Milkmaid," was distributed across the land. The cow belonged to Henry's mother, Mary. Ollie, a cultured teacher, boarded with Mary. Mrs. Starr operated a Tulsa café. Upon arriving from prison in January, 1903, Henry helped his mother in her business. He also married the boarder that year. They had a son named–what else?–Theodore Roosevelt Starr.

Henry entered the real estate business in Tulsa. In 1907, He, his wife, mother and sister acquired Cherokee allotments near Skiatook, and moved there.

On November 16 of that year, President Theodore Roosevelt signed the document combining Oklahoma Territory and Indian Territory creating the state of Oklahoma. Charles Nathaniel Haskell, native of Ohio, was sworn in the same day as Oklahoma's first governor. Henry and family were in the front of the crowd during the inauguration at the Carnegie Library. Henry held little Ted high so he could see Governor Haskell. Henry admitted that though he wasn't of the same politics as Haskell, he voted for him because Republicans arrogantly asked good folk to vote for carpetbaggers. Henry was proud of his vote when Haskell spoke of his support of Indian interests and chose the Indian Orphan Band to lead the parade. Adding to the euphoria, Robert Owen, a Cherokee, was sworn in as US Senator. The numerous Indians attending the ceremony suggested that they would be instrumental in guiding the state to greatness. George Henry Starr had a wife, a son named for the president who had freed him from prison, and an honest profession. Life was good, very good for a man who was free after being in jail for years and twice sentenced to death; and he was young–two weeks shy of 34. Pride and exuberance filled the upright and credible citizen of the new state of Oklahoma. Henry yearned to do something good for his fellow man. Benevolence swelled his heart. But the old shadow of Bentonville crept toward Tulsa. Henry's integrity notwithstanding, Arkansas authorities wanted to do something bad to Henry.

Within days of the inauguration, Henry learned that Arkansas requested the Oklahoma governor to ship one George Henry Starr to their barred hotel for the bank robbery 13 years previously. Starr sent a friend to tell the governor that he had lived honestly for five years and to please not turn him over to the state of Arkansas; nevertheless, he feared extradition; and knowing the type of injustice dealt by ignorant, backwoods juries, he rode into the Oklahoma outback and notoriety. Determined Starr preferred death to a prison farm. He was deeply ashamed of himself to learn that Governor Haskell refused to extradite him. He also learned, after he broke the law, that friends had been working in his behalf. But there was no turning back. Newspapers credited the renegade Indian with every robbery in three states, regardless of how illogical. Starr and a buddy (Stumpy) rode west. Henry had friends throughout the state and some in New Mexico.

They rode for two nights, then traveled by day. They enjoyed hospitality almost everywhere, taking meals and lodging with farm families and friends. They had ridden about 600 miles since leaving

Tulsa, when a storm chased them to a farm near Hooker, Oklahoma, on a Sunday afternoon.

The elderly couple had three attractive and refined daughters, the type that Henry preferred. They enjoyed camaraderie, discussed various topics. The eldest girl played piano while her visiting sweetheart accompanied her on the fiddle. The suitor played exceedingly bad. Henry took a turn with the instrument and charmed them with his skill.

On down the road, they haggled with a German family for breakfast. and feed for the horses. The teen-age boy translated and handled the offers and counter offers.

After several weeks in New Mexico, the pair robbed the bank in Amity, Colorado, in June. The job was bland and the chase grossly dull; so incompetent and desperate were the pursuers that they resorted to arresting a prominent rancher who knew Henry years ago in Oklahoma!

Back in New Mexico, Stumpy retired from crime and rode into obscurity. Starr headed for Eastern Oklahoma, some 800 miles distant, going by way of "No Man's Land," again. In Western Oklahoma, Henry was invited by a preacher to a supper of prairie dogs! An Indian relishes dog meat, but the aroma of those frying creatures was disgusting. Henry ate one piece, then they went to church.

Church turned out to be a foot-stomping, hollering revival, the preacher's wife rivaling the noise of her husband and four other ministers. Good heavens, prairie dog meat distressing his stomach and holy-rollers agitating his mind! It was enough to make a man vomit! Henry tried in vain to ignore the spiritual revelry. The pleasure of sitting with an attractive girl was overridden by older women tugging, begging him for a testimonial. He simply agreed with the previous fellow, who allowed that all had come up short; Henry neglected to mention the degree to which he had fallen.

The next day, Henry rode into a town and met his minister friend. The preacher was there to dedicate a new church. Henry ate with him and his host family, after which he donated a dollar to the church. We can safely assume they ate no prairie dogs.

Henry stayed for weeks in Eastern Oklahoma, then headed west again. One can only imagine how calloused his buttocks must have been.

The fugitive reined up for water at a way station several days ride from Clayton, New Mexico. A young boy was at the windmill.

An Anglo man and an attractive Mexican woman were bringing milk from the pen. When asked, the boy said the woman was his mother. Henry asked the whereabouts of his father. The youngster said he killed himself about a month ago, and he didn't know where he was.

Starr spent months of idleness with a friend in New Mexico. While roving about, more than fifty miles from his friend's home, he asked for a meal at a sheep camp. The Mexican cook said his boss–fresh from England–ordered him to feed no one; further, the boss always came about noon. Perturbed that the foreigner dared to counter customary hospitality, Henry told the cook to prepare him a meal, that he would teach the rude fellow appropriate manners.

Soon, the Englishman appeared in the distance. Henry turned his horse into feed stacked nearby. The boss bellowed and demanded answers. Henry furnished them, with pistols in hand and a fair cursing about the foreigner's abrogation of American custom.

January, 1909, found Henry in Arizona. A former official of the city of Tulsa owed him money; Henry wired him for it. Instead of paying, the man informed a detective named Fenton–a lowly whiskey detective—who joined Prowers County, Colorado, Sheriff Simpson–newly-elected by fewer votes than fingers on two hands. Fenton and Simpson left the arresting to Arizona authorities, while they remained about forty miles distant. But the cowardly pair told reporters how they bravely took the infamous and dangerous fugitive at gunpoint. Henry allowed as to how that was difficult at 40 miles. The sheriff's tale of tracking and capturing Starr got him reelected. Fenton's lies got him several promotions. All of this Starr added to his ample collection of hypocrisy and fraud by public officials–an extension of Judge Parker's chicanery.

Further, Sheriff Simpson, afraid of the fallout should Henry escape the county's new jail, got him put in solitary in the cell for the condemned in Pueblo. Bond was extremely high. Everyone, including Oklahoma friends, were denied access. Henry remained there until November 24. He pled guilty and was sentenced to seven to 25 years at Canon City.

Warden Thomas J. Tynan had the same kindly disposition as Warden E. G. Coggin in Ohio and Judge John Rogers. Tynan encouraged Henry to help himself. Tynan's policy was the honor system, allowing inmates to work on roads a long distance from prison. Henry was armed night watchman on such an assignment for more than a year.

Ollie, still in Tulsa, divorced him. Henry worked in the library, assisted the chaplain and learned law to the extent that officials believed he could easily obtain a license. With help from a newsman, Henry wrote *Thrilling Events, Life of Henry Starr; By Himself*, an extremely premature autobiography; but he threatened death to the newsman if he published it! Obviously, the threat was a marketing ploy. *Thrilling Events* was published in 1914 and sold for fifty cents per copy. At the end of the publication, Henry summed his philosophy: He had neither politics nor religion. His life had been improper, but was as good as that of some authorities. No, society hadn't gone to the dogs, because the two had never been separated. Yes, taking money from others is wrong, but lawyers and other big-time thieves took it from him, and remained free.

That publication plus the attributes that had won favor in other jails– polish, good behavior and education–again won Henry early release. He opened a restaurant. Another businessman's wife warmed for Henry more rapidly than did the grill; he swept her out of state, thus violating parole.

Again, Starr organized a gang. And, resuming the Henry Starr tradition, he scorned masks. He and his traveling troupe performed in 14 Oklahoma banks within a period of about four months. A victim recognized a photo of Starr, and the hunt was on.

Typically contemptible of the law, Henry and his lover lived in the middle of Tulsa. Among prominent citizens living within easy range of a Winchester were the mayor and Tulsa County sheriff. A church and school were even closer. Henry drove his new Dodge to movie houses at night.

A letter from Starr (supposedly mailed in Reno, Nevada, but actually posted in Tulsa) chided Governor Williams for offering a reward for an innocent man. Henry claimed to have been in Nevada for years. At the very moment the governor fumed over the letter, Starr and company performed identical acts simultaneously: They robbed the First National Bank and the Stroud State Bank in the town of the same name. No one had ever successfully held up two banks at the same time. Almost 23 years previously, the Dalton gang attempted the feat in Coffeyville, Kansas. Starr and Lewis Estes were wounded by 17-year-old Paul Curry. Estes soon fell from his mount and was captured. He and Henry were taken to Dr. John Evans' office over the First National Bank. Henry had a severe hip wound. A posse in automobiles pursued the other five bandits. The bandaged prisoners were taken to the Chandler jail. Starr was sentenced to 25 years in the state penitentiary at McAlester.

Again, Henry's demeanor, behavior and a dedicated advocate came to his rescue. Kate Bernard, Oklahoma's first superintendent of asylums and prisons, wrangled a parole for the perpetual robber; parole was authorized in mid March, 1919. Henry had served three years and seven months of his 25-year sentence.

Incredibly, the old Arkansas charge raised its ugly head again. Twenty-six years after the robbery in Bentonville, Arkansas authorities demanded Henry's presence! Oklahoma's new governor, J. A. B. Robertson, wasted no time in rejecting the demand.

Tulsa had become popular with moving picture companies. Somehow, Henry got a 25 percent interest in the Pan-American Motion Picture Company of Tulsa. "Debtor to the Law"–a re-enactment of the double bank caper–was Henry's first production; it was filmed on location, utilizing banks, bank clerks and other Stroud citizens, even to having Paul Curry–who had shot Henry–pretend to do it again. Henry, of course, was the star. Despite the movie's success, Starr received no profit. While promoting "Debtor to the Law," Henry met Hulda Starr–unrelated. They soon married. She was 23, he, 46.

Fearing extradition to Arkansas–the officials of which seemed to make careers based on Starr's ancient crime–he declined to go to California to create a bank-robbing scene for a company there.

Henry owed production expenses. An attorney told Kate he would get Henry's money for him or call on the governor to revoke the company's license; however, Henry was never paid.

Ted Starr was in his last year in a Muskogee high school when his father visited. Henry warned his son against a life of crime and confessed that he had always expected to die violently. Henry went home to Claremore and got his wife's assurance that should he die she would properly bury him. He tried to soothe her and walked out.

Starr and three associates stole a large touring car and drove to Harrison, Ark., and the People's National Bank. W. J. Myers, who had an interest in the institution, caught Henry during an instant of distraction, grabbed a rifle near the vault and shot Henry through his spine. The others escaped without money. Henry refused to identify them.

Henry's mother, wife and son came to his side. Four days after being wounded, the curtain banged down on George Henry Starr's final act. He was buried the next day at Dewey, Oklahoma.

Kate Bernard bitterly blamed society for Starr's fall. But perhaps the clue to that which repeatedly lured him back to the outlaw trail is in the title of his autobiography: *Thrilling Events.*

Unlike Coleman and Jim Younger—released from prison in 1901 from sentences for the ill-fated Northfield, Minn., murder and attempted bank robbery in 1876–who had lived uprightly, Henry threw away several rare opportunities to become honest. Frank James, pardoned, teamed with Cole to travel about warning against a life of crime. Perhaps if that preacher hadn't fed Henry prairie dog meat, he could have converted him. While dying, Henry bragged that he had outdone any robber in the nation's history.

There were no fewer than 30 crimes of record, numerous thefts of horses, saddles, food and other items notwithstanding. During his career, Henry had twice been sentenced to death, and 65 years and seven days imprisonment, of which he served 19 years and ten months. He was pardoned once and paroled twice.

It took 30 of Henry Starr's 47 years to do all of that.

3
Robert Potter, First Secretary of the Texas Navy and Mrs. Page

Robert Potter was born to serve the state of North Carolina, the United States Congress, the Republic of Texas and himself–priorities not necessarily in that order. The date of March 2 would prove significant no fewer than eight times in Potter's life from Congress's declaration of war against Algeria in 1815 to his death in 1842.

Ironically, William Pinckney Rose, also born in Granville County, North Carolina, was destined to be instrumental in Potter's life and death, years hence and far away.

The Potter home was in the Brassfields community south of Oxford. Though the Brassfields featured the lower rungs of society, the Potters were farmers of both good repute and circumstances. Perhaps it was Potter's adulation of Revolutionary War Naval hero, John Paul Jones, that prompted him to join the United States Navy on March 2, 1815, when he was 15. He gave his birth as June, 1799. He received an appointment as midshipman. The Naval Academy did not exist; therefore, the program required on-the-job training and studies onboard. Potter was a good student and a poet having a natural affinity for the classics. His home community must have been proud of him–a short-lived honor.

During his six years of service, Potter served onboard four ships, one of which was the *USS Congress*, commanded by Commodore William Bainbridge, hero of the War of 1812 and the Tripolitan War. Potter's initial duty was on revenue cutters off of Massachusetts and Maryland. After three years, he received six months leave, followed by an extension of one year. This generous leave is unexplained and surely beyond comprehension for current military personnel. Upon returning to duty, he sailed off the coast of South America intercepting slave traders. For unclear reasons, he resigned onboard the frigate *United States* in March, 1821. Potter's parents died young, leaving four children at home. There is conjecture that Potter left the Navy to aid his siblings; some figure he was disappointed never to have gotten a promotion; after all, his pay was only 28 dollars per year.

Former midshipman Robert Potter went to Halifax and studied law under the esteemed Thomas Burges. Ironically, and fittingly, the Willy Jones family–foster parents of John Paul Jones–gave residency to Potter while studying law. Willy was an affluent planter whose plantation, "The

Groves," was famed for its high society socials and opulence. Several lawyers studied in its huge library. Jones had no use for convention, desiring no grave marker or religious insults mouthed over his body. Considering Potter's subsequent life, one might wonder whether he learned from Jones's philosophy as well as his library.

Potter was appointed to the North Carolina House of Commons in 1826 and in 1828. He was elected twice to congress; this political rise was abruptly blunted in 1831.

According to the April 18, 1828, edition of the "Raleigh Register," Potter married Isabella A. Taylor of his home county on April 9.

Prior to 1800, a group who resisted authority and taxation with violence called themselves the "Regulators." Those opposed to their methods organized and called themselves the "Moderators." Then as in Potter's time, moneyed people were in control of virtually every aspect of society. Opposing factions of the same titles warred in California during its lawless gold rush era. Regulators were a lawless mob, while Moderators fought their excesses. Potter would eventually become involved in that situation in his last home at Potter's Point on Ferry Lake (Caddo Lake) in Northeast Texas.

Potter was granted a license to practice law. He strongly argued before the North Carolina Supreme Court that his client had been unjustly convicted by a justice of the peace instead of a jury. He lost the argument. In one particular murder trial, half of the jurors had themselves been on trial for their lives.

Potter, a Jacksonian Democrat, opposed Jesse A. Bynum, a Whig, for a seat in the state General Assembly House of Commons. Potter lost. The rivalry became bitter, with Potter charging fraud and challenging Bynum to a duel. The latter refused, saying that Potter was no gentleman. Potter posted a note on the courthouse door proclaiming Bynum a coward. Bynum refused but challenged Potter's second, Thomas Burges. Burges declined. Potter challenged Bynum's friend, John R. J. Daniel. This absurdity brought North Carolina politics to high boil; but the foolishness continued.

At a social gathering in January, 1825, Potter claimed that he was insulted by Bynum putting a hand on Potter's shoulder. Bynum denied doing it. A bloody fight evolved with other participants. Potter and Burges left. Potter charged that Bynum, John J. R. Daniels and William Amis followed, cursing him.

The following morning, Potter, armed with various deadly weapons, walked to a tavern, Bynum's haunt. Battle was done with a smorgasbord of weapons. Bynum received a head injury. Potter was run through with a sword. Potter again challenged Daniels to a duel, again to no avail. The election was cancelled, leaving Halifax with no representation for 1825. In 1826, Potter unseated Bynum.

Potter polished his poetic bent by maligning his enemies in verse.

Assemblyman Potter pushed for radical reform, including a free college for poor boys. The landed gentry opposed, fearing educated people and taxes. Potter's argument that investment in education would eventually benefit the state many fold fell on closed ears. The mass of commoners were to be kept ignorant and subservient. Potter fruitlessly argued for abolishing the state bank, alleging that the constitution did not authorize the bank to make money out of paper.

Mrs. Potter's cousins, the Reverend Louis Taylor and Louis Wiley, often visited the Potter home; the minister was in his mid-fifties, the latter a teen-ager. Potter hated the cousins and accused his wife of adultery with both. When the preacher visited again, Potter castrated him, then went to the youth's home and did the same to him. The act became known as "Potterizing." The victims were surely innocent, while it was reported that Robert was keeping intimate company with a woman in Washington, D. C.–another characterization that his subsequent actions would evidence.

Potter got off with a conviction of maiming the younger man, and was sentenced to six months in jail and fined 1,000 dollars. The assembly legislated that anyone committing such a crime would be put to death without religious consultation.

The inmate hurled curses between the bars of his cell window. He also published a booklet of 80 some pages that urged his constituents to support his actions against those who shamed him with his allegedly adulterous spouse.

In 1834, Isabella divorced him, took her maiden name for herself and children. She died the same year. Young daughter Susan, who enjoyed a prominent position in social circles, died of a respiratory ailment. Robert, Jr. was mentally retarded. In that year, Robert had the unmitigated gall to campaign for election to the legislature that had decided the death penalty for the crime of castration. The campaign became known as "Potter's War." The "Potterites" and the "anti-Potterites" were lashed into fury by the glib orator's fiery tongue and his booklet. They fortified themselves in stores and fired volumes of shot at one another. Potter was elected, but his enemies were in control. They refused to duel, but were no match for his oratory. He was expelled for allegedly cheating at cards, which Potter charged was merely an excuse to get rid of him.

North Carolina was the only state that allowed free Negroes to vote. It was said that this privilege was taken away in Granville County because of their support of Potter. Isabella's brother shot at Potter and missed; with that, "Potter's War" closed. The sun had set on Robert Potter's North Carolina political life. The disgraced former legislator, without a family or constituency, and unforgiven by many for "Potterizing" his wife's cousins, was desperate for a new climate. He looked westward; out there, years later, he would give his copy of the booklet he wrote in jail to Mrs. Page in explanation of his crimes.

* * *

Dr. Francis Moore practiced medicine in his home in Nashville, Tennessee. A dapper young fellow rushed in complaining of an injured hand. The man paced, waiting for the physician to finish wit a patient. The doctor's daughter, 17-year-old Harriet Ann, often greeted patients. She tried to calm him. He exuded a certain charm, considerably disarming the girl. He was elegantly dressed. Solomon Page was a wholesale distributor–his family business. Dr. Moore dismissed his patient and met Mr. Page–an occasion he would regret.

Mr. Page returned several times for follow-up treatment and continued to charm Harriet. She was overwhelmed by the successful and handsome gentleman, and was excited when he requested permission to court her.

Page was generous with gifts for the family. Eventually, he came in a fine carriage drawn by a pair of matched horses.

Solomon and Harriet were married in the Moore home. Solomon had a wonderful surprise for his bride–a large home with furnishings.

Doctor Moore and family decided to move to Texas. Fellow physician, Anson Jones, told him that doctors were much in demand in Brazoria, Texas, and free land was available. Harriet was unnerved by the prospect of her family moving so great a distance, though her step-mother, Sarah, had been cool to her for six years.

Harriet's father, sensing that all was not well in her marriage, took her aside and gave her money to be used only for herself in case of emergency. He told her she was welcome in her maternal grandmother's home in Kentucky.

Doctor Jones and his family visited Harriet and Solomon before departing for the west.

Solomon's hours were erratic, which he blamed on business. It soon became obvious that he had money problems–especially when a man came for the carriage and horses. Solomon explained that he sold them. Finally, he became frantic, admitting gambling losses. He was indebted to a "Mr. Howard." He begged Harriet for her money, but didn't get it. Further, she informed him that she was pregnant, which upset him to the extreme.

Mr. Howard became obsessed with Harriet. He soon suggested that they maneuver Solomon out and away, leaving Harriet and himself to live and love together in comfort. Harriet flatly refused.

Shortly thereafter, Solomon came home and exuberantly announced that they were free of debt to Mr. Howard, for he had been murdered, his safe plundered and all papers burned. Solomon swore off of gambling.

Harriet's grandmother came from Kentucky for Joe's birth.

Solomon returned to gambling.

One day, Solomon burst in and told Harriet that they were going to New Orleans. He met a man who told him of the wonderful opportunities there. He had already sold their home and most furnishings without consulting her. He finally persuaded her that little Joe, though only a few months old, would endure the trip just fine. Besides, he had secured a good carriage and acquired several paying passengers.

* * *

After several months, the Pages and passengers arrived in New Orleans in the summer of 1830. Reports of the bustling economy proved true. Solomon resumed the family business, but attended it poorly. Harriet determined to learn the business and did so with considerable difficulty. She soon had the business solvent. Virginia Page was born in 1831.

Harriet disposed of the wholesale material and opened a dress shop. Solomon continued his habit of absence and indifference. Even though she prospered and enjoyed independence, she kept a spark of hope for Solomon's redemption.

* * *

Virginia, Aug. 22, 1831: Nat Turner, the slave who claimed to be guided by visions, began a murdering rampage. His kind master–Joseph Travis--and his family were the first of 55 victims–including numerous women and children--to be hacked, bludgeoned or shot to death. Robert Potter's home state of North Carolina also suffered a slave rebellion. Turner was hanged and skinned on November 11.

* * *

Yellow fever, the scourge of New Orleans, felled Harriet. Dr. Anson Jones happened to be in the city and tended to the brave shopkeeper. The physician sensed Harriet's situation. He offered to escort her to her father's home at Brazoria or see her aboard a boat that would take her up the Mississippi River to her grandmother's home in Kentucky. She preferred to stay with her shop. He warned her that a person needed more than hope. Actually, she preferred independence to being dependent upon either her grandmother or father–especially considering her step-mother's disposition toward her.

Uncharacteristically, Solomon burst with enthusiasm, startled his poor wife. He excitedly announced that they were going to Texas and take advantage of free land and cattle. A ship captain had just told him that fabulous news.

* * *

Perhaps the robust economy of New Orleans drew Robert Potter in early 1835, about the time Solomon Page told Harriet they were leaving that city for Texas, which was actually Mexican territory. Some considered New Orleans the richest city in the entire country. It was on the edge of the frontier. Between the Sabine River and sundown lay vast open spaces; Stephen F. Austin and several hundred of his colonists were there. Nacogdoches, San Antonio de Bexar, LaBahia (Goliad) and Galveston were the only significant Mexican settlements in Texas.

After winning independence from Spain in 1824, Mexico continued the policy of inducing settlers who would pledge allegiance to Mexico; this was to discourage French and English designs to intrude on Mexican territory. Land was granted to empresarios who brought settlers. The democratic constitution of 1824 and the exemption of tariffs induced settlers.

Empresario Stephen F. Austin assumed his dying father's place in 1817. Four years later, he landed several hundred pioneers at Old Velasco, where the Brazos River kisses the Gulf.

Nine years later, there were about half a dozen empresarios in Texas. Then, in 1830, the government reinstated tariffs to finance personnel at ports of entry. Settlers and merchants strongly opposed at Anahuac, Trinity Bay, and Velasco in 1832. Mexican authorities at Anahuac jailed William Barrett Travis and his attorney partner, Patrick Jack. Because the Mexican authorities were outnumbered by protestors, Nacogdoches commander, Jose de las Piedras, ordered the prisoners released.

Texians were charged with several assassinations in Nacogdoches. Mexican Secretary of War Jose Maria Tornel y Mendivil termed illegal trade as routine. Also in 1830, President Anastacio Bustamente took action to stop settlers from entering the province of Texas. He feared eventual dominance by settlers from the states; however, Europeans were permitted. Naturally, impresarios Austin, and Edwards in Nacogdoches, frowned on the decree.

Santa Anna campaigned for states' rights and was elected president April 6, 1833. The newly-elected president promptly declared himself dictator, dissolved the Federalist government and abolished the democratic constitution of 1824. The very day Santa Anna was elected, delegates to the convention at San Felipe de Austin asked for relief from former President Bustamente's harsh decree. They prepared a constitution that provided for democratic government as well as separate statehood. Henry Smith from Brazoria became governor; Attorney James W. Robinson of Nacogdoches was elected lieutenant governor; Nacogdoches had the added distinction of Sam Houston's becoming major general of the army. All of this when Texas was merely a province of Mexico, having no other official status, and certainly no army, notwithstanding that the constitution of 1824 forbade states to form military units. Stephen F. Austin, who presided over the convention, took the bold and shocking proposal to Mexico City. Though the brash visionary favored Texas remaining part of Mexico, he was promptly tossed into jail on January 2, 1834.

* * *

Trade was brisk between New Orleans, Mexico and settlers in Texas. New Orleans merchants sold to any entity with money. Ships carried various cargoes, much being contraband. Adventurers, investors and rogues low and high flowed into the thriving port and gateway of the sea path to Texas. The constitution of 1824 forbade slavery; but Stephen F. Austin–personally opposed to slavery, but deeming it necessary to the agrarian economy--obtained a waiver in 1829. Texians imported slaves from Cuba and Africa and sold them in the United States cheaper than they could be purchased within the states. Pirate Jean Lafitte stated in his journal that he sold slaves for virtually nothing in Texas and Louisiana. Adolphus Sterne of Nacogdoches noted in 1843 that many slaves could be sold there at high prices.

Adah Isaacs Menken was born, June 15, 1835, reportedly in New Orleans. She would become an internationally famous actress and a legend in Nacogdoches, Texas, lore. Robert Potter arrived about the time of Adah's birth, and rested from his North Carolina trials and tribulations in New Orleans' Bank's Arcade. The Arcade, a popular watering hole, drew adventurers of all sorts and from all over. Friction between Anglo settlers and Mexico drew greedy opportunists–some of whom had grandiose plans for personal fiefdoms between the Sabine and Rio Grande Rivers. Upstairs was the war room for dreamers and schemers. With whiskey and cigars in hand–and often with ill-gotten currency in pocket–they sweated over St. Denis's map of Texas and plotted empire. Potter gravitated to that nest of intrigue; it would have been unnatural for him to ignore the visionaries. Regardless of whether he contemplated grabbing a piece of Texas, Fate persuaded him to enter that promised land. Fate was in the form of the twenty-year-old wife of a prominent Austin resident.

The intermediary sharing drinks with Potter offered him the job of escorting the lady to Nacogdoches, where her husband would meet them.

Obviously the agent–typical of Bank's patrons–neglected his charge to contract a responsible party. The offer of employment was fully consistent with the erstwhile senator's experience with married women in Washington. And to be paid for it? Of course he would be ecstatic to deliver the fair lady to her beloved! But he couldn't guarantee her virtue; after all, goods were commonly soiled during the rough trip up Red River to Natchitoches, Louisiana, and overland to Nacogdoches. His fee would be an incidental bonus. His service to the Texas Revolution and the resulting republic would eventually bring a bonus of gigantic proportions in an unknown industry to the state of Texas in perpetuity.

The lady's husband met them, took delivery of her and thanked the honorable Robert Potter for his arduous duty. The date was July 1, 1835. Sensing further opportunity, Potter stayed on and, at a meeting in the Stone House, was elected as a delegate to the Constitutional Convention.

* * *

Nine days before Potter's arrival in Nacogdoches, Cullen Montgomery Baker was born in Weakley County, Tennessee. Cullen would grow up in Northeast Texas and become the most notorious of the multitudes of renegades in that lawless area. He would proliferate the bloody outrages that caused Potter's murder more than a quarter century previously. Potter's paradise fell short of that lofty description, and would suffer bloodshed far beyond the Republic, statehood, the Civil War and Reconstruction.

* * *

Nacogdoches' population was about 500–only a fraction of its previous number. Stephen F. Austin was still in prison. He had been brought from jail into the presence of the Mexican council in October, 1834, and told that former President Bustamente's law barring immigration would be repealed, but the province of Texas would remain a part of the state of Coahuila.

Nacogdoches attorney, Thomas Rusk, was captain of the Nacogdoches Independence Volunteers. Robert Potter joined the group, and somehow gained the honorary title of "Colonel," which he would wear to the end of his short life.

* * *

Solomon's excitement filled his wife's little shop. The captain, he explained, regularly carried passengers to Brazoria, Texas, some of whom had gotten rich from a single season of agriculture. Harriet, finally recovering from shock, reminded him that they were city people with no understanding of pioneering, ignorant of agriculture and ranching. She preferred the security provided by her shop. He continued to rave about the potential for wealth. Surely, he argued, she could continue her business in the new location.

Harriet wondered whether a new place and different way of life might change her husband into an honest and dependable provider; God knew he had been neither.

Then he reminded her that her family was there. Wouldn't it be great to live near them?

Well, yes, if they didn't have to lean on her father and step-mother–especially her critical step-mother--for sustenance. The grief of bidding farewell to them in Nashville had not worn off. Perhaps Solomon had truly decided to turn his life around.

Yes, she would go.

* * *

They boarded the *Amos Wright*, the vessel of the captain who had convinced Solomon that his fortune awaited down the coast and a brief journey up the Brazos River. Though she was upset over Solomon's gambling during the trip, perhaps she savored a hint of romance in the bellowing sails, gentle swells and the breeze in her pretty face.

Upon reaching Velasco at the Brazos's mouth, some passengers obtained horses and rode to Brazoria. One of them told Dr. Anson Jones of the Pages' arrival in Velasco. Jones met them at the dock in Brazoria. Still mindful of Harriet's precarious lot, Jones allowed that they had brought too much furniture and bought a piece for a generous sum.

Harriet's brother, John, came riding a horse and leading another with a sidesaddle. Solomon would stay and protect their property. Harriet pled with him to not gamble it away. John would return for Solomon and the stuff tomorrow. John hoisted the children onto his horse, and with Harriet in the sidesaddle, they enjoyed the wonderful April weather and fresh countryside for the few miles to Dr. Moore's home. But her enthusiasm lost its edge upon finding her father ill.

John took a wagon into Brazoria the following morning. Dr. Moore and Harriet watched diligently for his return–Harriet with great trepidation–fear that proved to be well-founded: The wagon brought John and Solomon and one barrel of flour–not another item! Her husband blandly told her that he lost her things in a card game. John, extremely angry, assured his sister that he and Dr. Jones would get her property back on the morrow. John and Dr. Jones retrieved the furniture.

Dr. Moore suggested that his daughter get rid of Solomon. Harriet preferred to stay with her husband than to rely on her father. Sarah, her step-mother, had become even more embittered by frontier life and didn't hesitate to verbalize her feelings. Dr. Moore convinced Harriet to stay until he recovered, then they would find a solution to her situation.

Solomon rode a horse about, supposedly seeking work. During his rambling, he picked up talk of pending war with Mexico, which he favored. Stephen F. Austin remained in prison in Mexico City.

Dr. Moore had become a citizen of Mexico and favored peace instead of revolution. He had gained thousands of acres from Mexican policies and desired working out something short of war with the dictator Santa Anna. Solomon, however, having no investment, apparently felt no more allegiance to the country of his choice than he did to his family.

Late summer of 1835, Dr. Moore told the family he would move to one of his Chocolate Bayou properties. He offered Harriet several hundred acres near that place, and a generous herd of cattle. Sarah exploded, reminding him that Solomon was responsible for his family. Harriet assured her that she would accept nothing from her father, could manage on her own as she had been accustomed. Solomon blasted Dr. Moore, accused him of unjustly treating him badly. He would move his family. He walked to town.

Several days later, Solomon returned with a rented wagon. He explained they were moving to a house on Chocolate Bayou. Dr. Moore had a house in the area; he warned that the house Solomon had in mind was badly dilapidated. Brave, resourceful Harriet said they would make do.   They picked up a meager supply of food in Brazoria and set out. After traveling miles across trackless prairie, guided only by a compass, they came upon the derelict shanty; it had been crushed and corrupted by nature. Refuse of wild life abounded in piles and heaps. They more or less camped in the ruin.

Next morning, a neighbor saw the smoke from the fireplace and came. He told them of a fellow–a Mr. Merrick--up the bayou who needed help. They moved to Mr. Merrick's tenant house. The trip required a couple of days. En route, they stayed overnight with an elderly and wise lady, who counseled Harriet on the philosophy of life. She told Harriet that the nearest house from Mr. Merrick's tenant house was Mr. Merrick's home place, some twenty miles distant.

The wagon rolled across more trackless grassland that appeared to have no end. They met a horseman. When they told him of their destination, he despaired. He told them the family that lived there after Merrick moved out, had died: The man died in an accident, his wife and children starved to death. Noting the Pages' city aura and scanty provisions, he wished them luck and rode away. They found the house and moved into it. The wagon's owner rode out to get it. He told of growing tension between Santa Anna and colonists. Sure looked like war. Solomon rented the man's steed to find Mr. Merrick and get settled into his duties. Harriet paid the man and gave her husband several dollars for food, warning that they would be completely without in a few days. Solomon promised to return soon and rode away. Suddenly, Harriet, Joe and Virginia were alone–so very alone in a silent and empty land with plenty of game and her with no weapon; if she had owned one, she wouldn't have known how to use it.

Within a few days, the food was gone. Solomon had not returned. Harriet gathered parsely hawthornes to eat. They ate haws for days and grew weaker. Still Solomon did not come. Hunger gnawed and twisted their stomachs and spirits. They ate more haws. Hunger kept them scanning the faceless prairie for husband and father; surely even the lowly, self-centered rascal would not leave his family to literally starve. The former tenants had perished that very way–stomachs dried and lines etching their faces. After more than a week of growing weak to the point to where they scarcely moved, Harriet was shocked as in a dream. Then he came. Solomon returned–dressed in the rough clothing of a frontiersman.

He brought no food. Instead of going to Merrick, he had ridden to a settlement and gotten fired up by talk of war. Everyone volunteered, he said; so as to not be thought a coward, he offered his services. He spent Harriet's money for appropriate clothing for a fighting man.

Harriet cursed him for every sin that soiled his soul. She asked why he came back. There was no reason for him to come. He brought no food, had no statement except he was going to fight Mexicans; that put no food in their bodies. Didn't he realize his family should be given priority over dead Mexicans? Then she realized he had come in hopes of getting money. He finally mounted his horse. She loudly dismissed him. He merely stated his confidence in her management and rode from their lives.

Harriet and children continued the woefully inadequate diet of haws, and grew increasingly weak.

One day as the family rested, conserving strength, a man's voice called. Harriet struggled to her feet and went out. Mr. Merrick introduced himself and dismounted. He asked whether Mr. Page was present. He had come to find out why Mr. Page hadn't shown up for work.

Harriet, though almost too weak to talk, warmly greeted him as a savior of her and her children.

He brought basic foodstuff and liquor. She cooked a turkey that he shot. Harriet and children attacked it with little more decorum than would animals. With satisfied stomachs, Joe and Virginia fell asleep. Harriet and Mr. Merrick talked over cups of liquor.

His wife had died there, and he had bad dreams about the place–dreams, he told her, that a family might be there in serious trouble.

Thank God, Mr. Merrick! He asked her about herself, and she told him everything. And she was sure Solomon would not come back.

He believed Solomon would return, explaining that given distances and roadless stretches of that vastness, nothing happened quickly. He refused to believe that any man would leave his family to starve. He bedded down in the shed room.

Next morning, Merrick killed and dressed game and told Harriet how to best preserve the meat. She thanked him. He sadly rode away, still confident that Solomon would return.

And Harriet was confident that he would not.

Finally, a young preacher found Harriet and children. Just before the wise woman--with whom they had spent a night--died, she got him to promise he would find them and take her food to them, for, being on her deathbed, she wouldn't need it. The minister searched the empty land for miles, praying to find the way, when he saw the smoke from a fire that Joe had started to relieve the monotony. Given information by the dying old woman, he had tried to find Harriet's father; he learned that he and her brother, John, had joined a military encampment. He promised Harriet he would send a teamster to take them to Brazoria.

* * *

When Adah Menken was exactly two months old, August 15, 1835, a meeting was convened at Columbia to form a provisional government and plan for war. They agreed to issue letters of marque and reprisal for privateers; thus establishing preliminary steps for building a navy. Percentages of booty for the government were established then changed. Mercantile dealers prompted the government to act to protect their goods from Mexican sloops of war, though there was doubt of serious threat at the time. A founder of Houston, A. C. Allen, was one of the first applicants; he proposed an armed vessel with a specific number of men and arms. Privateering on the high seas was to be permitted, but Governor Smith objected, deeming it simple piracy; he also objected to the five percent of spoils for the government. Finally, the council of naval affairs scrapped the proposal and authorized a cut of twenty percent of spoils and a separate ordinance for establishing a navy. Every privateer was required to fly a flag with 1824 on it, supporting the constitution of that year; the provisional government conveniently ignored the fact that the document forbade slavery and states forming military forces.

Governor Smith granted Major Samuel Whiting's request for blank authorizations for captains, as he was in a hurry to get ships built in New Orleans and had no one in mind.

Mexico had, years ago, furnished citizens of Gonzales a cannon for protection against Indians. Colonel Domingo Ugartechea, San Antonio commander, ordered them to give it back. They refused and the revolution that was sparked at Anahuac, blossomed into battle; that was October, 1835.

Potter resigned from the army on November 21, 1835, in hopes of entering the navy. The provisional government accepted his application and, citing his naval experience, granted his application for a letter of marque and reprisal. It was granted, December 1, 1835, but neither privateer Potter nor the government owned a ship! Within a week, Ben Milam died–the sole fatality in his force--leading Texians in driving Mexican forces from San Antonio.

* * *

A teamster and his helper moved Harriet Page and her children back into Brazoria–back from the empty vastness where Solomon had deserted them–left them to certain death by starvation. Harriet had made it clear that she was through with Solomon, never expected to see him again. It was after Christmas when she moved into a small cabin.

Harriet's brother, John, came from the army camp, bringing his new bride, Amy. John furnished them a cow and other provisions that proved invaluable. Harriet welcomed her sister-in-law to live with her. John returned to rejoin his father. Amy, being a country girl, taught Harriet much about coping with the frontier. Amy was pregnant.

* * *

Friction increased between Governor Smith and the council. Smith accused the council and privateers of seeking personal profits rather than serving democracy. In January, 1836, the naval affairs committee received orders to review all letters of marque already issued. Potter obviously desired to keep his commission, but, feeling obligated to his friend, Smith, got Smith a hearing. Smith adjourned the meeting until March 1, 1836. The council gave a committee the responsibility of dealing with the governor; the committee replaced the governor with Lieutenant James Robinson of Nacogdoches. An election was set for February 1, 1836, to elect delegates to a constitutional convention to be assembled on March 1, 1836. The navy ordnance was adopted. Four warships were recommended.

The Nacogdoches election was held in the Stone House, an ancient, two-storey structure on the northwest corner of the square. The main topic–and cause of bitter argument--was whether to work for return to the constitution of 1824 or become independent from Mexico; native inhabitants, preferred the former, newcomers the latter. Soldiers, being newcomers, strongly favored independence. Potter argued against troops voting. After arguments, voting and threats of violence, the election committee reversed the popular vote and let the soldiers cast ballots.

Four delegates were to be elected from a field of seventeen candidates. Potter came in fourth with 235 votes. Sam Houston, long a resident of Nacogdoches, ranked next to last with fifty-five votes. Not to be outdone by the polished orator, Houston got on the ballot in Refugio and was elected to represent that district. The Independence or "War" party sent the majority of delegates to the convention to declare Texas an independent nation.

Potter's win over Sam Houston as a delegate from Nacogdoches set the stage for a long feud: Houston the rough frontiersman, who had lived with Indians and rawhide versus Potter the smooth orator from the east- -the poet and quoter of classics; Houston ridiculed such interests as frivolous and silly–unmanly. Real Texians reeked of horse sweat and liquor and shunned men of letters--especially one who named his horse Shakespeare!

March 1, 1836, Washington-on-the-Brazos, a settlement of less than fifty log cabins: The constitutional convention convened. Robert Potter and Sam Houston were the only delegates present from their districts-- Nacogdoches and Refugio, respectively. The group rented an unfinished blacksmith shop for three months, but fled in less than three weeks. The weather was horrendous; a norther blew through window openings and a doorless entry to sink temperatures to almost freezing, for which some delegates were poorly clothed.

Domestic animals and poultry dashed into the building seeking shelter. Potter nominated John Hizer as doorkeeper to keep swine and poultry out. Speculators and the curious—and not unlikely, Houston, himself—briefly wondered whether Potter referred to them. By acclamation, delegate Hizer became pig kicker and chicken shooer.

The rules-of-order committee included Potter and Houston.

Henry Smith, the former governor of a non-existent provisional government, and James Robinson, who had replaced him as head of the same non-entity, argued as to which was governor of the present delegation. Actually, the only entity with authority was the body of shivering delegates huddled in the crude structure. Surely, they wished the shop were finished and equipped with a glowing forge.

Shortly after midnight, Smith wrote a strong appeal for patriots to come to arms and share the fight for independence. He dispatched a rider to race about with the message.

Also on that day–March 2–Sam Houston wrote the "Proclamation Concerning the enemy's Occupation of Bexar." In a tone similar to that of Smith's, he called on patriots to answer the challenge to freedom.

Potter and Houston were on the framing committee. Potter moved that a regiment of rangers be authorized and moved that Colonel Jesse Benton and Lt. Griffin Banes be authorized to organize it. The moves were approved.

S. Rhoades Fisher—former privateer, and R. R. Royal—both delegates from Matagorda, quibbled about the election for the similar reason that beset the election in Nacogdoches: It was alleged that some soldiers voted more than once, and some voted after legal hours. Childress moved that all delegates be seated. Rusk and Potter objected, but lost.

Potter signed the constitution on March 2. There was a motion that Sam Houston be appointed commander-in-chief of all segments of the Texas Army. Naturally, Potter voted nay.

Sunday morning, March 6, 1836: The sergeant of arms rounded up the delegates to hear a dispatch that had just arrived; it was dated March 3 at the Alamo. Colonel William Barrett Travis stressed their untenable position defending the old mission against great odds, and made an impassioned plea for reinforcements.

Potter moved that they adjourn and rush to Travis's aid. Rusk and others objected. Houston said it would be foolish, for their present predicament resulted from the lack of organization. A government must be firmly established. Houston's advice was heeded. As commander-in-chief, Houston and several others left for Gonzales. Upon arrival, Houston found fewer than 400 ill equipped and poorly trained volunteers.

Potter moved for regulations against fraudulent land titles and greedy land speculators, and wrote a bill invalidating certain tracts, some of which had been under valid title for a hundred years or more. In 1830, James Bowie brought from Saltillo numerous land grants that Mexicans transferred to him. Dr. James Grant, when killed in 1836, had several hundred leagues in questionable certificates. Sam Houston represented the Galveston Bay and Texas Land Company, which sold hundreds of thousands of acres in the Nacogdoches area for five cents per acre during the early 1830s. Potter's motion was defeated. He moved that every citizen of the Republic receive a league and a labor of land; that was tabled. He succeeded in establishing a land committee, himself being a member. Potter convinced the majority to set the voting age at 21 instead of 18.

Potter moved that armed forces be segregated. The constitution stated that the Mexican army and the priesthood were enemies of liberty; therefore, Potter feared that Mexicans in the Texas Army might fight with less vigor than expected. The motion was defeated. Potter agreed with the accepted provision that no one be imprisoned for debt.

About the middle of March the delegation got word that all

defenders of the Alamo had been killed and burned, and that Houston was fleeing eastward.

Finally, after being in session all night, the government of Texas had been established. The date was March 17. Potter nominated Lorenzo de Zavala for Vice President. Rusk beat Potter for Secretary of War. Potter won over S. Rhoades Fisher for Secretary of the Navy. President David Burnet swore in the officials about 2:00 a.m. Burnet ordered Potter to prepare Velasco for defense. With Santa Anna's army rushing eastward, the convention dismissed and the delegates scattered in various directions.

Potter, who hadn't received a promotion after six years in the United States Navy, now had a Navy of his own. He might have been the only Secretary of a Navy in history addressed as "Colonel." Colonel Potter set out to vigorously administer his new office.

* * *

Amy Moore's terrified parents fled their home near Gonzales, the Mexican Army being close. They arrived breathless at Harriet's cabin. They begged both Harriet and Amy to go east with them, for they would surely be killed or worse by Mexican soldiers. Amy protested mightily, sure that John would arrive ahead of any danger; but her parents prevailed and they left, reminding Harriet of her folly.

Now that Amy was gone, Harriet desired to get acquainted around. She and Joe and Virginia set out on foot. Very soon, the town drunkard ran past warning that Mexicans were right behind him. Didn't they hear musket fire? Indeed, they heard loud popping noises. The entire settlement panicked. Many fled with no more than they could carry. Harriet and family sloshed through mud. After trudging many miles, the bunch made camp of sorts. Some men returned to see if, indeed, Mexicans had overrun Brazoria; they hadn't. Abandoned slaves had fired homes and cane fields, the burning cane making the loud popping noises.

Secretary of the Texas Navy Robert Potter, Colonel Hall, commander of Velasco, and several servants rode up. Potter told them that the new government had moved to Harrisburg and that he was directing people to go to Galveston for safety. Harriet had met Colonel Hall in her father's home. Potter, gushing with chivalry and waxing poetically, took Harriet on his horse, instructing a servant to put the children upon his; then they continued toward Velasco.

At Velasco, Potter took families aboard his flag ship, the *Flash*. Harriet and children were perhaps quartered in his own cabin, which resulted in scandal and legal problems throughout their relationship and even after Robert's death; all of this piled upon Potter's inescapable scandal that pursued him from North Carolina. For several days Potter and Hall tried to build defenses for the port at the mouth of the Brazos, then gave up.

The only news trickling into Velasco was bad news: Mexicans were rushing eastward, killing and burning a clear path. Fannin and his men had been massacred at Goliad on March 27. General Houston retreated up the Brazos–a fact that Potter trumpeted loud and often. His old enemy was a joke–a cowardly one at that. Potter reasoned that Santa Anna gave priority to capturing the officers of the new republic. The Secretary of the Texas Navy would save them and the republic! He ordered the *Flash* to sail for Galveston.

Amy and her parents were in a refugee camp when pregnant Amy became ill and died.

The *Liberty* and *Invincible* had destroyed much shipping meant for the Mexican army. Potter expected to find the *Brutus* and the *Independence* at Galveston. He told Harriet that the Texas Navy would win the war by rescuing the republic's cabinet from the mainland and destroying Mexican ships in Galveston Bay.

Robert Potter made romantic overtures to Harriet. She reminded him that she had a husband, though she would never again live with him. Under his persistence, she admitted that if she were free, she would marry him. They embraced and kissed. This was a strange departure from reality, being torn between imagination and hard facts. Robert had been very kind to her and Joe and Virginia; he was the extreme opposite of Solomon Page–the wastrel, gambler, deserter of his family. But she was the one who would bear the curse of runaway wife; already, she was rumored to be Colonel Potter's woman.

The *Brutus* and *Invincible* were indeed at Galveston as was *Cayuga*, a steamboat. Presently the *Independence* brought in the captured *Pocket*. The *Pocket* was an American vessel with a Mexican crew carrying war supplies. The Secretary of the Texas Navy and his captains celebrated.

Potter brought wine to Harriet's cabin–wine destined for Santa Anna, taken from the *Pocket*. He told her they were moving onto the captured ship. She told him that Virginia was feverish. He was concerned, but directed romantic hints at her. Again, she discouraged him. He promised to have a doctor look in on Virginia tomorrow. Harriet wept.

The physician told Harriet that the child was worn out from neglect of various means, including lack of nutrition and fear and probably wouldn't live but a few hours. She begged Potter to do something for Virginia, but the situation was futile.

A man at New Washington told Potter that Solomon Page was killed in the Grass Fight. Before General Cos was whipped out of San Antonio, Jim Bowie led troops against a Mexican mule train, reported to be carrying bags of money; it proved to be grass for the stock. Of course, Potter might have concocted the tale for his own purposes.

Strange feelings came over Harriet; the person she most hated–her husband–was dead. Potter again stressed his love for Harriet, emphasizing that she was free to be his. But Virginia was dying–that's where her thoughts lay.

The next day, Potter had men bury Virginia Page–age five--in Galveston's sand.

Colonel Potter calculated that Santa Anna would drive hard to catch the Republic of Texas cabinet headquartered at Harrisburg. The dictator found Harrisburg abandoned except for several printers. He burned the town and pursued the officials to Morgan's Point (La Porte), but again, he was too late; he watched the *Flash* sail away with the hated rebels onboard. The government relocated to Galveston. President Burnet promoted Potter to commandant of Galveston.

Harriet agreed to marry Robert. He described the beautiful place on Caddo Lake in Northeast Texas that he would claim as his headright. They would build a comfortable home and enjoy a garden and domestic animals and–most of all–each other. Harriet and Joey fantasized about their future with the compassionate and courageous Colonel Robert Potter.

Headquarters learned on April 19 that Houston's army was located on Buffalo Bayou. Ernest G. Fischer writes in *Robert Potter: Founder of the Texas Navy* that the "Biographical Directory of the American Congress, 1774-1949" has Potter participating in the battle at San Jacinto, but Fischer states that Potter was actually on the *Cayuga* on April 19, taking supplies and volunteers to Houston. The distance between Galveston and the battle site is roughly twenty miles by sea. The *Cayuga* had ample time to deliver its cargo and return to Galveston before the battle on the 21st. It seems unlikely that Potter would linger after unloading. It is also improbable that Potter would stay in camp with the hated Houston a minute longer than necessary. One can only try to imagine arguments of strategy between the Commander-in-Chief of the Army and the Secretary of the Navy–each having hotly declared the other's incompetence.

On April 26, several worn men brought word to the *Invincible* that Houston had defeated Santa Anna. President Burnet felt insulted that he had not been the first informed. He ordered all officials to immediately board the *Yellowstone* for a trip to the place of victory at San Jacinto. Potter felt upstaged by his old enemy–the man who had ridiculed his ships as tubs and Potter a counterfeit sailor; he was eager to put a damper on Houston's imminence.

While Potter was gone, Solomon Page came to Harriet's cabin aboard the *Pocket*. After she recovered from shock, she told him she heard he was killed in something called the Grass Fight. They argued. He had been with the volunteers at San Antonio, joined Houston at Gonzales and was one of perhaps two hundred who were ill or stayed with the army's baggage at Harrisburg during the decisive fight at San Jacinto; he himself had been ill. He explained his absence as due to various hardships. He had come for his family. Though he had heard of her adultery with the good colonel, he forgave her for the children's sake. When he asked to see his children, she told him he had none; Virginia had died because of his neglect, and Joe had no thought of him. Bitter accusations continued. Harriet gave better than she received, rebutting his attempt to act superior. Solomon, very distraught, finally left. And good riddance!

The *Yellowstone* returned. Colonel Potter told Harriet of General Houston's perfidy. Houston had the audacity to share Santa Anna's gold with his troops. Potter and Burnet said it should have been turned over to the republic's bare treasury. Potter argued for dismissing Houston from the army he had just led in securing independence for Texas, but Secretary of War, General Rusk, defended Houston. Potter was among those who advocated hanging the dictator. Houston and allies defeated that notion. Some suggested taking Sant Anna to the scene of the massacre at Goliad and shooting him. Also, Houston suffered an ankle wound, which Potter termed insignificant–perhaps because he had rather Houston die of complications. Nevertheless, he said it was Burnet who refused Houston passage on the *Yellowstone*, in order that he continue from Galveston to New Orleans for medical care. The ship's captain would not sail without Houston. When Houston's doctor insisted upon accompanying him, Burnet dismissed him from the army of the Republic of Texas. Harriet was appalled to learn that the hero of San Jacinto was onboard the dirty and decrepit *Flora*, sailing to New Orleans. Potter allowed that Houston was unworthy of decent accommodations.

Potter happily told Harriet that he had navy business in New Orleans, and they would be married there, then travel to Nacogdoches and on to Caddo Lake to establish their home.

Harriet finally broke the awful news that Solomon lived, had visited. She was not, after all, free to marry. Potter was beside himself, swearing he would find a legal means for matrimony–an issue that would demand much of his time and maneuvering. After much arguing, she said she was going to her grandmother's in Kentucky; that declaration triggered another row.

Harriet pleaded for him to be patient, that she loved him and would wait in Kentucky should fortune remove obstacles to marriage.

Colonel Robert Potter was not a patient man, demonstrated by summarily and angrily castrating his former wife's cousins.

Occasionally, someone from North Carolina happened into Potter's presence. All of them knew about his "Potterizing," and spread the word. Potter was exasperated that he could not outrun that demon from his past.

The travel-weary seat of government was moved yet again, to Velasco. Some cabinet members accompanied Santa Anna there. On May 14, an agreement was reached with Santa Anna. Potter was highly displeased. A week later, the *Pocket* carried Harriet and Potter to New Orleans. Potter was chagrined that he had scarcely been noticed, while Houston was much celebrated–and that after Potter arrived on a ship appropriate for the secretary of the Texas Navy, while the general of the Texas Army came on a wretched boat. Providence was unfair!

* * *

May 19, 1836: Comanches attacked Fort Parker and captured several women and girls, including nine-year-old Cynthia Ann Parker, who became the mother of the famous Chief Quanah Parker. Potter, hater of Indians, later boasted that a Comanche village of several hundred were killed with the exception of two young boys, one of which he intended to enslave at Potter's Point.

* * *

Potter brought thirteen-year-old Martha to Harriet, explaining that she was the daughter of a friend, who prevailed upon Potter to see that she went to her grandmother's home in Kentucky. Since that was Harriet's destination, perhaps they could travel together. Harriet and the girl got along fine.

They left New Orleans. Robert tried again to charm Harriet into marriage. Given the romantic setting--the boat, river and the moon, her resolve weakened to a frightening degree; but she broke away and fled the moon and his presence.

One morning Harriet awoke to find themselves on a narrow stream. Potter casually explained: They were on Red River instead of the Mississippi. A yellow fever epidemic was expected, and this was the last boat leaving New Orleans. He did it for their protection. Harriet suspected that she had been tricked. She informed him that she and Martha would go ashore at Alexandria and arrange for travel to Kentucky. Potter promised to help them do that. Dr. Anson Jones had nursed Harriet through yellow fever acquired in New Orleans and it was no fun. An epidemic? Well, perhaps. Gradually, she granted Potter benefit of the doubt.

After hours in Alexandria, Potter returned to the boat. Travel east from there was, he learned, hazardous and rough. But he had an alternative plan: He met a family–the Turners–who were going east, who would travel with Harriet and Martha. At Bennet's Bluff (Shreveport), they would outfit a wagon with provisions and head east on a well-traveled route.

In 1836, Texas was a vast and uncharted expanse of forests, plains, desert, hills and swamp. Savages would rape, steal and murder for another forty years. Indians raided Austin in 1858. The Comanche-Kiowa attack on Jacksboro in 1876 was the last Indian raid in Texas. Existent maps were crude and inaccurate to a large degree. Even if Harriet had seen one–which is doubtful–she would likely have remained ignorant of geography and distance. Informed, she would have realized that the Red River angled westward in the general direction of Potter's promised paradise on the body of water to become known as Caddo Lake in Northeast Texas; nevertheless, his intentions since plucking her from the mud during the Runaway Scrape–his proposals, delays and excuses–should have been obvious. Upon reaching Velasco, he had put her and her children into comfortable quarters aboard the *Flash*. Why her, when there were hundreds of women with children whose men were either dead or chasing about the country. Those other women, probably with rare exception, were plain, homespun, weathered, stooped, worn and hungry. Those who were basically attractive had no means of showing their beauty, for it was masked with dirt and anxiety. And there was his story about a yellow fever epidemic.

Potter attempted yet again to win Harriet for his wife. As the boat plied the waters of Red River, he admitted that which she should have realized--he had maneuvered every turn to hold onto her. He outlined his plan to enter government and introduce laws that would legitimize their marriage, as the new Republic of Texas had no laws governing divorce and marriage. He pressed her to let the ship's captain marry them immediately. All she had to do was say she had no husband, which in effect, she didn't, the colonel rationalized. She refused and he walked away, perhaps contrasting this trip with the one last year when he escorted the young, married lady up this river.

* * *

At Shreveport, they bought horses, tools, wagons and other supplies. Potter hired Mr. George to go along. They and the Turners set out for a spot Potter located the previous summer. About twenty miles into Texas, near the junction of the Sabine River with the Shreveport-Nacogdoches road, Potter halted the group and announced this was where they would settle for a while, calling the small stream branching off the Sabine "Potter's Creek." This move was one more step in the colonel's scheme; Potter's desired headright was only 40 miles north, bordering Caddo Lake. He was gradually edging Mrs. Page there; one more short move would do it.

Mr. Turner and two sons started building a cabin. Mr. George took a wagon and pack horses to Nacogdoches to get the colonel's furniture and personal things. One way was about 50 miles. He was to send word from Nacogdoches to Martha's family. Potter scouted the land he coveted. George returned with the colonel's goods. He also brought word that hostile Indians were troubling small groups of travelers along the road east. He had arranged for word to be brought when a safe caravan was available. This was likely another delaying maneuver of Potter's.

The cabin was finished. The men brought livestock, and a garden was planted. Life was good; too good–pleasant enough to lull Harriet into a strong sense of contentment.

But no word came from Nacogdoches. Harriet asked more than once. Finally, he told her there would be no caravan going east, and the Turners had decided to stay in place. Harriet expressed disappointment. He told her he would arrange for her to leave by way of Shreveport. She asked about Martha getting to her family.

Now Robert Potter–the gentle romantic poet and student of the classics, the polished orator who charmed many, the gentleman who showed great compassion toward Harriet, Joe and Amy–burst with a character flaw that anyone not blindly in love with him would have questioned immediately. He coldly told Harriet that he wasn't concerned about Martha's family. We don't know whether Harriet properly considered the flaw. Perhaps she was becoming accustomed to and accepting of his deceit.

Harriet surely enjoyed life in the one-room cabin shaded by beautiful pines, oaks and magnolias. Potter was no charmer for nothing. The clever colonel finally connived a way to blind Harriet: He asked whether she and Solomon were married by a priest upon settling in Texas? Well, no. Didn't she know that in order to get land, couples had to become Catholics and be married by a priest? But they hadn't filed for land. Never mind, their marriage in Nashville wasn't recognized in Catholic Mexican territory; therefore, she wasn't legally married! Couldn't she see that? Well, perhaps he was right–being a lawyer, he should know. He further explained that they could make a bond marriage, a common practice in localities far removed from clergy.

Three surveyors agreed to witness a signed document establishing the bond marriage. According to *Love Is a Wild Assault*, this occurred on September 5, 1836. Witnesses were George Davis Torents, Joe Miller and Paddy Roling.

It seems that Robert Potter had not resigned from the navy, simply left it behind. He knew very well that Sam Houston would become president of the republic and replace him. Indeed, Houston was elected in September, and he appointed a former skipper and competitor for the office, Samuel Rhoades Fisher.

If any place in the world could protect Robert's secret, this sparsely settled wilderness should be the perfect vault; it wasn't. A family lived in the general neighborhood. The lady told Harriet of Robert's scandal in North Carolina. At home, Harriet asked her husband about it. He explained that he hadn't thought it necessary to bother her with the account. His family had left him and taken another name. Anyway, he said the boy wasn't his son. Perhaps he disowned him because he was mentally impaired. Potter gave her the eighty-six page booklet he wrote in prison : "Address to the People of Granville County." It was signed "Robert Potter, Hillsborough Prison, 1832."

This was the booklet that ignited "Potter's War" between his supporters and the opposition. Excerpts quoted in *Love Is a Wild Assault*, by Elithe Hamilton Kirkland, are verbatim as taken from the whole copy.

Upon reading the publication, Harriet decided that Robert wasn't such a bad fellow. After all, he served two years in prison and was reelected to the assembly, though forced to resign. Though he had deceived her, she considered his many fine qualities, for which he was grateful.

Robert Potter had grandiose plans. His stature and law practice would grow with the population of Red River County; he would represent them in court and in congress. Shreveport, only a short distance downstream, was a commercial and transportation hub that served the Northeastern Texas area. Potter's Point was an ideal location for the future politician's home and base of operations. A paradise, he told Harriet many times.

In December, they moved to Potter's Point. The Point was a high peninsula jutting into Lake Caddo. The view proved to be spectacular. The log buildings that Rob had constructed waited snug and inviting beneath protective trees. When Harriet paused in her excitement, Robert told her that a trader named Ames in Shreveport had shown him the area on a map.

In June, 1837, Rob, Mr. George and hired help shoved off with a flatboat of products from field and forest to market in Shreveport. Robert said he would return in a week with a woman to help Harriet in childbirth. The child wasn't expected for several weeks.

Soon after the men left, Harriet gave birth to a son, who died immediately. She and Rob anticipated a girl to name Lakeann. She told Joe to leave. She hoped she had removed all evidence of the birth, hiding the body. Should she send for her squaw friend to bury the baby? Perhaps someone would happen by. Someone came.

Charles Ames stood in the doorway. The electricity between them was much like that which linked her and Rob when they met in the Runaway Scrape. He brought word from Robert that he was prospering and would soon be home. She quickly told Charles what happened and to please hurry and bury the infant; Joe must not know. With quiet assurance and understanding–and with tears–he did as asked.

Though there was something intangible but positive linking Harriet and Charles, neither could possibly guess that they would have thirteen children together.

* * *

Charles performed chores until Robert returned, then he insisted that he had business in New Orleans and left. Robert brought a servant girl, Delia, to help Harriet; she belonged to a client in Shreveport, who loaned her in exchange for legal services. Robert took the news of his infant son's death in stride, assuring Harriet there would be others. Besides, another issue lay on his mind–a legal challenge.

While in Shreveport, he learned that new law legislated by the Congress of the Republic of Texas did not recognize their marriage. Harriet legally remained Solomon Page's wife. Having served in the Texas Army, Solomon was entitled to the headright of a married man, which was 4,605 acres. A single man was entitled to only 1,476 acres–a devastating reversal for Potter. Further complicating the issue was the stipulation that to qualify for the family headright, the man had to have been a resident of Texas before March 2, 1836. As previously stated, Potter came to Texas on July 1, 1835; however, his North Carolina divorce was years past. Also, recording their bond marriage would convict Harriet of bigamy. What to do?

Of course, he had always planned on entering government; but he must do so as quickly as possible to enact legislation to legalize his and Harriet's situation.

In 1838, Potter's hatred for President Sam Houston and Indians–all Indians–boiled over. Potter railed against Indians at every opportunity; they were all savages, rapists and everything else no good. They should be driven from the land, he said. It isn't clear where such a place would be. Caddos and Coushattas lived all about Caddo Lake; they were peaceful, but sometimes stole horses.

In 1835, the Caddos in Louisiana made a treaty with the United States to forfeit all land and leave the states within a year in exchange for eighty-thousand dollars in goods, animals and cash to be paid in yearly installments for five years. Texas was the only place they could go; this posed a problem for some, especially Robert Potter. A meeting was called to deal with the Caddos. Potter's fiery denunciation of Indians and Houston's consort with them worked up the ignorant–early-day rednecks.

The Caddos had gone to Shreveport to collect some due compensation. The mob–a lynch mob, for that's what they had become under Potter's blistering oratory–planned to ambush and annihilate the natives as they returned home. The young man–Lt. John Salmon Ford-- selected to lead the bunch, wisely persuaded the would-be assassins to seek a more peaceful path. (John "RIP" Ford, young physician and lawyer from South Carolina, would become prominent in government). To murder the Caddos would likely cause widespread war. Potter conveniently had business elsewhere when the ambush was supposed to take place. He was very unhappy about the turn of events.

Sec. of War Thos. Rusk came to the area and persuaded the Caddos to give up their guns. Texas government would take care of the Caddos, he promised. The weapons, part of their annuity, were returned to the U. S. government agency in Shreveport. Now, of course, the natives were defenseless against hostile white settlers who considered the only good Indians were those who had departed for the happy hunting grounds.

* * *

A desperate young man rode hard to Potter and begged him to save his father from a lynching at Clarksville. Potter had met the accused, who was surely innocent of murdering a friend. Obviously Indians did it, the boy said. His father was to be hanged without a trial at sundown tomorrow. The sheriff was too cowardly to uphold law. Potter arrived shortly before the execution, but even his oratory failed to sway the mob.

The areas of Northeast Texas, Southwestern Arkansas, and Northwestern Louisiana was called the Neutral Strip; it was a haven for all kinds of outlaws and riff-raff. Justice had been put on hold. Corruption reigned supreme in and out of office. Honest men were hard to find and were quickly put in their places when identified–places often being graves, or victims were simply left for wild animals to devour.

Potter mistakenly accused local Coushattas of stealing his horses. A firefight left several Indians dead–including the chief and his son–two white men dead and Potter with a head wound. Potter, fearing retribution, hastened to Shreveport with Harriet, Joe and Delia. Robert bought a congenial elderly slave, Hannah. Harriet was pregnant. She was sure this would be the Lakeann they desperately wanted. And she wanted to give birth at the lake; that was very important–for the baby to enter the world at her beautiful namesake.

Charles Ames visited briefly with Harriet in Shreveport. Rob was out at the time. Ames promised Harriet that he would visit Potter's Point and report on the animals and such. Ames didn't return; instead, he sent a letter. Everything was fine and the Indians were gone.

In January, 1839, Lakeann was born at home.

Potter received ownership of several slaves as payment for legal services, and an extended loan of Delia. Potter became exuberant about the potential of the area. Jefferson, strategically located, would surely become a thriving port. Potter's friend and political ally, Mirabeau Lamar, was inaugurated as President of the Republic of Texas on December 10, 1838.

* * *

Summer, 1840: Robert Potter was elected Senator. He learned that Solomon Page had filed for divorce. Harriet asked many questions about what they should do about their own union; after all, she was pregnant again, and, of course, wanted the child to be legitimate. Robert bamboozled her with legal jargon and told her to trust him to take care of the situation appropriately. He took his Senate seat in Austin in November, 1840.

William P. Rose, as mentioned earlier, was, like Potter, a native of Granville County, North Carolina. Rose, his clan and Negroes settled in Jefferson and on land in the near vicinity of Senator Potter's estate. Rose was known for his violent methods of eliminating outlaws--methods that also eliminated trials. A vicious character known as Moorman led the Regulators (vigilantes) in Shelby County. Captain Rose organized his own bunch of ruffians to install lynch rule in Red River country.

Robert occasionally hired Charles Ames to help at Potter's Point. While plying his usual trade, Charles heard numerous tales about Robert and Harriet, especially in the southern part of the republic. Rumors bloomed with exaggeration and outright fabrications. Charles was en route to Potter's Point in January, 1841, when he took up with a peddler. The peddler had also heard the stories, some true, and the peddler knew that Solomon Page had claimed a headright in February, 1838, and immediately sold it; he had been a witness to that transaction. Ames knew that Potter's certificate was issued in March of that year. He also knew that the Traveling Board of Land Commissioners were checking certificates for validity, for there was much fraud. Charles settled in

Potter's guest cabin and kept silent about the legal threat.

Senator Robert Potter returned home in February. He told Harriet he had legislated law that superseded the marriage law of 1837. Additional good news included the fact that he and another Congressman, Isaac Van Zandt, had become law partners. Also, Van Zandt was instrumental in blocking Sam Houston's (a legislator in the House) Cherokee policy, and supported bonuses for Texas Navy veterans.

Potter was considered an expert on land issues and expected upon reelection to become chairman of the Committee of Public Lands. He seemed blissfully unaware of impending doom to his domain, even told Ames that he was proud of the results of the Traveling Board of Land Commissioners! He boasted of legislation that made settlers secure in their homes. But those swindlers in Shelby County! Mercy! Those villains were regularly murdering one another over fraudulent land certificates! And good riddance to that trash! They were no better than savages, who had no right to land!

Davis Torents, the map-maker who had signed the marriage bond, was with Ames and Potter, when Ames said he was going to make furniture in Clarksville. Torrent revealed that he was also taking up another business. Potter was disappointed that they were going away, not to return when the farm needed their help while the senator was in Austin. After everyone else had turned in for the night, Robert assured Harriet again that their marriage was—thanks to the special act of Congress he engineered—perfectly sound and legal in every respect; nothing more need be done. Harriet was jubilant.

Their son was born that month, February. Robert strongly insisted he not be named after him. He probably feared that his sordid past would follow his son–and surely would have. Of course, he might have objected because his retarded son by Isabella Taylor was named Robert. They settled on John D., Harriet's brother's name.

Robert's friend, Amos Morrill, told him the committee had rejected his headright claim. He had not qualified as head of a family as of March 2, 1836. Potter suspected enemies of causing the trouble. Old Rose, Amos told him, loudly proclaimed that Potter was single and acted as such–flirting with Rose women; he was not entitled to all that prime land; not surprisingly, Rose wanted some of it. Amos advised Robert that he had a good chance of winning his case in court. Both agreed that it would not be appropriate at this time to bring up the bond marriage. Good legal talent would emphasize Potter's service in the revolution and resulting republic. Potter's partner, Isaac Van Zandt; John B. Denton and Thomas Rusk would represent him.

Potter won his case in April. John Denton became a candidate for

Potter's senate seat. Captain Rose supported Denton, and resumed bellowing outrages against Potter.

Harriet's brother Abraham came to live at Potter's Point. He brought word that brother John and their father and family were well. Dr. Moore had recovered from the debilitating illness that beset him in 1835.

Robert hosted a huge barbecue at home. He sent to Shreveport for a large supply of tobacco products, and miscellaneous items for guests. Potter smothered about two hundred guest with silky oratory and his fiddling. Of course, he was reelected to the Senate.

Congress convened in November, 1841. Potter was indeed made chairman of the Public Land Committee.

Captain Rose murdered three citizens of Panola County—the county sheriff in January and two people the first week in September. Former President Sam Houston had been elected again to the presidency. Outgoing President Lamar offered a five-hundred dollar reward for the capture of Rose. The man was too dangerous for such little money; nonetheless, the senator announced to one and all that he would arrest Rose himself, as soon as Congress dismissed. Potter and Van Zandt introduced a bill for the creation of Marshall University.

Potter had the dubious distinction of arranging incoming President Houston's inauguration and doing courtesies for Houston and wife. Potter held his hatred in check and performed his official duties with dignity. There is no record of ulcers following the ceremony.

President Sam Houston signed Potter's land patent in January, 1842. Also that month, the *Weekly Texian* published a complimentary article about the senator.

Potter made a deed on February 8, a will three days later, then headed for home. He and several others from Austin arrived in Nacogdoches where he and Judge-Elect John Mills had tea with Nacogdoches postmaster Adolphus Sterne on Feb. 21. Robert left for home on Feb. 23.

Charles Ames had returned to Clarksville. Robert gathered between fifteen and twenty men and went to the Rose home. Harriet believed Rose to be near, but hidden. Potter dismissed his group and went home, as it was near dark. Harriet pled with him to keep some men around the house. She knew very well that Old Rose wouldn't hesitate to kill him; it is incomprehensible that Potter didn't realize the danger; nevertheless, he would hear none of her reasoning.

Come morning, the servants went out to do their chores. Rose and his bunch captured them. Mr. George went out and was felled by a load of buckshot. Robert sprang awake. Someone called for Robert to come out. Harriet begged him to fight; she had learned about firearms and would keep the many weapons loaded and hand them to him. And there was the cannon fastened to a table and aimed at the door. Potter chose to run from the house. Despite Harriet's plea, he dashed out, shotgun in hand. Several shots missed him. At the lakeshore, he leaned his gun against a tree and dived into the water. Harriet was outside and saw the action. Rose tried to drag Harriet inside, but she insisted upon staying. She saw John W. Scott, Rose's son-in-law, grab Robert's gun. When Robert's head appeared, Scott fired. The men left. Many of them were Potter's friends; he had helped them in many ways, including free legal work. Their fear of Old Rose proved them actually to be craven cowards. Their images and names were imbedded in Harriet's mind as they slunk away as whipped dogs. They would pay!

This was March 2, 1842. Harriet and a couple of friends spent the day in a canoe searching the lake, hoping that Robert had escaped.

A violent thunderstorm hit that night. The search continued the next morning. They found him, a huge hole in the back of his head. Scott's reputation for marksmanship proved true. They buried him in the spot he had chosen long ago.

The nearest magistrate was in Daingerfield, about fifty miles distant. Harriet knew Rose would kill her if she left home. She knew that he posted spies day and night. She rearranged sleeping arrangements and armed the hired help at night. She also spread the word that she intended to leave the country, put all this behind and forget it. Perhaps Rose would relax vigilance. But the only route was the road that ran by Scott's home. Nobody could pass there unseen.

Finally, after much planning and preparation, Harriet, her young brother, Abraham and another man disguised themselves and with several pack horses and left in rain. The men on Scott's porch saw them, but had no idea they were being fooled.

Harriet finally prodded the magistrate in Daingerfield to have Scott and several more brought in. Scott convinced the official that they had a trespass warrant and Potter fired upon them. Despite Harriet's protest, the matter was dismissed.

Shortly after, in camp, a fellow came and told Harriet of a new district judge in Boston. The ride was long, but Judge Mills issued orders for the arrest of all the murderers. Harriet rode to Clarksville and delivered the charges to Sheriff Edward West. West rounded up those charged. But Clarksville had no jail.

During the week the prisoners were in chains awaiting the grand jury indictment, Old Rose sent someone to try to hire all lawyers so that there would be no one to represent Harriet; her friend and ally, Amos Morrill and an associate refused Rose's hire. Rose loudly cursed both Harriet and the jury; finally, the sheriff threatened to kill him with a knife. Of ten men charged, seven were indicted.

A long entourage set out for the nearest jail, which was in Nacogdoches, approximately 200 miles distant. Rose secretly got someone to go ahead and hire Thomas Rusk and J. Pinckney Henderson. Sheriff David Rusk–Thomas's brother–declared his jail not fit to hold the prisoners. Of course, that was an excuse not to inconvenience the murderers, a favor to his brother, former general of the Texas Army.

Sheriff West rode to Shelbyville to seek help from District Judge William Ochiltree. (The judge's son, Tom, would become a prominent character in the legend of Adah Isaacs Menken). Judge Ochiltree decreed the Nacogdoches' jail indeed capable of accommodating Rose and gang. Rusk and company delayed and maneuvered and shifted arguments about until Ochiltree freed himself of the Regulator mess and came to Nacogdoches. All this time, Harriet suffered abuse by local residents. Rusk had documents from Austin—a deed and a will—that Robert penned only days after President Sam Houston signed the patent for his headright in January. Amos reluctantly read them to his client.

Senator Robert Potter deeded three sections of land (1,920 acres) to a Sophia Ann Mayfield, which included his residence; he bequeathed to her this parcel in his will as well. It seems that he meant to preclude any possibility that the land could ever be denied her. Mary Chalmers was named beneficiary to more than two sections, some bordering the place of residence. Both women were being rewarded for bestowing much happiness upon the good senator, and he so stated in the documents.

Harriet had never heard of these women! Who are they?

Amos explained that Sophia Mayfield was wife of Robert's fellow congressman, Colonel James S. Mayfield. Mary Chalmers was the spouse of Dr. John Chalmers. Potter was often seen in the company of the women–a common observation in Austin.

Nor was Potter ungrateful to Colonel Mayfield—perhaps out of gratitude for the good colonel's forbearance or blindness—for he willed to him his favorite horse, Shakespeare.

Of course, Harriet was stunned. Her mind reeled trying to rationalize her late husband's possible motives. Surely, it wasn't as it appeared on the surface. But what? The answer sank in the lake with Potter, but unlike him, it would remain there forever.

But Robert didn't completely forget Harriet; though her home had been left to a married lover in the capitol, Harriet was given the kitchen ware, some animals, three slaves and some property–one hundred acres of which she was to convey to her brother, John. Potter bequeathed a Negro girl, Mary, to his good friend John Crunk.

Dr. Chalmers, spouse of Potter's lover, Mary, was generously remembered; he would receive all of the estate personal and real not bequeathed to others. Though Harriet was willed the silverware, It is questionable whether she got the table, much less the cannon attached thereto; perhaps Dr. Chalmers was destined to carry away that weapon. Maybe Colonel Mayfield would lend him Shakespeare to haul it.

All of that business doomed Harriet's case, for Judge Ochiltree, after reading the deed and will, refused to hear her testimony. Perhaps most damning of all, Robert Potter had addressed her as Mrs. Page in the documents! Whether she considered the bond marriage certificate worth producing, or whether it still existed, is conjecture. She chose to drop the murder charges and go home to Potter's Point. Her children waited there, and she had been away for weeks in the grueling process of trying to convict Robert's murderers. Yes, home to Lakeann, Joe and baby John.

Robert's Texas sojourn had come full circle in only seven years; here in Nacogdoches he had delivered the young wife from the wilds of New Orleans in Jan., 1835; here joined Capt. Thomas Rusk's Independence Volunteers. He was elected delegate to the convention in Columbia, Aug. 15, 1835, to form a provisional government and plan for war.

Indeed, Harriet was eager to go home–to leave Robert's first home in Texas and his treacherous murderers. Charles Ames, Amos Morrill and several others accompanied her.

Lakeann had been scalded to death by a kettle of boiling soap that Hannah was making contrary to Harriet's orders. Delia had run away screaming and remained gone. Harriet grieved long at Lakeann's grave. It was the ideal time for Charles to tell her that which she had always suspected: He loved her, always had.

Soon after Harriet and Charles married in August, 1842, they asked the probate court in Bowie County to distribute Robert's estate, and asked for the three sections bequeathed to Mrs. Mayfield. The land was turned over to them and John D. Potter, the infant by Robert.

In 1852, both James and Sophia Mayfield died. Fayette County administered her estate. The administrator sold the sections Robert bequeathed to her to Samuel K. Lewis and Edward McGinnes, who sued the Ames for title in 1857. The trial was held 15 years later.

Harriet testified that she believed her husband, Solomon Page, had died at San Jacinto. As previously mentioned, he was one of about two hundred who guarded baggage and the sick at Harrisburg during the battle; Harriet's brother John was there in the same company. The judge awarded two sections to the Ames and one to plaintiffs.

The Supreme Court received the case in 1875. The case was a tangled legal morass. To consider were marriages, divorces, separations, children, co-habitation, Harriet's polygamy status under the republic's law of 1837, a bond marriage, marriage laws of Texas, the province of Mexico, and the Republic of Texas. Also, laws governing land bounty. Witnesses testified that she and Robert lived together aboard the *Pocket* and elsewhere. She admitted they meant to marry while in New Orleans while there on navy business, but had been too busy. Harriet and Robert's marriage bond certificate was missing; considering Robert's treachery, it wasn't unthinkable that he destroyed it. Nor was a witness produced. Many years had brought the demise of friends and acquaintances. And yet again, there was the matter of Robert officially referring to Harriet as Mrs. Page; that was clearly a clever means to officially deny that he considered her as his wife, and it surely strongly leveraged Chief Justice Oran Roberts to rule that Robert Potter's will was valid in every respect.

Harriet and Charles lived in the house for many years and had 13 children. Harriet bore 18 children: two by Solomon Page, three by Robert Potter and 13 by Ames. It wasn't only the home and improvements that the Ames' had to give up: Young daughter Lakeann, the son who died immediately at birth, a slave girl and Robert were buried at Potter's Point.

Eventually, widow Harriet lived with Adeline–her youngest daughter and one of only four survivors of her eighteen children--and Adeline's husband, Dr. Frank Marreo in New Orleans. In deep contrast to her ordeals in raw Texas–Harriet lived in comfort and security. In that wonderful environment, at the age of 83, she wrote her autobiography, "The History of Harriet A. Ames during the early days of Texas." While researching land titles, Texas lawyer J. H. Benefield found the manuscript among Harriet's relatives in 1936. In 1951, a Texarkana lawyer, A. Burford furnished a copy to Dr. George Salmon.

Upon that manuscript, Elithe Hamilton Kirkland built the wonderful and appropriately-titled, *Love Is a Wild Assault.*

* * *

Robert Potter: midshipman, lawyer, North Carolina legislator, Independence Volunteer, delegate to the provisional government convention in Columbia, delegate to the convention at Washington-on-the-Brazos, signer of the Declaration of Independence, first Secretary of the Texas Navy and senator of the Republic of Texas. A man of many facets. He championed free Negroes in his native Granville County, NC., and reaped their votes. He strove in vain against wealthy planters to make education available to poor people. Heavy odds against him didn't deter him. He gave Sam Houston as much as he received in rival politics. Sam got the last word, making a negative remark on Potter's character after his death. As mentioned, Potter wanted Houston discharged immediately after the battle of San Jacinto. Nor did Houston admit that the navy enabled his victory by denying Santa Anna supplies and troops.

Potter had no use for Indians and delighted in their massacre. He owned several slaves. He helped, without fee, his neighbors at Potter's Point to secure their land claims–lent them equipment, horses and other supplies. And they murdered him. Perhaps this is the source of the saying that, "No good deed goes unpunished." He was a man of contradictions and deceit–secretive. A noted orator and practicing poet. Named his stud horse "Shakespeare." A man of the classics, indeed. Mighty proud of that horse, or nursed a low opinion of the great bard. Regardless, it was decided that his service to Texas earned him the right to rest in the State Cemetery in Austin; his remains were exhumed and buried there in 1928.

March 2 was a prominent date in Robert Potter's life: On that date in 1815, he joined the United States Navy; he was in Texas prior to that date in 1836 to qualify for a headright; Potter signed the Declaration of Independence in 1836; Houston issued "Proclamation Concerning the Enemie's Occupation of Bexar;" Dr. James Grant authorized by the provisional government to raid Matamoros; the court ruled Potter's land claim legitimate, 1836; Potter was murdered, 1842; and even more ironic, his perpetual enemy, Sam Houston, was born on March 2, 1793.

Potter's greatest contribution to Texas was surely unforeseeable during his lifetime. Vast oil deposits were discovered beneath Gulf waters. States' mineral rights were limited to three and one-half miles offshore. The Republic of Texas proclaimed ten and one-half miles. This became controversial during the mid-20th century. Courts finally ruled in Texas's favor for two reasons: Texas was not bound by the rule of states' uniformity upon annexation. Also, contrary to Federal contention, Potter's Texas Navy had indeed roved wide and often in Gulf waters—the equivalent of hostile possession of land—capturing Mexican ships and supplies as Santa Anna's army swept across Texas. Ironically, Potter's heirs did not benefit any from the oil discovered on his headright.

Fittingly, the last congress that Potter attended removed the stigma from children born out of wedlock, if parents married after the fact, offspring were then legal and rightful heirs.

During the years of the Texas Republic, 1836–1845, the Texas Navy fought Mexican ships, even hired out to Yucatan rebels in 1843. But the four stalwarts of the initial flotilla–the *Brutus*, *Invincible*, *Independence* and *Liberty* were lost to various misfortunes in 1837. Briefly after 1838, Texas had no vessels, but others were soon acquired. After annexation, Texas turned over her navy to the United States in June, 1846.

Robert Potter's Texas Navy must be given credit equal to General Sam Houston's Texas Army in securing independence from Mexico– even if neither admitted the fact.

In 1846, Adah Menken was eleven years old and learning to dance.

4
Adah Isaacs Menken, naked on a horse

Not really. As "Mazeppa," Adah *appeared* to be naked, an illusion that packed patrons–mostly men–into theaters and opera houses on both continents. Lady Godiva was an equestrian sans clothing, but Adah, sporting skin-hued tights, was strapped to the back of the "Wild Horse of Tartary."

Adah Isaacs Menken; William Clarke Quantrill; Phineas T. Barnum; and the carnival huckster who promoted the "Wild Woman from Borneo" in my hometown of Lindsay, Oklahoma, shared a common denominator–outlandish prevarication. Adah's particular brand of hokum was wilder than her "wild" mount that leapt from the footlights and over papier mache mountains.

As a teenager in 1949, I paid twenty-five cents to see the "Wild Woman from Borneo." That creature was swathed from head to foot in a mass of filthy tatters; his or her face was blackened and barely visible among the shreds. All of that was, of course, to disguise the "geek" beneath who bit the head off a chicken while ranting within a cage. A young carnival tout mingled with the crowd and exhibited scars on her arms that she explained resulted from the two-day struggle to drag the wild woman from the jungle and onto a boat. The late Frank Buck, who could assemble a boatload of lions and tigers in much less time, might have marveled at their inefficiency.

William Quantrill, brutal guerilla leader during the Civil War, told his followers that he and his brother were ambushed on their way to the California goldfields. His brother was killed and William left for dead. Friendly Indians rescued him, and a squaw nursed him back to health. Quantrill died near the war's end. Some of his surviving guerillas pursued honest labor. One, a cobbler, repeated the Indian story to William Elsey Connelley, author of *Quantrill & the Border Wars* (1909). The biographer informed the cobbler that Quantrill never had a brother, nor a sister for that matter. Cobbler became indignant, saying he knew Quantrill was truthful, because he had heard him tell the story many times! Obviously Adolph Hitler didn't originate the idea that an oft-told lie is as good as the truth. P. T. told us that a sucker is born every minute.

A Quantrill biographer included in the title to his book the "true" story of "Charles" Quantrill. It isn't often that a title betrays the entire book as worthless. No few writers erroneously spell his name "Quantrell." Accurate references to that infamous villain are readily available. But Adah spun an Indian tale no less wild than Quantrill's nor more credible than those of his lazy biographers.

Adah claimed to have been captured by Indians while hunting near Port Lavaca, Texas, and held for three years. Fortunately, an Indian girl captured from another tribe helped Adah to escape; they happened onto a camp of Texas Rangers (how convenient!), but Laulerack was mistakenly killed. Adah composed a poem in her honor. This fib has been trundled through decades by numerous biographers. Then there's her version that she persuaded a young buck to take her away. Had the story basis in fact, it would have been entirely appropriate for her to charm a "buck" of any age to abscond with her.

Adah's numerous biographers offer many "facts," never mind the disparities. Eminent historian Walter Prescott Webb has her born in Memphis, Tennessee; some say she was born to Richard and Catherine McChord in that city. Another wrote that Adah was born in Memphis, her father being Ricardo Fuentes, a Spanish Jew. Others tell us she was born to an American Indian and a French woman in Arkansas. Perhaps New York or Havana. Or did she enter the world near New Orleans, the offspring of the free Negro, Auguste Theodore and creole wife, Marie? Paul Lewis says she is registered as Adah Bertha Theodore in St. Paul's Parish church. Yet another tells us that she was born in Nacogdoches, Texas, to one James McChord. James was either an indolent wastrel or the proprietor of a dry goods store that adjoined Nacogdoches' Old Stone Fort on the square. To further complicate matters, Adah often thrust forth a new identity for her parents and herself.

In 1860, Adah told an interviewer that her father was Dr. Josiah Campbell. The next year, she identified Campbell as her stepfather, and herself as Adelaide McChord. She said her father was James McChord of Dublin, heavyweight champion of Europe. Some say it was Campbell who owned the clothing store instead of James McChord. In *Notes of My Life,* (1862), she gave her name as Marie Rachel Adelaide de vere Spenser. Though Paul Lewis says Adah is registered in St. Paul's parish church, and virtually all biographers agree that she was born on June 15, 1835, near New Orleans, no supporting document has been produced. The Louisiana State Archives for Orleans Parish lists only one father named Theodore between the years 1820-1845. Auguste Theodore and Madeleine Jean Louis Taneany had three children, whose birth years were 1834, 1836 and 1839. None were named Adah, Ada or Adelaide. Further, there is no St. Paul's Parish.

Accepting June 15, 1835, as Adah's birth date, this is about the time that Robert Potter fled family, politics and his crimes in North Carolina, and paused to determine direction in New Orleans. Though thirty-five years separated Adah and Robert, they had much in common. Adah was destined to be a poet, sculptor, a famous actress and a reckless lover. Potter became a poet, and a prominent player in both the Texas Revolution and married women's boudoirs. Both were hot-tempered, and both died young. One can scarcely imagine the combustible results that might have resulted had their lives coincided and mingled. Potter and Adah's father died about the same time. Adah was seven.

When she was fourteen, Adah and younger sister, Josephine, danced in the New Orleans French Opera house. Adah is said to have learned several languages while in her early teens.

An entity in New Orleans sent her to Texas to fill a role with a traveling theatrical company, but she found it filled. Whether she met musician Alexander Isaac Menken on the stagecoach returning east, or in Galveston or Liberty or Livingston, Texas, is anyone's guess.

Beginning during the early 1980s, Lucille Fain wrote a series of studies on Adah in the *Redland Herald*, Sunday supplement to *The Nacogdoches Sunday Sentinel*. Ms. Fain researched Adah for more than forty years. In the *Herald* edition of July 5, 1981, she quotes Joyce Calhoun, director of the Sam Houston Regional Library and Research Center in Liberty, Texas, stating that she had a photocopy of the marriage license issued by Polk County Clerk K. W. Kennedy to Adah H. Theodore and Alexander I. Menken on April 3, 1856, and filed for record two days later. Justice of the Peace D. D. Moore performed the ceremony. Calhoun said the original license is lost.

August 29, 2002 Darlene Mott, Librarian/Reading Room Supervisor, Sam Houston Regional Library and Research Center at Liberty, furnished this author a photostatic copy of a marriage license issued to Alexander I. Menken and Ada B. Theodore on April 3, 1856, by "L. S. McMickin, Deputy Clerk County Court PC." The "Rites of Matrimony" were "celebrated" by D. D. Moore, J PPC., on April 3, 1856 in Polk County, Texas. "I certify that the foregoing License and Certificate thereto were this day recorded in my office in Record Book B of Marriages on page 77 at 51/2 o'clock P. M. Witness my hand & seal of office April 4/56. L. S. McMickin, Depty. Clk. CCPC." Librarian Darlene Mott also furnished this author copies of *The Liberty Gazette*, dated October 8, 1855, which gives notice of Adah's four upcoming Shakespeare readings, and her poem lauding a brother's love, "To My Brother Gus." Interesting, for she supposedly had a brother "Joe," a compositor in Ohio. The poem was signed "ADA BERTHA. Washington, Texas, October, 1855."

Wanda Bobinger of the Polk County Memorial Museum kindly furnished the author copies of photos of Adah and related newspaper articles. She also sent a list of many who were married by Justice of the Peace D. D. Moore during the period that Adah and Alexander married, but no record of that couple:

"Microfilm Reel #1006875

a) Index to Marriage Record Polk Co. TX

b) Volume B–1849-1863"

Atascosita was a Mexican municipality founded about 1830; it was named Liberty in 1837; it was an important port on the Trinity River prior to the Civil War. Sam Houston had a law office there; and it boasted an opera house.

It seems most likely that Adah entered Texas from Louisiana with a traveling company. During the 19th century, there were no large settlements in Texas. Dallas was founded in 1846; its population in 1872 was approximately 3,000. Houston was laid out in 1836; as the capitol of the Republic of Texas, it had about 1,200 residents when incorporated in 1837. Opera houses were commonly built as permanent structures on main streets of tiny settlements during the 1800s.

Calvert, Columbus, Nacogdoches, Livingston and Liberty are typical of towns that prided themselves on culture provided by opera houses. The old Nacogdoches opera house is on the northwest corner of Church and Main Streets.

The Marx brothers singing group were performing in Nacogdoches when mules running away with a wagon drew their audience downstairs. When the people trickled upstairs, an indignant Groucho informed them that "Nacogdoches is full of roaches! " Their laughter caused a career change that has the world still laughing. That opera house dates to 1889, twenty-one years after Adah's death; however, Nacogdoches, being the oldest town in the state, probably followed the tradition of other small settlements and had an earlier playhouse. Their current one—the Lamp-Lite Playhouse–is on the West Loop. The author, a Nacogdoches resident for 16 years, enjoyed many performances in that wonderful icon of culture. Many opera houses have been rescued from decay to enrich every aspect of their communities.

A lady in her 90s wrote librarian Joyce Calhoun that as a young child she saw Adah in Galveston and Liberty. This might have been Mimmie Hardin, who will be featured later.

Alexander Isaac Menken is described as a musician, whose family had a mercantile business in Cincinnati or Nashville. Seems likely that he and Adah met while performing at the same theater, and the circuit took them to Galveston, Liberty, Livingston and, plausibly, Nacogdoches. She adopted Menken's Judaism. Later, she claimed to have been born a Jew.

The marriage lasted three years while Adah acted in various plays: She was Pauline in "The Lady of Lyons" in Shreveport, 1857; Bianca in "Fazio" in New Orleans; and Widow Cheerly in "The Soldier's Daughter" in her New York debut. She claimed to have published her first collection of poetry–"Memories"–as Indigena, and contributed poetry to the Cincinnati *Israelite*. As to Adah and Alexander's marriage, consider the following accounts:

Alexander was not content to be a bit player basking in his wife's success. He was jealous of the adoration heaped upon her. He wanted to join his father's clothing business in Ohio and desired Adah to be a society matron. The disgrace of her smoking cigarettes in public drove him away. Her in-laws disapproved of her career. One version says that Alexander publicly scolded Adah, creating a scandal; another has it that he, being a gentleman, quietly divorced her.

After divorce, she adopted Alexander's middle name, added an "s" and forever after called herself Adah Isaacs Menken; however, in 1859, before the divorce became final, she married boxer John Heenan "Benecia Boy" of Benecia, Cal. The Rev. J. S. Baldwin married them at Rock Cottage, NY. Adah claimed to have learned boxing from John, but reportedly not well enough to defend against his brutality. She was pregnant with his son when he left her. The child died shortly after birth—or was he quietly given to a couple never to be heard from again?

Following divorce from the pugilist, Adah continued with minor roles and writing poetry. She performed with brothers John and Edwin Booth. Then the gateway to fame and fortune opened with her role as Mazeppa in "The Wild Horse of Tartary" at Albany's Green Street Theatre in June, 1861.

How Mazeppa came about offers yet another futile search for truth. Bill poster, J. Smith found himself in possession of the Albany Theatre and at a loss as what to do with it. Adah's manager, James Murdoch, suggested that Adah perform in "Mazeppa," also known as "The Wild Horse of Tartary," Coincidentally Smith hit on the idea simultaneously. Adah strongly objected, but finally agreed. Another version has Adah begging for the part. Previous promoters ordinarily strapped a dummy resembling a male to the horse, but Adah chose to do it herself and became a pioneer stunt actress. The play proved controversial but very successful for its week run.

Ivan Mazeppa was a Russian Cossack leader, born about 1640. According to legend, a jealous husband stripped him, lashed him to the back of a wild horse and dispatched him into the steppes. The play was taken from Lord Byron's poem, "Mazeppa," published in June, 1819, exactly forty-two years prior to Adah's debut as the unfortunate Cossack.

"Mazeppa" had been staged before, but Adah's portrayal in skin-colored tights gave it new life and brought her fame and fortune; she was paid hundreds of dollars per performance. Audiences crammed theaters across the nation, including those in New York, New Orleans, San Francisco, and Virginia City. In 1862, she married journalist Robert Newell. She supposedly reached San Francisco by ship and returned east by stagecoach. This latter leg would have been extremely dangerous, considering marauding Indians and the Civil War; however, adventure was an integral part of Adah's life. Being strapped to the back of a fleeing horse is not for the timid.

In August, 1863, Adah opened as "Mazeppa" in Tom McGuire's opera house in San Francisco. The city was mesmerized. Local firemen made her an honorary member of their brigade. Virginia City, Nevada, named a street for her. Luminaries, especially thespians, artists, musicians, literary lights and European royalty flocked to her performances and her apartments. She claimed Mark Twain, Bret Harte, Walt Whitman and Henry Wadsworth Longfellow as friends. In San Francisco, Samuel Clemons (Mark Twain) supposedly asked her to critique his work; however, none of his voluminous papers mention her.

"Mazeppa" dazzled London, Paris and Vienna. Adah often sailed to and fro between the U.S. and Europe. Robert Newell traveled with her for a while, then divorced her. Not one to long lament the loss of a husband, Adah soon married affluent James Barkley. The bride, a spendthrift with her own money, waded into Barclay's fortune with reckless abandon. They stayed at a fancy hotel in London and entertained lavishly and almost perpetually. In addition to "Mazeppa," Adah performed in "The Soldier's Daughter," "The French Spy," "The Child of the Sun," "Dick Turpin," and "Three Fast Women." Adah and James parted company. Perhaps she spent all of his money. She went to Paris and bore Barkley's son, Louis Dudevant Victor Emanuel Barkley. As had her son by John Heenan, Louis died in infancy.

* * *

Perhaps the most controversial question of Adah's life is whether she was associated with Nacogdoches, Texas; this uncertainty has been grist for numerous biographers, some of whom insist that her presence graced that historical city whose roots reach into antiquity; and no wonder they desire it to be true! That ancient and romantic place hosted the likes of Davy Crockett; Sam Houston and lady friend, Anna Raguet; the Marx brothers; Robert Potter; Louis "Moses" Rose, deserter of the Alamo; the first newspaper in Texas, *Gaceto de Tejas*, and several adventurers who tried to make Texas their personal fiefdoms. After relishing Lucille Fain's series on Adah in the *Nacogdoches Sunday Sentinel*, I wrote to her how appropriate it would be to find evidence in a Victorian attic linking Adah to the city. Now to examine some claims:

Paul Lewis published *Queen of the Plaza* in 1964; it was heralded as being well documented, even contained Adah's diary. Lewis has Adah performing at the Tacon theater in Havana, hence the title of the biography. My acquaintance of many years, Pamela Lynn Palmer, while Special Collections assistant at Steen Library, Stephen F. Austin State University in Nacogdoches, wrote an article for the Texas Folklore Society. She contacted Paul Lewis, whose actual name is Noel B. Gerson, a resident of Connecticut. Gerson admitted that Adah's diary quoted in his book is a hoax. Gerson had the unmitigated gall to write in "Queen of the Plaza" that Adah lied profusely in her diary! This information courtesy of Lucille Fain's article in *The Redland Herald,* a supplement to *The Sunday Sentinel*–Nacogdoches County, Texas–Sunday, April 12, 1981. Not even Lewis's bogus account places Adah in Nacogdoches. Nonetheless, at least one other story has her born there.

Linda Nicklas, Director of Special Collections, Steen Library, found an interesting story in their files about Adelaide McChord and Tom Ochiltree. The story was published in the *St. Louis Globe Democrat* in 1902. The piece is signed "Brazos."

Thomas Ochiltree was the son of William Ochiltree, the last district judge of the Republic of Texas. William, a native of Alabama, settled in Shelbyville, East Texas, soon after the Revolution, with his wife and very young son. This is the judge to whom Harriet Potter appealed to aid her in her struggle to punish William P. Rose and accomplices for the murder of her husband, Senator Robert Potter, in 1842. "Brazos" has Adelaide and Tom growing up together in Nacogdoches, and this is the tale he or she spun in the St. Louis paper:

Tom became a Texas Ranger at an early age. On a Christmas Eve, the rangers gloriously dispatched a band of Comanche marauders and returned to Nacogdoches. The captain's wife and other women had prepared a feast for them in the former Spanish military building on Pilar Street. They gorged themselves and danced until early morning–this following a day of hard riding and combat with savages! The captain's wife insisted that the rangers spend the night and hang their socks for Santa Claus. Prolonged dancing wore holes in Tom's socks, but he was persuaded to hang his boots.

Upon waking, Tom's comrades found presents in their socks, but his boots were gone. He wasn't to despair for long, for he saw Adelaide wearing them! With much joy, he hoisted his sweetheart–the best Christmas present of all!

"Brazos" presented this tale as so obviously authentic, he couldn't understand why it had not been previously published! Of course, it is obvious why the author used a pen name! Adah had been dead for 34 years, else it could have been appropriately attributed to her. Tom, himself a windbag, spun his own yarns linking himself to the renowned star of "Mazeppa." To his credit, Tom served as a Ranger, became a lawyer, served in the Confederate Army, and in state and national politics. But neither he nor his father practiced law in Jefferson or Marshall as some claimed. Tom was four years Adah's junior, and the dates given for their association are scarcely plausible, and at best a far stretch. As with the stories that Belle Starr rode with Bill Quantrill, there is neither documentation nor probability that they ever met. Nevertheless, there is an Ochiltree Street in Nacogdoches; whether it is named for Tom or his father or simply because of the legend, it adds color to the city's many charms.

Perhaps it would be a courtesy to the romantic legend to name a parallel street "Adah" or "Menken."

Regardless of her background, she enjoyed fame and fortune before poverty and death. Following are quotes received from Wanda Bobinger of the Polk County Memorial Museum. The author(s) uncertain. They are apparently from a reporter and an author's comments on his review:

"That woman in tights Adah Isaacs Menken revealed the shape of things to come in burlesque while strapped to a horse (left). Below, she clutches a sword and shield for protection in another role."

This by another unknown writer in an unknown publication:

"Scandal! Preachers piously fulminated against loose women in tights (a contradiction if you ask me). But Adah had brought something new to burlesque, and it didn't take theatrical promoters long to grasp the idea. Soon there appeared the most notorious burlesque of its time, The Black Crook, featuring 'The Amazon Parade of Legs.' This was almost too much for one of the critics of the day. 'All for what?' he wrote. 'A display of brilliant costumes, or rather an absence of them; crowds of girls set in array and posturing so as to bring out every turn and play of the limbs. Throughout it was simply a parade of indecency artistically placed upon the stage, with garish lights to quicken the senses and inflame the passions.' Sounds to me as if that critic was 'quickened' and 'inflamed' himself. I can always tell.

"'The Begar's (sic) Opera,' John Brougham, Adah Isaacs Menken, and 'The Black Crook' were just a prelude. Burlesque in America at the time was just a small off-shoot of show business. The girl whom everyone credits with the establishment of burlesque as an instilation (sic) was about to arrive. She came from England, and her name was Lydia Thompson. One hundred years later, I want to salute Lydia and her gorgeous, bouncy British blondes. Without her, I might not be writing this book today, for there would be no story to write.

"Villainy is foiled in 'The Black Crook.'"

The *Houston Chronicle*, Sunday, March 7, 1976, states that the striptease was introduced on Broadway in 1860 when Nacogdoches actress, Adah Menken, appeared nude in "Mazeppa."

* * *

Let's consider Mimmie Hardin's story of boarding with Adah in 1856. Her account is taken from *Seven Pines, Its Occupants and Their Letters, 1825-1872*, by Camilla Davis Trammell. (SMU Press)

The Hardins lived in the country near Liberty, Texas. This family has the dubious distinction of being related to one of the American West's most notorious killers--John Wesley Hardin. Fortunately, John operated mostly in West Texas. He was murdered in an El Paso saloon.

In 1916, when Mimmie Hardin was 76, she vividly recalled Adah. In 1856, Mimmie, age 14, enrolled in Mrs. Fatheree's school for girls in Liberty. She boarded at The City Hotel, taking a room upstairs. A fellow guest, an actress known as Adelaide McChord (Adah Bertha Theodore), fascinated Mimmie. Mimmie wrote often to her family and often mentioned Adelaide. Adelaide's age is given as 18, but she was probably 21. Mimmie described Adah as graceful and having a melodious voice. Curls to her waist. (Imagine what a sacrifice to cut her hair to portray a male in "Mazeppa"!) Mimmie said that Algernon Swinburne's poem, "Dolores," exactly described Adah, even to her polite manners and blue/ grey eyes. Swinburne was one of Adah's many suitors after she found fame. Adah reciprocated Mimmie's adoration.

Adah had acted in Havana prior to coming to Liberty to read Shakespeare. Henry Shea, owner of *The Liberty Gazette*, called upon the actress to write a column, which was titled "Vaporings." She wrote in praise of books, noted men's ingratitude toward women and urged women to become a power themselves rather than rely on marrying into wealth. With Adah in Liberty was her younger sister, Josephine.

Mimmie goes on to write that she saw Adah and Josephine perform in Galveston when Mimmie was nine years of age–five years before sharing the hotel in Liberty. The girls' parents, the McChords, are named as their managers. A footnote says that Josephine wasn't Adah's sister, nor the McChords her parents.

Mimmie lost respect for Adah when she married the boxer, John C. Heenan (Benecia Boy).

As previously noted, no birth certificate for Adah has been produced; however, someone (page 113 of *Seven Pines*) determined that the document lists Adah's father a free, colored wheelwright living at 35

Bagatelle Street, New Orleans. Speculation being that her sad countenance was because of her parentage, unknown to any Texan–nice details, those!

Mimmie recalled that her first boyfriend often socialized with Adah and Henry Shea as a couple.

"The Liberty Gazette" was first published early in 1855. Within two years, Henry Shea sold it and went to Houston. He surely took the nude photo of Adah that decorated his office wall, for Mimmie searched for it in vain. Shea hadn't been in Houston long when Adah sent Josephine home and followed Henry. Within days, she boarded a stagecoach for Livingston. Alexander Isaac Menken–a Jewish musician--was a fellow passenger. Following a brief courtship, they obtained a marriage license in Livingston on April 3, 1856, and were united the same day. Adah adopted Judaism and clung to it for the remainder of her short life.

* * *

After numerous performances in theaters across Europe, Adah returned to London and tried to resurrect "Mazeppa." She found that audiences had changed. Her last performance was in Sadler's Wells Theatre in May, 1868. She went to Paris and attempted to breathe new life into "Les Pirates de la Savane." But her own breathing was difficult, ravaged as she was by tuberculosis and riotous living. Her managers were anxious when she didn't show for rehearsal. With gendarmes in tow, they burst into her poor apartment several flights up in Rue de Bondy, opposite the stage door to Porte St. Martin, and found her body. That was August 10, 1868. She was thirty-three years of age. She died with a Hebrew Bible in her bed. Death, as had life, bore its variations: It is claimed that American poet Thomas Buchanan Read was the only person with her at death. Another account has a Jewish rabbi attending her last moments. She was buried in the Jewish section of Pere La Chaise Cemetery in Paris.

Adah's last poetry collection "Infelicia" was published posthumously. Some of her literary friends are suspected of writing some of her poems; however, the fact that sadness is the common theme in all of her poetry and pervasive in her column "Vaporings" indicates that she is indeed the author. Mimmie Hardin wrote that Adah's sad countenance at the City Hotel in Liberty was noted by the other lady guests. As with Adah, Edgar Allan Poe's poetry mirrors his troublesome life. Ironically, Poe began editing literary journals in Richmond, Virginia, in the year of Adah's birth–1835. He lived but 40 tormented years.

In New Orleans, marriage between people of color and whites was illegal. Perhaps her parents were never married. It is suspected that Adah had all her life tried to escape her color. On tour, she lived extravagantly as a white woman, captured many white lovers and married several. But a pall remained. She was chained to color, but attractive by most accounts.

It is ironic that Adah lived and loved without restraint as had Lord Byron, the author of "Mazeppa." Byron died at age 36; his daughter Ada--a mathematical genius–also died at 36. Adah Menken lived but 33 years. Both Adah and Byron chased phantom happiness. Consider the irony of Byron's diary entry of January 21, 1821, the day before his 33rd birthday:

"Through life's road, so dim and dirty,
I have dragg'd to three and thirty.
What have these years left to me?
Nothing–except thirty-three."

Adah's death was virtually ignored. The numerous benefactors of her generosity were focused elsewhere. A token obituary appeared in a Paris newspaper:

"Ungrateful animals, mankind; absent
Walking his rider's horse behind,
Mourner-in-chief her horse appears,
But where are all her cavaliers?"

Those who benefitted from Senator Robert Potter's kindness were even less grateful; with their shot in his head, he sank in Caddo Lake. His wife and a neighbor dragged his body from the water and with no cavaliers present, buried him in a crude grave in his yard. He was forty-two. His remains were eventually moved to the State Cemetery in Austin, where numerous of his esteemed contemporaries rest. Adah's remains were moved from Pere La Chaise to Mount Parnasse to company numerous fellow celebrities.

Success as Lord Byron's "Mazeppa" might have induced Adah to read all of his works. In his play "Cain," Adah tells Cain—her brother/ husband—regarding the consequences of the fall of their parents, Adam and Eve:

"Thou Know'st,
"Ev'n for our parents' error."

Adah's grave marker at Pere La Chaise reportedly was inscribed with "Thou Knowest." Perhaps Adah borrowed that for a final expression of rebellion against her parentage.

Biographer Wolfe Mankowitz in *Mazeppa* (1982) credits the eight foot monument in Mount Parnasse as having the epitaph, but writes that the monument is gone. Lucille Fain writes in *The Redland Herald: A Weekly Supplement to the* (Nacogdoches) *Sunday Sentinel*, December 5, 1982, that the monument was there in April, 1982, but the epitaph is not.

As if to settle controversy as to Adah's birthplace, her monument credits: "Louisiana."

5
Cullen Montgomery Baker, Neutral Strip nemesis

Cullen Baker was a bad seed; he sprouted early and evilly, the antithesis of compassion and justice. Hate and destruction were his themes. He went about with cloven hoof, strewing widows and orphans in his murderous wake. Whoever coined the notion that something good can be said of anybody, never met Baker; if he could whistle well, no one recorded the fact. The black seed was born to a poor but honest family, a weed in a garden of decency. Law officers, soldiers and agents of the Republic of Texas, Arkansas, Louisiana and the Federal government cowered before his wrath. The general area where those entities joined was called the Neutral Strip; it was anything but neutral. Lawless factions fought one another and government forces in the region from 1836 until well after the Civil War. Cullen Baker's ruthlessness peaked during his campaign against Reconstruction.

Cullen Baker's five feet, nine inches and approximately one hundred and sixty pounds belied his power over people; however, his muscles and sinews must have been strong, for he routinely toted no less than four six-shooters, several derringers, numerous knives, a large bore shotgun and a bellyful of whiskey–all of which probably weighed at least fifty pounds– the latter item not being insignificant. Even more weighty was his reputation for terrorizing Northeast Texas, Southwestern Arkansas and Northwestern Louisiana. Slaves, freed slaves and those who assisted them perished by Cullen's bullets, knives and ropes. Neither were imagined enemies spared plunder, arson and summary execution.

Cullen was born to John and Elizabeth Baker on the Obion River, Weakly County, Tennessee, June 22, 1835, one week after famous actress Adah Bertha Theodore (Adah Isaacs Menken) was born in Louisiana, and one week before the former North Carolina politician, Robert Potter, arrived in Texas. Cullen was the second of three offspring and the only son. John was born in South Carolina between 1805-1808. His reason for moving to Tennessee is unknown. The Republic of Texas granted headrights of 1,280 acres to family men who moved into the Republic before October 1, 1837. Single men could claim 640 acres. Families arriving between October 1, 1837 and January 1, 1842, could get 640 acres. In late 1839, John and his family made a rough journey to take advantage of this provision. After reaching Texas, they moved a time or two before settling near the south bank of the Sulphur River and northeast of Linden, the county seat, 1843-1844. The Bakers struggled mightily to carve a living from the harsh country. President Sam Houston signed John's land patent shortly before leaving office in 1860.

Citizens of the United States came to the area early in the century. The 1840s saw many immigrants from the upper south. During the 1850s, people from the Deep South came with their slaves. Slaves were soon the majority. Between 1821 and 1846, more than 100,000 people moved to Texas.

Adolescent Cullen quickly became a hard drinking, cowardly ruffian-- vulgar and temperamental. He often behaved outrageously. As did most boys of the time, he learned his way about the woods and became adept at hunting. He often went shoeless. While working in a grist mill, a bully stepped on Cullen's bare feet and, of course, a ruckus followed.

Though Cullen had no means of support, he married Mary Jane Petty in January, 1854, when he was nineteen. Nine months later, he could have brought a life into the world; instead, he took a life.

Cullen nonsensically accused a boy of plotting to kill him. Cullen almost killed the the lad with a whip. One of the witnesses, Wesley Baily– a prominent citizen--testified against Cullen. An hour after the trial, Baker went to Baily's residence and blasted him in his hips and legs with both barrels of a shotgun. He died several days later. Baily, 52,left a wife and seven children. Baker fled to his Uncle Thomas Young's farm in Perry County, Arkansas, fearing revenge from Baily's son.

After Baily's murder, Cullen's neighbors considered him a pariah– not that he cared. He often courted trouble and usually found it. The Sulphur River swamp, measuring approximately five miles by twelve miles, became his main refuge. Once Cullen and his hardy black mule, Nell, entered that primitive region, pursuers became quickly discouraged.

Cullen and Mary Jane's daughter, Louisa Jane, was born in May,1857. Mary Jane died three years later, and was buried in the Nooner Cemetery in Perry County, Arkansas. Cullen left his daughter with his father-in-law, Hubbard Petty, and saw little of her thereafter.

John F. and Mary E. Warthan were neighbors of Baker's Uncle Thomas Young. Mrs. Warthan was outspoken about Baker's rowdy ways. Baker got drunk and cut switches with which to chastise the woman. John went to his wife's aid. Baker stabbed him through the heart, then rode into the Red River country. Warthan was 37-years of age and, like Cullen's first victim–Wesley Baily–the father of seven children; the eldest was fourteen.

Baker eventually returned and said he had changed and wished only to live in peace and be a good citizen. Six years had passed since he murdered Baily, and he was still wary of the law. Instead of promptly arresting the murderer, many foolishly accepted his stated intentions. Thomas Orr, Baker's first biographer, said that Baker was peaceful and industrious.

Baker became a member of the Confederate Army; whether he volunteered or was conscripted is unknown. He first served with a cavalry unit at Jefferson, Texas, during the fall of 1861. Records are confusing, but it appears that Cullen deserted, then enlisted again.

Sixteen-year-old Martha Foster of Bright Star, Arkansas, married Baker in July, 1862, two years after his first wife's death. Baker's frequent absence from military duty seems to have been of little consequence to his superiors. He eventually fell ill and was discharged.

During 1863, Cullen's pure hatred of Negroes exploded into action. There is no evidence of an incident that might have driven him to murder them. In Sevier County, Arkansas, Baker encountered a wagon load of people headed for Texas. The area was ravaged by troops and guerillas from both sides; perhaps someone was moving his slaves to safer territory. Baker is said to have shot a black woman in the wagon.

During 1863-1865, two groups warred against one another and all who supported them. Union sympathizers were known as "Mountain Boomers." The "Independent Rangers" were irregular Confederates, deserters, and outright criminals who murdered, burned and pillaged at will. Of course, Baker joined the latter group.

In an event known as the "Massacre of the Sabine," Baker and company encountered about ten Unionist who were fleeing Arkansas and executed them. Afterward, they shot half a dozen more people and burned as many homes. They occasionally collected tribute from Confederate supporters. But the rag-tag group was no match for disciplined troops; therefore, by the end of 1864, Baker had reorganized a band of villains. He posed as a Confederate officer and led raids on Union posts, scouting parties and even stabbed at Federal headquarters at Natchitoches, Louisiana. They defeated two groups of Mountain Boomers and slaughtered all prisoners. Whiskey fueled all of Baker's crimes.

Outrages of every description were visited upon the country. The aged, crippled and innocents were robbed, murdered and their property stolen or burned. Citizens begged the Confederate Army and the state to eliminate the brigands; that effort merely spurred Baker and company to increase depredations. They headed south with wagons loaded with loot. Some Arkansas militia and enraged citizens pursued them, forcing them to abandon their loot and flee. Baker again headed for the Sulphur River bottom.

Baker's second wife, Martha, lived with her father when word came that Federal authorities captured her husband. On February 5th, 1865, she left for Perry County, Arkansas. Legend has it that she rode for thirty-six hours–without food or sleep for herself or her horse—through swamps and across rivers. Having ridden two hundred miles to Cullen's Uncle Thomas Young's place, she found her husband safe. If Martha made the journey, this account of it is obviously wildly exaggerated–much more so than the myth of Belle Starr's cross-country dash to save her brother from arrest.

Baker never traveled far from Cass County, always returning there. As previously noted, officers of the law did not make sincere efforts to bring him to justice, even for unspeakable crimes. Some thought he had rendered the Confederacy honorable service. Baker never accepted defeat of the Confederacy, but remained largely inactive for approximately two years after the war ended.

Cullen and Martha settled into a normal life following the war and tried to establish a ferry on the Sulphur River, but could not compete with the Line and Petty ferries.

Cullen became incapacitated with an unspecified illness and he and Martha moved in with her parents. He recovered early in 1866 and worked for the Line Ferry for about one year. Unfortunately, Martha became ill. There is speculation that her exhausting ride a year previously might have induced the malady. She died in March, 1866.

Cullen's depression and shock drove him to near insanity. He lost all values and reason, and never regained the semblance of normality of the past two years–probably the only such period of his adult life. Nevertheless, a couple of months after Martha's death, he proposed to her sixteen-year-old sister, Belle. Belle wisely declined. Neither did her parents approve, for Cullen had been less than a reputable son-in-law. Cullen became angry. The fact that Thomas Orr was courting Belle, infuriated him. Orr's right hand was crippled with rheumatism; in Baker's estimation, that made him inferior.

Thomas Orr, born in Georgia in 1844, taught a one-room school near Bloomburg, Arkansas. He and Baker were initially on good terms. Orr boarded with the Fosters.

Baker lost a bid to operate the Line Ferry, and threatened to kill anyone who used it. He established a ferry several miles from the Texas border and continued to drink heavily. He still chaffed about Belle's refusal and her parents' disapproval, but focused his anger on Thomas Orr.

Cullen had either gained control of the Line Ferry or was an employee, when Orr approached the Sulphur in June of 1866. Baker falsely accused Orr of saying derogative things about him, hit him with a limb and fled, leaving his mount.

Orr, head bleeding, rallied and mounted the bay mare on which Martha Baker was said to have ridden on her legendary journey. Orr had been in the area only a few months and only now learned of Baker's nefarious reputation. He was shaken to learn that his enemy was extremely evil and intransigent. Orr found it incredible that the community would tolerate such a demon. He knew that he would have to be extremely cautious.

Several weeks after Baker assaulted Orr, Baker went to Orr's school and demanded the ferry fee, which Orr paid. The students were horrified at Baker's threats and cursing. Further, he warned that if he ever caught him on his dead wife's horse again, he would blow his head off. Some students were so affected, they quit school. One of those students brought Orr an illiterate warning letter from Baker.

Aroused citizens met and discussed how to deal with Baker, even considering violence. Elderly William Foster thought a committee should talk with Baker. (This Foster was not Baker's father-in-law). Baker was hostile and threatening to the group, but relented somewhat, even swearing to not bother Thomas Orr. With naked blasphemy, he declared that his word was as good as that of Jesus Christ–this in July, 1866.

In a crude letter–the only type of which he was capable--Baker berated his in-laws for no longer being his friends and favoring Thomas Orr. A clear insight into Baker's twisted mind was revealed in that letter in which he admitted to evil, but vowed loyalty to friends. He graciously promised to leave Orr alone until the end of the school term, which ended during the first week of November, 1866. Baker promptly came to the vicinity the day after school finished. That both the county sheriff and the justice of the peace refused Orr's request for a warrant is significant of why Baker would continue his nefarious ways relatively unmolested. Orr continued his career and was always heavily armed.

Despite Baker's harsh treatment, Orr attempted to renew friendship. Baker did not respond. Finally, Orr attempted reconciliation through an open letter in a Jefferson newspaper in the spring of 1867. In a sense of revenge against Orr and supporters of the school, Baker embarked upon a dog massacre in a community near Bright Star, Arkansas. He stole a horse and shot challenging dogs. When the owner awoke and came out, Baker shot up the house. He killed other dogs in the area and Mrs. Pugh's lame goose. The 1860 Census listed Mrs. Pugh as a farmer and widow with five children. Her estate was valued at little more than one hundred dollars. Deranged Baker was never deterred by the poverty and grief of others.

Baker routinely took supplies from stores without paying. During the summer of 1867, the brigand stopped at the Rowden store near Queen City, Arkansas, and bid Mrs. Rowden to gather supplies; he then told her to bill the Confederacy. When Mr. Rowden learned of the incident, he roundly denounced Baker as a thief and drunkard. Baker went to the Rowden farm and shot him. Young James Clements saw Baker leave; upon investigation, he saw the man dying from buckshot in his chest. Baker vowed to unmercifully murder any man who blamed him for the murder! How dare anyone accuse him of such a foul deed!

Shortly before the war's end, the federal government provided for the "Bureau of Refugees, Freedmen, and Abandoned Lands" to help former slaves adopt to freedom. This organization was called "Freedmen's Bureau." The first agent came to Texas in the fall of 1865, and was ill-received. The Texas Bureau and District of Texas military combined to insure implementation of the program; nevertheless, resistance continued to build. Baker's depredations began in earnest in mid-1867.

Obstinate former slave owners and most whites vowed to defeat Reconstruction and restore the South to its old way of life. Emancipation was rarely if ever mentioned without curses and sometimes with bloodshed. Cullen Baker resolved to continue the war and, given that too few troops were posted in Texas, succeeded to a horrifying degree. Typical of diehards was the intransigent woman who exclaimed that she had rather shoot niggers than teach them to read.

"Carpetbaggers," who grabbed property and freed Negroes, who ravaged and pillaged white people, were credited far beyond their numbers and deeds, but they furnished excuse for brigands like Baker to clear the country of such trash.

Summer of 1867, Baker and probably one or more accomplices abused a freedwoman and killed a peaceful freedman (probably her husband) for trying to earn an independent living.

In July, 1867, William G. Kirkman, former Union infantryman from Illinois, became a Bureau agent based in Boston, Texas. His pursuit of Baker and his chief aid, one Rollins, was hindered by local people who favored the outlaws. After all, some employers hired Baker to murder their former slaves or to be rid of ones they blamed for poor crops.

No one in the area–black or white--was safe. White men other than Baker simply rode up to freedmen and free women and shot them. How dare they strive for independence and dignity! And to aspire to education was certainly worthy of summary execution! Uppity "niggers" would not be tolerated; they were born to fields and mules, and there they would stay.

Shortly after assuming office, Kirkman, DeWitt Brown and several cavalrymen, failing to find Baker, headed back toward Boston. Baker and gang ambushed them near a ferry crossing on the Sulphur River. It seems that no one was killed. Later that morning, Kirkman and soldiers exchanged fire with Baker in an alley in Boston. Kirkman wounded Baker's arm and Baker's hat was shot off, but he escaped. Twenty-two-year old Albert Titus–a soldier and veteran of the war from Maine--was killed by buckshot.

Kirkman's request for additional troops was denied–a decision that became common, causing agents to resign and encouraging outlawry.

Even troops near to depredations weren't called into action, such as Baker's attack on a wagon of supplies destined for Kirkman's 20th Infantry escort. Two cavalry companies posted at nearby Mt. Pleasant had never searched for Baker. Commanders simply did not seriously approach the situation, though Baker slaughtered scouting parties and Negroes and whites who guided them. Baker murdered Freedmen's Bureau agent Hiram F. Willis of Rocky Comfort, Arkansas, and threatened to kill agent Kirkman. Kirkman was assigned several additional guards. Though the chase for Baker obviously required cavalry, infantry was often deployed to little effect.

Perhaps the yellow fever epidemic at Galveston affected military assistance to some extent. Texas District commander Charles Griffin died during the outbreak. Governor E. M. Pease posted a $1,000 reward for Baker's body delivered to the sheriff of Bowie County, but suggested to the Clarksville Bureau that it not be published! Cowardly leadership at the top certainly did not encourage subordinates. Some authorities argued that a much larger reward was necessary, because no one dared to attempt to get Baker for a mere $1,000. As much as $25,000 was suggested.

The Howell Smith family of Bright Star, Arkansas, housed and employed a family of former slaves. Hiring freed people wasn't to be tolerated, but worse, the blacks lived in one room of the Smith home. Separate quarters were planned. There were four Smith daughters. Rumors of interracial sex abounded–an abomination to social mores and the final insult to the Old South, and all that's white and holy! Even Howell was rumored to be sleeping with a black woman! How anyone could know that is a mystery; however, proof is of no concern to the ignorant and prejudiced. Baker and between fifteen and twenty desperados bought whiskey on Christmas, 1867, and attacked the Smith home that night. Many rounds were fired into the house. Four Negroes were hit, two fatally. The outlaws attacked the Smiths, fracturing Howell's skull until he was insensible. It is unknown whether all four daughters were present, but grown daughters Emily and Sally tried to protect their father. They were stabbed and severally beaten.

The gang set fire to beds. Baker had been shot in a leg by one of his own men. The house did not burn as intended, and the family escaped. Howell, in addition to his head injury, had a badly burned foot.

The murderers went to the Fosters--Baker's in-laws, who lived nearby–where Baker demanded aid for his wound.

Two days after the outrage, Captain N. B. McLaughlin, commanding the post at Jefferson, learned of it. On December 28, the officer and twenty men rode for more than forty miles to the Smith place and verified the account. He learned the identities of several of the band, and that they were camped only a few miles distant. Upon finding the camp freshly vacated, they went back to the Foster home. Neighbors gathered there were eager to have Baker captured, but so feared for their lives they refused to act as guides. Captain McLaughlin made every man in the settlement arm himself and accompany him in pursuit of the gang. They picked up a new trail. Several miles farther, they saw the camp just across the Black Cypress River. The gang escaped the attack, leaving behind numerous supplies. The pursuers scoured the wilds for several days, capturing Meredith McAdams, one of those present during the Christmas murders.

McLaughlin was satisfied that forcing the local population of men to join in the hunt would hasten Baker's end. Realizing that their self preservation depended upon dispatching Baker, they vowed their assistance. The captain knew and they knew that Baker would hunt them down and kill every participant. That they were forced would make no difference to Baker. McLaughlin auctioned the captured supplies–except for a shotgun, which he gave to his troops. The proceeds of the auction went to the extremely destitute Smith family. Howell Smith had died from his beating.

Faithful to Captain McLaughlin, citizens led by John S. Jackson, joined the hunt for Baker. They captured Baker associate, Matthew Kirby, but released him when they learned he had been too drunk to participate in the crimes at the Smiths. Lee Rames was one of Baker's group. His younger brother, John Howard "Seth" was caught by several men, who tortured him in an effort to extract information. He was finally shot. Seth was eighteen years of age.

Baker's actions were practically identical to Ku Klux Klan atrocities. Both hated those who took up the cause of freedom for blacks. Through terror and murder they sought to return their idea of civilization to the South. Most Klan chapters materialized in Texas in 1867. They first appeared in Travis, Anderson, Collin, Panola, Robertson, Tarrant and Hays Counties. Viciousness increased after Congress assumed direction of the Freedmen's Bureau and removed Texas government, headed by elected Governor James W. Throckmorton. The Red River area received its first Bureau agents. The Klan reacted violently.

While Baker recuperated from his wound, rogues, including Benjamin F. Bickerstaff, John Duty, Bob Lee and Elisha P. Guest continued to ruin the lives of innocent people. Halfway through 1868, Baker reappeared astride his mule and resumed leadership.

Some authorities were in collusion with employers to control Negroes. Baker was hired to keep them in line. He shot some because they worked for Unionist planters. Black people were no better off than when in slavery. Baker threatened the whole population of black people around Bright Star, Arkansas, if they voted for a Republican convention. Employers promised to fire blacks if they voted.

Election day was November 5,1867. The Bureau agent at Lewisville, Arkansas, reported that blacks turned out for the vote, the Bright Star area being the exception. The agent, outraged that people were abused, tortured, shot and threatened with more of same if they voted, said that the government ought to offer a reward for Baker and levy a tax on the residents of his county to fund it for allowing him to raid as he pleased and limiting his depredations to Union citizens, soldiers and Negroes. Blacks in Texas voted only once while Baker lived–February, 1868, while Baker recuperated from his leg wound. In some areas, a greater percentage of blacks voted than did whites.

One story has it that Coke Stevenson's grandfather lived in Baker country. He recalled that a union man with two daughters lived near Jefferson. One Sunday, two black men offered to bring the daughters home from church. Their father had no objections. Baker happened along and killed both Negroes, threatened to murder the girls' father if he ever again consented to such an arrangement.

Andrew Hall lived for a century. He knew Baker well. Baker was employed to chase down Negroes who had completed their labor contracts and bring them back for further labor. Hall said Baker's mule Nell seemed to have absorbed her master's hatred for black folk, and could follow their scent.

Albert H. Latimer had signed the Declaration of Independence, been a legislator for the Republic of Texas, and legislator for the State of Texas. He became a civilian agent for Clarksville and the adjacent Red River area. He found it incredible that the area remained oblivious to the Union's victory. Denied military assistance, Latimer resigned.

C. S. Roberts replaced Latimer. He told headquarters that no area of the United States suffered from more criminal activity. He suggested that the districts be merged and Brevet Brigadier General James Oaks of the Sixth Cavalry put in charge. His suggestion was refused. Roberts suffered attacks and humiliation, for renegades increased control and terror. Roberts was replaced by Charles F. Rand. Districts were reorganized and DeWitt C. Brown installed in the new office in Paris.

Violence boiled over into 1868. Agents Roberts, Brown and DeWitt were constantly in fear of their lives. John Henderson made an attempt on Rand's life in Clarksville. The military and Rand killed one desperado. So great was the danger, disguised soldiers escorted Rand from Clarksville.

After Baker and a large band failed to kill Brown in the countryside, Baker led even more men into Paris for another attempt, but failed to find Brown. But by fall, Baker had chased the Bureau from his area.

Delegates to the Republican-dominated constitutional convention of 1868 resolved to appropriate a $25,000 reward for the governor to administer for the apprehension of desperadoes. But the money could be spent only when criminals were tried by military commissions. Unionist called lackadaisical military officers "copperheads."

The Arkansas governor declared martial law and sent General R. F. Catterson with 500 men to restore order in the area. They captured three killers and hanged them at Rocky Comfort, Arkansas–the name surely being ironic to the condemned.

Two companies of cavalry led by Captains T. M. Tolman and A. R. Chaffee operated out of the often besieged Sulphur Springs. They were hard-riding soldiers noted for severe methods. Brevet Major General Joseph Reynolds chastised Tolman for his harsh discipline of his troops and severity with citizens of Sulphur Springs. Chaffee, as ruthless as Tolman, and his company rode a great many miles in a few months in a successful purge of outlaws. The unit became known as "Chaffee''s Guerillas" for their brutal methods. They dispatched outlaws Ben Bickerstaff and Bob Lee.

Agent Kirkman had long warned that his life was in danger. The Freedmen's Bureau in Texas was being dissolved even as Kirkman's cavalry escort was withdrawn. Kirkman's commanding officer removed him from office, telling him that he should no longer be at risk.

One night during the first week of October, Kirkman was finishing Bureau business in his office when he went out to investigate a noise. He was felled with multiple buckshot and bullets. Kirkman had fired once. Everyone was afraid to approach the body. Later, it was determined that his money and a watch and chain were missing. Kirkman's horse and pistol were also gone. Later that morning, several men, including Baker and Elisha P. Guest, had the nerve to prowl through Kirkman's office while the entire population stood still.

Baker had not been in Cass County since his crime at the Smith farm, but he returned with a handful of men to kill those who had helped Captain McLaughlin chase him. Also to avenge Seth Rames' death. But mainly to murder the hated Thomas Orr, who had married Belle Foster–the girl who had spurned him. There was a wagon load of murder on his alcoholic mind. The Baker band roamed the country killing defenseless blacks and whites. Baker took James Salmon from his home and murdered him, even as Salmon's wife begged them. A newspaper reported several months later that Mrs. Salmon was a mentally and physically wasted hulk.

Tragically and ironically, Baker murdered the elderly William Foster, who had convinced a committee to reason with Baker rather than kill him. No harder evidence could prove Baker's character.

Arkansas Governor Clayton Powell offered $1,000 reward for Baker. Baker posted a $5,000 reward for the governor. However, Baker sensed a pinch. His gang had dwindled and more pressure was on him; therefore, he arranged for a parley with three prominent men: R. M. Stewart, county commissioner who owned a farm in the Linden area; F. M. Henry, a Linden lawyer and owner of the future site of Texarkana which he helped to develop; and R. P. Crump, a former Confederate colonel. They met late in 1868.

Baker agreed to their plea to leave the country forever. He had a letter of his intentions published in newspapers. With unmitigated gall, he reserved the right to punish those who committed crimes in his name and demanded that no civil offices be allowed in the counties in which he stayed! Further, he vowed to uphold law and order administered by legitimate officials–which he surely meant those who underwrote the Confederate cause. He cited his good character by telling of rescuing a party of Negroes being plundered by white villains and returning their goods and roundly denouncing the culprits before sending them away.

The "Weekly Austin Republican" ridiculed Baker's claim to uphold law and order and protect peaceful people. Baker's arrogant implication that he was a power within the state to be reckoned with also got short shrift. Further, that Crump, Stewart and Henry took Baker at his word was considered disgraceful. While men scoured the country for the rogue, this trio should have captured him and delivered him to the nearest jail. Or killed him outright.

Negroes, believing they were covered by the truce, believed at their peril.

Baker found George Barron, the one who told him that Thomas Orr planned to ambush him, and hanged him to his gate beam for participating in Captain McLaughlin's hunt. However, he was cut down by Lee Rames and survived. They proceeded to other homes, only to find that the residents had fled. As Baker approached the Dempsey home, the couple ran out and hid in the woods. The outlaws searched for supplies then killed the dog.

Belle Foster had married Thomas Orr in 1867. He continued to teach school. The winter of 1868, they moved in with her parents. On Dec. 7, a Monday, Baker's bile reached fever pitch. He and fellow brigands ravaged the neighborhood and surrounded the Foster home well before midnight. Baker ordered his followers to burn the house if a shot was fired at them. Men knocked the door down and entered with cocked pistols. Baker ordered Orr out. Orr complied, hoping the family might be spared.

At dawn, a detail was dispatched to bring in an elderly gentleman, Joe Davis. Why Baker sent for him is unknown. Orr was put on a horse behind Alfred Elliot, a mere boy. A rope was put around Orr's neck. They rode westward a little way. Baker fastened the rope to a limb and ordered the boy to ride forward. Orr dangled. A vote decided that the old man should also die. They had no other rope, so Orr was taken down and dragged aside. Orr's neck had not been broken. He feigned death on the frozen ground. Joe Davis somehow survived, too. Orr and Foster plotted to kill Baker.

Upon learning that Orr survived, Baker swore to kill whoever was responsible for his survival. Lee Rames said he was responsible, for he had noticed that Orr was not dead, but said nothing. He offered to shoot it out with Baker; not surprisingly, Baker, whose only courage came from whiskey, declined. Rames and others went their own way. Baker's only associate now was the notorious Matthew Kirby.

In December, 1868, E.R.S. Canby took over the Fifth Military District from Gen. Reynolds. Gen. George Buell became commander of the Jefferson post. Canby ordered Buell to use the cavalry to bring down Baker. Buell gathered a force of more than 600 men. Reliable citizens suggested that Buell's troops take enough supplies to stay in the field for more than a few days.

Under command of Capt. Wirt Davis, almost 50 cavalrymen headed into Bowie and Cass Counties. Buell asked Arkansas Gov Clayton Powell and Gen. Catterson to be alert should Baker flee in their direction. Five days later, Capt. Davis had captured one of Baker's rogues.

John Chamblee proposed to Gen. Buell that Chamblee organize a group to hunt Baker, if the military would help. Buell said he would, but, typically, nothing came of it. Troops returned empty-handed to Jefferson after weeks of searching. John Chamblee and company decided to act independently.

Baker's former father-in-law, Foster, and others were butchering hogs on a neighbor's place when Baker and Kirby approached. Baker forced Foster to come along to Foster's home. Orr saw them coming and dashed out the rear and ran to where Frank Davis and teenage son, Bill, were working less than a mile distant. They planned to get the aid of those butchering hogs to help get Baker. Orr and a group armed themselves and hid in woods near the Foster home.

Baker said he came to conclude financial business with his former-father-in law, but wanted whiskey first. Foster gave him whiskey. Kirby ate spare ribs. Both men slept. Fittingly, Joe Davis–whom Baker intended to hang with Orr–shot Baker through his head. Just as appropriately, Kirby died by Billy Smith's bullet. Billy was the son of the murdered Howell Smith. Additional shots were fired–undoubtedly with great satisfaction if not outright glee. Cullen Montgomery Baker and Matthew Kirby died an hour before noon on January 6, 1869; and citizens of three states breathed a collective sigh of relief. The "Swamp Fox of the Sulphur" was no more; he would soon return to the dust that was soaked with the blood of his victims.

In 1926, 57 years after the event, Bill Foster's son, Hubbard, said he was about 12 years old when he saw Baker and Kirby killed. According to Hubbard, his father put strychnine in the whiskey he took to Baker. Foster had often poisoned whiskey in preparation for Baker's visit.

Baker died as he had lived–drunk and heavily armed. In his possession was a heavy shotgun–his trademark weapon, four six-shooters, three derringers and about half a dozen knives. His pockets contained more than twenty-five keys and an empty wallet. One wonders how he meant to settle financial accounts with his former father-in-law– perhaps as he did with numerous others who displeased him, even in the most trivial issues. And Baker certainly didn't consider trivial Foster's refusal to contribute a second daughter to marriage with the rogue. Also in Baker's possession was an article from the *Courier Times*, dated December 16, 1868, which allowed that Baker had joined the Cuban expedition. The writer added that the area would "enjoy peace and prosperity," if Governor Clayton Powell's militia followed Baker anyplace. Those who wondered whether Baker was a Klan member were probably satisfied to find a paper with the Klan oath on Baker.

Orr and company borrowed a wagon to take the bodies to Jefferson. They covered the corpses with corn stalks and began the 35-mile journey. The Line Ferry/Jefferson road ran close to Atlanta and Queen City and crossed Big Cypress Creek by ferry. Edward Stevenson–whose nephew Coke Stevenson would become Texas governor–operated the ferry.

Edward knew Baker for a long time and identified the bodies. On January 7, Orr and associates delivered the bodies to General Buell.

The two Jefferson newspapers expressed delight at Baker's demise. Marshall's *Republican* and Galveston's *Flake's* also rejoiced. Other newspapers in the three-state region surely agreed.

Much controversy ensued as to who was due the reward money. Buell decided that Orr and Chamblee were entitled. Baker's corpse was delivered to Little Rock, probably for identification to qualify that state's reward. However Governor Powell's reward stipulated that it be paid to either civil or military authorities for capture; of course, Orr and Chamblee were neither. Following much bureaucratic wrangling, the military paid them. Texas was a larger problem. Much correspondence between prominent men and officials, including at least one affidavit, seemed to account for nothing. Texas records do not show that Orr received the reward.

John Chamblee gave power of attorney to Orr and moved to Georgia.

Orr deducted expenses from the Arkansas reward and distributed the remainder among his group, though they forfeited claims.

The Army rounded up Baker confederates through 1869-1870, including his lieutenant Frank Rollins. Gangs of cutthroats and the Ku Klux Klan were wiped from the area. Residents could once again enjoy peace in the pursuit of earning a living.

Exaggerations are part and parcel of legendary people. Though Baker probably murdered some whose deaths escaped wide-spread publicity, or who were merely dispatched into a river or remote gulch, never to be mentioned, it is unlikely that he killed nearly as many as were credited to him. Barry A. Crouch and Donald E. Brice, authors of *Cullen Montgomery Baker: Reconstruction Desperado*, concluded that "Fifteen largely innocent deaths constitute the provable Baker legacy."

Thomas Orr became a prominent citizen, surveying boundaries of Lafayette and Miller Counties and determining the site for Texarkana, of which he became the first mayor. He is credited for the opera house, the streetcar system, and enhancing the culture and civic aspects of the city. From 1880-1882, he was Miller County judge. Thanks to Cullen Baker's inefficiency with a rope and Lee Rames aiding his survival, Thomas Orr contributed a great deal to society. He was the absolute antithesis of Baker, the wholesale destroyer of all things good and proper.

Thomas Orr was born in Henry County, Georgia, February 10, 1844. He died July 10, 1904, and is buried in Texarkana, Arkansas. No one knows why he came to Arkansas and sought a teaching job.

Cullen Montgomery Baker is buried in Oakwood Cemetery, Jefferson, Texas, and society prays that he stays there.

Chapter 6
Gail Borden, Jr.'s Terraqueous Machine

Gail Borden was similar to Thomas Edison in that both were prolific inventors. Borden is readily associated with dairy products, but his accomplishments went far beyond processing food. Borden was born in Norwich, New York, in 1801. The family moved to Indiana when he was fifteen. When about 21 years of age, he was instrumental in rescuing a free black man from the grasp of those who held him as their property. He wandered to Mississippi. Despite having less than two years of formal education, he became a surveyor and school teacher. Later, he went to Texas and became surveyor for Austin's Colony. When friction developed with Mexico, Borden became a delegate at the Convention of 1833.

During the fall of 1835, Borden, Joe Baker and Thomas Borden–Gail's brother and predecessor as surveyor–published the *Telegraph and Texas Register* in San Felipe; naturally, the paper urged independence from Mexico. Mexican dictator Santa Anna moved against the rebels, causing the Runaway Scrape. The publishers fled with their press to Harrisburg in March, 1836. After operating briefly, the publishers again fled, this time without their press; the Mexicans tossed the offending equipment into the bayou.

Several months after Texas became a republic, Borden bought a press up north and began publishing in Columbia. Even later, in 1836, he helped to survey the site for the new city of Houston. During the spring of 1837, he moved the *Telegraph* and *Texas Register* to that bustling town on Buffalo Bayou–the same waters that had drowned his equipment a few miles east at Harrisburg. Even though a new settlement, Houston had a reputation as a sweltering, malarial and crime-infested place. The *Telegraph* had no shortage of bad news to report. But, of course, it had a social obligation to lure settlers to the rich soil, suitable for orchards and a moderate climate! The *Telegraph* published only a few months before Jacob Cruger bought Gail's share.

President Sam Houston appointed Borden collector for the port of Galveston. President Mirabeau Lamar fired him. Houston, elected again in 1841, returned Borden to the position; however, friction developed between Sam and Gail and Gail resigned. Borden vigorously supported the civic community. He promoted real estate for the Galveston City Company, and helped to run vice from the island. Gambling and prostitution would eventually return to the extent that major reform became an issue more than a century later. Borden and his spouse became devout Baptists, he serving in numerous capacities in the organization, including founding Baylor University.

Shortly after quitting as collector of the port, Borden experimented with methods to condense and preserve food. He and brother Tom had another idea far removed from diet: They built a wagon that was supposed to operate on land and water.

Upon treating friends to a late-night meal of his experimental food—of which he told his guests was composed of animal parts normally discarded—Gail announced another surprise. They choked down the food, followed their host to the livery and beheld the "secret" invention. The wagon of revelers was towed to the beach, the horses unhitched and the sail hoisted. Soon they were moving at an extraordinary clip. The women became hysterical; their clamor intensified in proportion to the speed until, just before they would have reached the lower end of Galveston Island, Gail lowered the sail and braked.

The second trip was in public and daytime–probably without women among the passengers. The machine operated so well that he decided to test its seaworthiness. To everyone's surprise, he steered into the Gulf. Pandemonium again ensued. Shrieks drowned the skipper's plea for order. As everyone swarmed to the side facing the shore, someone dropped the sail. The vehicle capsized, dumping all into the shallow water. Borden climbed atop the inverted wagon and continued to scold and explain. They hadn't known that the thing was unsinkable nor that wind power would make the wheels function as screws. Perhaps they didn't care. It isn't difficult to imagine that a tad of saltwater mixed with the ghastly meal resulted in an odorous flotsam.

Experiments with wind wagons continued for years, some with varying degrees of success freighting goods across the prairie from St. Louis to Westport (currently Kansas City). But overall they fell victim to treacherous currents and were abandoned. Had they been more successful, Gail Borden–who became our country's dairyman–might have delivered his products by terraqueous wagon.

He continued working with foods and in the latter 1850s received a patent for condensing milk. Previous years of failure to market a meat biscuit left him in poor financial condition. Soon after securing the patent for condensing milk, he built two plants in New England; both failed. With help from a new source, he established another factory. The advent of the Civil War brought success. Several more factories were built. With the war's end, he looked again to Texas. He built a plant for packing meat at Borden. At Bastrop, he manufactured copperware and built a sawmill.

Borden's philanthropic bent bloomed with his success. He invested much money and effort in educational and religious facilities. Both white and colored children and various charities benefitted from his generosity.

In 1828, he had married Penelope Mercer in Mississippi. Seven children were born to them. His second wife, Augusta Stearns, deserted when he lost most of his fortune experimenting with food. Emeline Church became his spouse in 1860, and enjoyed prosperity.

Gail died in his namesake, Borden, Texas, in 1874. His remains were transported by private railroad car to be interred in New York. Borden County, Texas, and its county seat, Gail, were named in his honor.

As with many pioneers who came to Texas during the nineteenth century, his life was filled with adventure, misadventure and eventual success.

7
Annie

John Whitmire donated land for a Baptist church and cemetery in 1856 and planned the town of Grandview, Texas. Soon, the settlement had several stores, a saloon, and a Masonic Lodge (1861), Johnson County's first. The town continued to grow. The railroad came through just down the hill in 1881; consequently, most businesses were located there within two years. As the settlement gravitated to the area of the railroad, the cemetery expanded to consume the original site.

The South labored under the constraints of Reconstruction. Life was hard for former Confederate states, especially Texas under the notorious Governor Edmund Davis. That economic situation complicates the legend of Annie.

Summer of 1867, a man and a woman came from the north and stopped at a general store in Grandview. The woman wore expensive riding clothes and mounted a fine horse. As they gathered supplies, they were overheard arguing. They continued to ride south.

The following day, the woman's body was found; she had been shot in her head. Her horse, money and jewelry were missing. The only clue to her identity was an embroidered handkerchief bearing the name "Annie." The community buried her and inscribed Annie on her gravestone. Soon after burial a spiral-like stone, unlike any in the area, was mysteriously placed on her grave. That stone disappeared long ago. Perhaps it rests in a backyard near the old town site, its significance unknown. Maybe it lies buried by nature in layers of earth.

The legend of Annie remains a mystery. The young people running Granny's Café say the story is a Halloween favorite, noted annually by the *Grandview Tribune*. One young lady was surprised to learn that the story is true.

Annie's affluence was surely noticed among the small and generally struggling population. There's no indication of her companion's economic status. Was he a mere cowboy she met on her journey? Her husband? Where was her home and where was she going? Obviously, she had a destination in mind and rode straight toward it. Given the lawlessness of the period, when Civil War deserters and bandits ravaged Texas, she was either strongly determined or naive. Annie would have been a tempting target for robbery that not even her companion could have deterred. Many would have killed her for her horse, alone. Obviously, her trail partner took everything but her first name.

8
Another Annie, "Diamond Bessie"

Annie Stone flaunted lots of stones–diamonds, courtesy of Abraham Rothschild. Abe was a traveling salesman for his father's jewel business in Cincinnati. Meyer Rothschild was related to the famed banking family of Europe. Abe's itinerary included bawdy houses, the residents of whom benefitted from his expense account.

He patronized Annie in a bordello–reportedly in Hot Springs, Arkansas--and was so enthralled by her skills that he took her along as his wife; beyond doubt, she was equally thrilled to flaunt his samples around her neck and on her fingers. Few gals afforded precious baubles from flat-backing. Annie's professional handle was "Bessie Moore," the surname being from her lover when she was in her early teens. As Abe's companion, she became known as Diamond Bessie.

Their business/ bliss tour took them to Texas and Marshall's Old Capital Hotel for a few days before boarding the train to the bustling port of Jefferson on Friday, January 19, 1877. They checked into the Brooks House under a fictitious name. Residents witnessed their frequent arguing.

On a mild Sunday, the couple, picnic basket in hand, walked into the woods and legend. Abe returned alone. When asked about his wife, he gave the lame story that she would meet him later. Two days later, he left alone by train, leaving his room bare of her apparel. Snow came immediately to Jefferson.

Two weeks after Rothschild left, snow melted revealing a woman's body–fashionably clad–in the woods just outside town. Her head bore a bullet wound and her jewelry was missing. Citizens collected money to bury her in Oakwood Cemetery. Investigation revealed that the couple had registered in the hotel in Marshall under Abe's real name and place of residence.

Abe, back in Cincinnati, ruined his right eye in a suicide attempt. He was arrested while recuperating. Rothschild money strenuously fought extradition, but eventually lost on March 19, exactly two months after Abe and Bessie stepped from the train in Jefferson. Perhaps the Rothschilds reasoned that their son should not have to answer for killing a mere prostitute; after all, that scarlet woman took advantage of their son.

Numerous attorneys rushed to participate in both the prosecution and defense. The defendant's money drew Jefferson attorneys Colonel

David B. Culberson and his son, Charles. David had a distinguished career in both Texas and national politics. Charles, recently admitted to the bar, would participate in politics at all levels, including becoming governor of Texas. Governor Richard Hubbard personally called upon two prominent lawyers to help the prosecution.

Legal maneuvering by all lawyers and their responsibilities toward their political offices, delayed the trial for more than a year. Following a lengthy, sensational trial, Rothschild was found guilty and sentenced to hang. On appeal, the trial was judged unfair.

While Rothschild was incarcerated, his jailer–William Fergusson and wife, Augusta, suffered the loss of their five-year-old son, John. Abe composed a poignant poem for them. The poem survives.

The second trial involved the testimony of one Isabelle Gouldy, who swore she saw the victim with a man other than Abe the day before her disappearance and several days afterward. Also, the defense argued that had Bessie been murdered on Sunday, her body would not have been so well preserved; never mind that the lengthy snowfall would have contributed to that. Nevertheless, in December, 1880–more than two years after the first trial--Rothschild was acquitted.

More than a decade later, a stranger placed flowers on Bessie's grave and left as mysteriously as he had come. Approximately 60 years after Bessie was interred, a headstone mysteriously marked her grave. Still years later, a local man confessed that he furnished the marker. The Jesse Allen Wise Garden Club eventually put a fence around Diamond Bessie's plot. The Garden club is the driving force behind Jefferson's historical restoration and preservation movement. The city has more than 30 historical designations.

During the nineteenth century, numerous Jewish families established small businesses in raw Texas. Jefferson's Jewish community built a synagogue; it is ironic that the building hosts the annual re-enactment of Jewish Abe Rothschild's trial–the "Diamond Bessie" murder play; the production is generously laced with music and hilarious comedy. Sometimes, actual judges and attorneys participate.

The circumstances of Annie Stone's fate generally parallels that of "Annie" at Grandview, Texas. Ten years separated the tragedies. Both women and their companions arrived as strangers. Grandview was a growing settlement on the new railroad. Jefferson was a bustling river port, sometimes hosting more than a dozen steamboats simultaneously at the wharf. Both couples were heard arguing. Both women were found shot in their heads just outside of town, and stripped of valuables. Both corpses were fashionably clothed. And both murders remain unsolved.

Chapter 9
Alabama-Coushatta

White men didn't bring civilization to the Alabama-Coushatta Indians. These closely-related natives of the Southeastern United States were an advanced society for centuries before Hernando De Soto met them in the sixteenth century. When he repaid their generosity by trying to enslave them, they responded as violently as did the Apache to the Spanish yoke. The explorer quickly decided to investigate other regions.

Coushatta means "cane." These tribes were mound builders and natural friends, commingling, but didn't commonly intermarry before the early 1900s. They are thought to have migrated from Yucatan by way of the Gulf of Mexico. Art objects found in their burial mounds are similar to those of Mayans. They believed in one God, and lived chiefly by means of agriculture and hunting. Paintings of animals were thought to attract animals. Bears and deer were plentiful; skins and bear oil sold in the ancient village that became Nacogdoches.

Corn, the chief crop, was celebrated with a festival. "Sofkee" was a drink made from corn. They put grains of corn in a hollowed stump and whomped it with the butt of a wooden club until it was finely-ground, then they cooked it in water that had been filtered through ashes. Hernando De Soto might have sampled sofkee, but probably didn't hang around long enough to cultivate a taste for it. Necklaces were made from seeds, dyes from roots and berries in the fall, roots being more permanent.

Settlers nudged the tribes westward. Being peaceful, they moved with little protest, many settling along the Trinity and Sabine Rivers. Spanish missionaries influenced them to forsake some customs. Eventually, they decided to revive and preserve old traditions, and brought in other natives to teach religious dancing. But tribal medicine men didn't vanish with the buffalo and the advent of Christianity. Some patients swear that the practitioners of old-time methods are sometimes more effective than those who wear white frocks and tote stethoscopes.

Their society greatly differed from that of the plains Indians. The world of the Alabama-Coushatta pretty much belonged to women. The wife was absolute boss in her house. ("So,"say some men,"that's not unique.") Family lineage was established through females. A divorced man went to live with a female relative, usually the closest kin; but he wasn't allowed to loll in the shade and sip sofkee instead of working. He hied himself off to the annual buffalo hunt with Caddo brothers or tilled the cornfield with a buffalo bone hoe. Perhaps that is where the term "bone tired" originated.

Finally, following abuse, neglect and government bureaucracy, the remnants of the tribe got their own reservation near Livingston, Texas. Even so, they were in poor circumstances. They were simply a poor, ignorant bunch eking out an existence. Buffalo bones had long been displaced by iron hoes; but a hoe is a hoe and blisters are blisters, and nobody ever won prosperity through blistered hands and tired backs. Leaders put their minds together and, with a government grant, began building their future. Tourism was big business in many parts of Texas, why not on the Alabama-Coushatta reservation? Arts and crafts were rescued from antiquity and marketed. Chief John Paul Battiste was instrumental in the movement.

Reservation improvements include recreation areas, tourist cabins, and a community center. Indian dances are demonstrated for visitors and at fairs and other events. Tourism has enabled them to upgrade their society tremendously. Education is stressed and accepted. Many professionals sprang from this once desolate tribe. Education's ripple effect filters down to boost everyone's welfare. The work ethic remains strong, and sofkee is preferred to white men's version of corn squeezings

10
Famous Oaks of Texas

I t seems that almost all "hanging trees" were oaks, the majority being "live" oaks. Remember Tom Dooley who was hanged from a live oak tree in Tennessee? Perhaps live oaks that were used for executions should be renamed "die" oaks. Or group them with "whipping" and "dueling" oaks and classify the lot as genus maximus miserous oakus. Texas has a number of famous and infamous oaks, some of which are marked with plaques.

Clarksville's "Page Oak" (post oak) permanently suspended the operations of numerous outlaws. The first rope was invoked in 1837. A fellow named Page, his son, son-in-law, and a hired hand were hanged for two murders.

The "Hangman's Oak" near Bandera might have produced the largest crop of human fruit on a single occasion. During the summer of 1863, eight men were traveling to Mexico to avoid Confederate conscription; soldiers from Camp Verde intercepted and hanged them. A boy with them was spared.

On September 12, 1879, The Hallettsville "Hanging Tree" served justice for a murder resulting from drunkenness.

Two teenagers were illegally hanged on legal grounds–lynched in the Shelby County Courthouse Square. The "Center Hanging Oak" (southern red oak) claimed one youth in 1920, the other in 1928.

Many hanging trees still shelter the graves of those whose lives they took. A huge, southern red oak marks the only remaining ancient Indian burial mound in Nacogdoches, Texas.

A live oak presided over John King Fisher's resting place for three-quarters of a century. Fisher–a former outlaw–was a family man, deputy marshal and tax collector of Uvalde when he was unfortunately ambushed alongside former Austin Marshal Ben Thompson in San Antonio's Vaudeville Theater, gambling hall and saloon in1884. Fisher's remains were among those removed to accommodate a new street in Uvalde. Workmen saw–through the glass section of the coffin lid–that Fisher's body and clothing were well-preserved after 75 years.

The "Suicide" tree in New Orleans probably never hosted a rope; those who perished beneath its branches chose poison.

All notable oak trees, however, are not tainted with the macabre. Live oak branches have witnessed the freeing of slaves, establishment of governments and legal courts that tossed "Judge Lynch" out of the shade.

Live oaks were often landmarks for Indians and pioneers. The "Treaty Oak" in Austin supposedly witnessed the signing of an agreement with Indians and hosted numerous other historical events. A mad man driven by a phantom voice poisoned the famous tree. Heroic efforts and much expense were applied to save it from total destruction.

And there is the "Kissing Oak" in San Marcos.

Those unfortunate in marriage might argue that "The Matrimonial Oak" at San Saba be classified in the aforementioned genus maximus miserous oakus.

In a sense, live oaks were midwives to the West. Maybe, upon reflection, "live" oak is the most appropriate designation.

11
Cynthia Ann and Quanah Parker

Cynthia Ann Parker's story of captivity by Comanches at age nine and her acculturation and marriage to Chief Peta Nocona is one of the most prominent legends of Texas frontier history. That story and the life of her son, Quanah, are probably second only in prominence to the saga of the siege of the Alamo. To put the story in perspective, let's return to the 1770s in Culpeper County, Virginia.

John Parker and Sally White were married in Virginia, and produced six sons: Benjamin, Silas, Daniel, Isaac, John and James. The Parkers were strict Baptists and clannish. "Elder John" got itchy-feet–which was often–and the Parker tribe loaded beds, spinning wheels and plows and teamed to northeast Georgia. They bought slaves and raised cotton. Shortly after 1800, they settled in southern Tennessee. A dozen years later, after the War of 1812, they migrated to Clark County, Illinois; Cynthia Ann was born there to Silas and Lucy Parker in 1827; during this period fever attacked all the Parker grandchildren, three of Isaac Parker's children died and young John was killed fighting Indians in southeastern Missouri. All this prompted Elder John to move on. He heard of free land in Texas; a married man could claim a great many acres.

Daniel wished to found a Baptist church in Texas, but learned that only the Catholic faith was allowed; nevertheless, the Parkers determined to be a congregation unto themselves and practice their faith there. With that issue settled, they aimed oxen and more than twenty wagons toward the Sabine River in 1832. Cynthia Ann was five years of age. Miscalculation put them in Logansport, Louisiana, from which they crossed the Sabine River into Texas. Indian trails and primitive passages finally led them to Stephen F. Austin's colony between the Colorado and Brazos Rivers. They occupied Grimes' Prairie for about 18 months.

Summer, 1833, Silas and others staked land in present day Limestone County. Some chose to build along the Spanish Trail that led from Nacogdoches to San Antonio. Others settled in present day Elkhart. Silas and others replenished supplies at Fort Houston, then crossed the Trinity River and forty-five miles of wilderness to the Navasoto's headwaters to establish Fort Parker.

Fort Parker was well-built. The gates were of heavy slabs of wood fastened together with wooden pegs. Strict discipline and rules assured safety.

December, 1835, Cynthia Ann and thirty-three other of her family lived in Fort Parker. Cynthia was now eight years of age. Indian trouble was so intense that the families lacked confidence in their formidable fortress. Also, trouble brewed between settlers and Mexico. Texans were demanding certain rights from Santa Anna, dictator of Mexico, who had abrogated the democratic constitution of 1824. The Parkers loaded up and headed for Louisiana; however, the Sabine was at high flood and they couldn't cross. Rumor reached them that Santa Anna had been defeated. Feeling secure, they returned to their fort and left the gate open. Perhaps they figured that men organized to fight Mexico were now available to keep savages at bay.

Of course, they quickly learned that Texas was not free of Mexico's rule–and certainly not safe from savage depredations. The "Consultation of 1835" granted Daniel Parker authority to form a company of Rangers; he now did that with Silas as captain. The "Consultation" was comprised of numerous prominent men, including delegates Sam Houston and Robert Potter. They met to work on future issues dealing with Mexico and to prepare for revolution. They were probably happy to have the Parkers deal with Indians, for Texans had enough pressure from Mexicans.

As though the vicious Comanches didn't demand full attention, Silas and his rangers dealt severely with all natives, killing some peaceful ones. White horse thieves plundered peaceful Caddos, prodding them onto the warpath.

Caddos were a confederation of agrarian tribes who had lived in East Texas, Northwestern Louisiana, Southeastern Oklahoma and Southwestern Arkansas for centuries. They were permanent planters, going west annually to hunt buffalo. Spanish explorers were warmly greeted as "Tejas"–friends.

Violence was pretty well limited to defense against marauding Osages from what is now Oklahoma. Eventually, settlers from the east forced the Caddos into north Texas; there, they learned warring ways from the indigenous Comanche and Kiowa tribes.

The horde who approached Fort Parker in the morning of May 19, 1836, was comprised of those three tribes. Some men were at work in the fields. The fort gate was open. Benjamin went out and talked with the Indians. They displayed a white flag and asked about a place to water their horses. Benjamin was suspicious, for their horses were wet from crossing the Navasoto River. The ruse was so obvious as to be ridiculous, for natives had known every place of water for centuries before white men arrived.

Nevertheless, against advice from his kinsmen, Ben took provisions to them, only to be slaughtered. Then the others–five men, ten women and fifteen children were attacked. Elder John, his wife, Sally, and

Elizabeth Kellogg were caught less than a mile distant. A tomahawk killed Elder John. Sally was forced to watch as he was scalped. Sally and Elizabeth were made to mount horses behind warriors. Sally deliberately fell. A warrior lanced her until he thought her dead. She dragged herself to a cabin. Some escaped into the woods and brush.

Lucy was forced to put Cynthia and Cynthia's younger brother, John, astride horses behind the killers. Warriors then attempted to kill Lucy and others, but two of the men with rifles kept them away. The following day, the badly wounded and wretched Sally were found. That day, eighteen survivors, including children from infant to twelve years, barefoot and virtually naked, started the trek toward Fort Houston, one hundred and fifty miles away.

Torn by vines and thorns and having eaten only several skunks and terrapins in days, they were too weak to continue. Somehow James Parker, who had given his share of the awful meat to others, forged ahead. It took only eight hours to walk thirty miles to the fort. He arrived on May 24, having not eaten for six days. Soldiers rescued the others the following day.

The next day, Luther Plummer arrived, believing there were no survivors.

L. D. Nixon and his bunch stumbled in the next day.

Nixon said five were captured and at least five killed. Captives were Elizabeth Kellogg; James's daughter and grandson, Rachel Plummer and her son, James Pratt Plummer; Cynthia Parker and younger brother, John. Sally died soon after reaching Fort Houston. James and others took her body to Fort Parker and buried her and the bodies sprawled about.

The captives were tied and beaten as warriors celebrated their great victory. Even James Pratt, only eighteen months of age, was beaten. For five days they had not been fed and were given little water. Elizabeth was sold to another tribe for about one hundred and fifty dollars. Within months, she was ransomed to General Sam Houston for the same amount. In August, 1836, James Parker met Elizabeth in Nacogdoches. She could offer no information about the other prisoners. She and James left for his new location about fifty miles from Fort Houston. On the road, they met a fellow who had just wounded and captured one of two Indians trying to steal his horses.

The shot had grazed the savage's head. Scars on his arms helped Elizabeth identify him as the one who had taken her and killed Elder John.

Of course, James killed the savage who had murdered and scalped his father. James followed rumors of white captives, riding many miles to distant trading posts and Indian campsites.

Rachel was taken to snowy mountains in late summer of 1836. She was worked hard, caring for horses, tanning hides and other work customarily done by Indian women; however, she suffered horribly because of little clothing. Rachel's overseer, an elderly squaw, often beat her. Finally, Rachel turned on her, thoroughly thrashing her with her own club. Instead of punishing her, the men showed respect for her courage.

In 1837, bands gathered at the headwaters of the Arkansas River and planned to drive settlers from Texas, then conquer Mexico! A warrior cursed Rachel in English–the only words she had heard in her language– and told her all white people would become servants. The all-out war was to begin within a year or two.

Early 1838, Sante Fe trader Bill Donoho ransomed Rachel from the frigid camp in the mountains and took her to Sante Fe–a trip of more than two weeks. After Rachel gained strength, Donoho and family took her to St. Louis. Her brother-in-law, L. D. Nixon, took her to Montgomery County, Texas, arriving in February, 1838. She was reunited there with her husband, Luther Plummer. Unfortunately, captives enslaved under brutal conditions often did not survive for long after returning to their own people; such was Rachel Plummer's fate; she died one year after being recovered, never learning the fate of son, James Pratt.

This was a particularly volatile period in Texas; President Mirabeau Lamar determined to clear the Republic of Texas of Indians; in this, he had many allies, including former Secretary of the Texas Navy, Robert Potter.

Former President Sam Houston, having lived among Cherokees in Tennessee–and having been married to one or two--tended to be favorable toward natives; this attitude increased friction that had existed between him and Potter ever since competing as candidates for the Consultation of 1835. Indians tried to pass word to the Texas government that they wished to talk peace, but were told that Texans intended to exterminate them. Perhaps traders were merely passing along President Lamar's intention or perhaps they told that in order to continue profiting from trade with them. Regardless, the situation made it more difficult for James Parker to get information about captives.

James Pratt Plummer, after six years with various tribes, was ransomed by the army and taken to Fort Gibson, Indian Territory, in 1842. He wasn't quite eight years of age. James Parker went to get him and found that his nephew, John, was also there. John was twelve. James Pratt went to his Grandfather James Parker's home in Anderson County, Texas. He lived in Anderson and Houston Counties until his death during the late 1800s.

A letter dated Dec. 10, 1842, from Sam Houston to Secretary of the Treasury, William Henry Daingerfield, cites authorization of ransom for captives, including John Parker. There was no mention of Cynthia. James continued searching for her and others. He went so far as southwestern Missouri in 1844 to see whether a released white woman might be Cynthia.

Romantic myth has John Parker growing into a prominent warrior. He was abandoned upon contracting smallpox. Juanita, a Mexican captive, elected to stay with him. He recovered, they married, he served in the Confederacy, and he and Juanita lived in Mexico. Quanah Parker, his nephew, is said to have visited him after the former accepted the white man's ways. Sam Houston's letter to Daingerfield and one written by James Parker (1844) to Mirabeau Lamar prove the tale to be false. James assured Lamar that of the five captives from Fort Parker, only Cynthia remained away.

On rare occasions when traders or soldiers saw Cynthia, they offered huge ransoms of horses, goods and money. Indian agent Robert Neighbors saw Cynthia with a band on Red River, but his ransom offer was refused. Indians always refused to consider offers for her. Further, Cynthia demonstrated that she didn't wish to leave. For all practical purposes, Cynthia Ann Parker was a Comanche.

Early in 1840, several Comanche chiefs met with Texas Ranger Colonel Henry Karnes in San Antonio to discuss peace. Karnes told them that such a treaty hinged upon all captives being released. Two months later, sixty-five Comanches came to the council house, bringing Matilda Lockhart and several Mexicans. Lt. Colonel William Fisher ordered the group seized pending release of other captives. One Indian lunged to escape, triggering a fusillade that killed thirty-five natives, including three women and two children. Twenty-seven were held prisoners. The incident gained notoriety as the "Council House Massacre." Consequently, Indian raids increased along the frontier, and thirteen captives were slaughtered.

In 1841, Sam Houston, again President of the Republic of Texas, affected limited communications with the natives culminating in a shaky peace. The natives simply did not trust Houston or any other Texan. Houston's position was a politician's nightmare—trying to get along with Indians while under pressure from those who agreed with Lamar that the republic should be rid of them!

During the 1840s, Cynthia married Chief Peta Nocona, who had led the attack on Fort Parker. Their first born was Quanah, then came Pecos and daughter, Topsanna (Prairie Flower). Historians disagree as to whether Pecos existed. Subsequent mention is based upon legend.

During the latter 1840s, cholera and smallpox–scourges brought by white people–decimated tribes to the extent that they again sought peace.

A small percentage–young warriors–persisted in keeping the frontier flaming; that situation killed any concessions from the state and federal governments.

John Baylor, former Indian agent, fired for incompetence, stirred trouble between natives and whites. He falsely charged that peaceful tribes were raiding. In 1858 Choctaw Tom and his small, harmless group were hunting on the Brazos when attacked by more than 20 men. Seven men and women lost their lives, and several others were badly wounded. The murderers boasted that they had the support of settlers. Famous Ranger Captain John Salmon "Rip" Ford didn't dare attempt to arrest them. Agent Robert Neighbors, who sincerely worked for the Indians' welfare, finally convinced the commissioner to order reservation natives moved to Indian Territory; this was accomplished during the summer of 1859. But those who never went to reservations, continued depredations throughout the upper Brazos valley and surrounding counties.

Peta Nocona and his band continued ferocious attacks; they burned, raped, murdered, and stole. Late in 1860, they swept into Lost Valley, northwest of Weatherford, Texas. They killed John Brown, scalped him and cut off his nose. Took his horses and rode to Ezra Sherman's place on Rock Creek. Finding pregnant Martha Sherman alone with two small children, they fastened her to the ground and repeatedly raped her. They fired three arrows into her and lifted her scalp. Miraculously, she lived for two days and detailed the crime. This incident spread the length of the frontier. Inflamed settlers screamed for revenge.

Even Sam Houston–friend of red men, twice president of the Republic of Texas, and now governor–was compelled to act. He sent Colonel Middleton Johnson and his rangers to quell Chief Nocona; they failed. Ranger Captain Lawrence Sullivan Ross replaced his inept predecessor. Ross drew scores of volunteers and borrowed more than twenty cavalrymen from Camp Cooper.

After tracking the raiders for days, the tracks disappeared into those of a buffalo herd–a common trick to lose pursuers. Young Charles Goodnight, future cattle baron, scouted until he cut sign* *(found tracks)* on the far side of the herd's path. The plunderers stole the books from the Sherman home to stuff into their shields for reinforcement. Charles found the family Bible on the ground. Shortly, he found Peta Nocona's camp on the south bank of the Pease River. The date was December 18, 1860. There were fewer than twenty women in camp, and fewer men.

Captain Ross reported to Governor Houston that most Indians were killed within minutes, while others managed to mount and ride for a mile or two before being overtaken and shot. Lt. Tom Kelliher chased the horse down and found its rider was a woman with a baby. He brought them back to the camp. Meanwhile, Ross had shot dead one of two on a horse, the dead one pulling the other off. The corpse was that of a young girl. The warrior hurled a lance at Ross, but missed. Ross shot him in the arm. Ross's servant and translator, Antonio Martinez, told Ross the wounded one identified himself as Chief Nocona. Martinez said Nocona had killed his family and taken him captive, so Ross gave him permission to dispatch the savage. He immediately did so.

Charles Goodnight revealed the Indian wasn't Chief Peta Nocona, but "No-bah," head of the hunting party; such functionaries were commonly called chief. Lt. Kelliher's captive woman had Anglo eyes. She was the long-sought Cynthia Ann Parker, captured 25 years previously at nine years of age. Her daughter was Topsannah, "Prairie Flower."

Captain Sul Ross reported that twelve Comanches were killed and three survived. H. B. Rogers, who wasn't proud of participating in the raid, said sixteen squaws and one or two bucks died.

Many varied accounts of the event abound in countless books and articles. It was reported that there were five hundred or six hundred Indians in the camp. Some authors believe that Chief Nocona and all his band were killed, when in fact, except for the one or two previously noted, they were away from camp. Some say that Quanah was captured along with his mother. Others disagree about Quanah's age. In an interview with Curtis Davis–Quanah's great grandson–in Olustee, Oklahoma, July 7, 2001--this author learned that Quanah was born in 1845, which established his age at fifteen at the time of his mother's capture. Eventually, Cynthia told an unnamed translator that thirty-five men had left camp before the massacre. Chief Nocona, sons Quanah and Pecos, age fifteen and twelve, respectively, were among them. Laura Birdsong, Cynthia's granddaughter, said that Peta returned to camp and gathered the survivors, including Quanah and Pecos. Actually, Cynthia and Topsanna were the only survivors. Laura said the servant that Martinez killed was Joe Nocona, and that Peta died years later of blood poisoning.

Peta Nocona had occasion to meet translator Horace Jones in Indian Territory, in 1862, and asked what happened to Cynthia. Jones filled the void of information that had plagued Peta ever since his wife disappeared. Peta told Jones that Quanah and Pecos were far away. Soon after this meeting, Pecos perished from smallpox.

Captain Lawrence "Sul" Ross made much capital of recapturing Cynthia and returning her to her white family. He fudged the truth here and there and his popularity got him elected governor. Sul's report glorified the massacre as a great victory, every man having fought with valor. He neglected to mention that virtually all of the dead were women. Captain Curetan's volunteer's were bitter that Ross attacked without them, falsely saying that their mounts were weak from lack of grass and unfit for battle.

When Ranger Colonel Isaac Parker arrived at Camp Cooper to get his niece, Ross claimed to have furnished his interpreter, Antonio Martinez. Charles Goodnight said Ross asked former captive Ben Kiggins to interpret. Further, Goodnight said that camp officials sent for Colonel Parker, not Ross as he claimed.

* * *

John R. Erickson, cowboy, rancher and author of the immensely popular *Hank the Cowdog* books is the great, great grandson of the aforementioned victim—Martha Sherman. John wished to find his ancestor's grave.

John learned of Weatherford businessman, Fred Cotton, Parker County's unofficial historian. Summer of 1969, John visited Cotton in his store. Martha Sherman had requested to be buried near a church in Willow Springs Cemetery. Cotton had found the barren grave and paid to have a marble marker erected. The state proposed to lay Highway 180 directly through the cemetery, because circumventing it would be too expensive. Fred Cotton gave state officials to understand that they had better forget that notion, for he would spend the last cent of his considerable assets to keep them in court long past their endurance. They wisely accepted his vow. The highway runs directly past the cemetery.

* * *

The Civil War drained manpower from the frontier, emboldening savages to raid with renewed vigor. Some settlers became as savage as their enemies, indiscriminately slaughtering the natives.

A dubious version of the interview with Cynthia at Camp Cooper appeared in a Galveston newspaper, in which Cynthia is quoted as saying her brother John died of smallpox. As mentioned earlier, Sam Houston ransomed him during the early 1840s.

Several weeks after being taken, Cynthia went with her uncle to his home near Birdville, county seat of Tarrant County, on condition that if her sons were captured, they would be brought to her. On their journey, they stopped at the studio of A. F. Corning in Fort Worth. Corning made the now famous picture of Cynthia with short hair and Topsanna at her breast. The short hair signified mourning. Birdville became the site of Haltom City.

Cynthia could not adjust to her new life, and tried many times to run away. During the spring of 1861, Cynthia's kin and neighbors dressed her appropriately and took her to the succession convention in Austin. She feared the legislators were chiefs deliberating her fate, and tried to flee. While in town, she again sat for a photographer.

In April, 1861, legislators voted to give Cynthia one hundred dollars per year and a league of land. Isaac and Benjamin Parker were designated temporary holders of the title. In another attempt to pacify Cynthia, she went to live with her brother, Silas, Jr. and his wife, Mary, near Tyler. Early in 1862, the legislature appointed Silas as her guardian. The family promised that she could visit the Comanche and look for Quanah and Pecos, but the war intruded. Mary was uncomfortable with Cynthia and Topsannah in her home. Cynthia, still depressed from the moment of her capture, moved in with sister Orlena and husband, Ruff O'Quinn.

Topsannah got feverish, which progressed into pneumonia; she died on December 15, 1863. She was buried in Asbury Cemetery eight miles south of Ben Wheeler. Cynthia, heart-broken beyond measure, moved into the O'Quinn's sawmill near the Henderson-Anderson County line. Having no knowledge of her husband and sons for ten years, and her daughter dead, Cynthia had no will to live. She neglected her health and mourned until expiring of influenza in 1870. She was buried four miles south of Poyner in Foster Cemetery, near the Henderson-Anderson County line.

Cynthia Ann Parker's life was torn, patched, and torn again. She surely witnessed fellow captives, brother John; and Rachel Plummer and her infant, James Pratt; and Elizabeth Kellogg beaten and otherwise abused. Perhaps she herself was abused. However, she fully acculturated into the Comanche life, marrying and giving birth to three children. Then, in one way or another, she was stripped of her family. Nor did joining her original family heal the pain. Her life came in three parts, each with its degree of pain. It is not unthinkable that her last wheezing breath was welcome.

* * *

Chief Peta Nocona died of blood poisoning during the 1870s, having never again seen Cynthia. Quanah attached himself to the fierce Quahadi Comanche tribe, and soon became a chief. They declined to attend the Medicine Lodge Treaty in 1867. The very thought of life on a reservation was anathema to these wild and free natives. Quanah led his people on hunts and raids for years. The frontier was aflame. Efforts to stop depredations proved futile. The young and brilliant Colonel Ranald McKenzie was selected to either capture or eliminate Quanah's band.

McKenzie drilled his troops to be as much like Comanches as possible. They were driven to exertion, surviving on meager rations and little water. One could imagine them as current special forces on horseback.

After weeks of training, the unit proudly and boldly rode into the Comanche domain. In October, 1871, McKenzie's scouts spotted Quanah's camp in Blanco Canyon. The colonel, much pleased at the thought of victory, settled his camp to rest for attack come morning. About midnight, the Indians rode through the camp, whipping blankets and stampeding the cavalry mounts.

McKenzie's elite cavalry had been reduced to ordinary infantry with no enemy in sight.

In spring of 1872, McKenzie's soldiers killed more than twenty warriors and captured one-hundred and twenty-four. Nine months later, the captives were released as a token of peace–a fatal gesture.

McKenzie, now a general, surprised a Comanche camp in Palo Duro Canyon in the fall of 1874. He massacred everyone, burned lodges and food, and killed horses numbering about 1,500. This raid devastated the Indians. The Comanche were famed for their natural equestrian skills. From the very beginning, since Spaniards introduced horses to the New World, the Comanche mastered the beasts as probably no Cossack ever did. But with 1,500 horses dead, they found themselves in worse shape than Quanah left McKenzie's cavalry three years earlier. Aggravating their situation was the wholesale slaughter of buffalo.

Buffalo hunters kept on stabbing into the Staked Plains; their powerful rifles decimated herds–animals that were the staff of life for Indians.

A group of hunters were so brazen as to set up shop at Adobe Walls in the Texas Panhandle, not far from the Canadian River. Formerly Bill Bent's trading post–established in 1843 and abandoned the next year–the several buildings hosted two stores, a saloon, twenty-eight men and one woman. A young and ambitious medicine man had a vision that Quanah and company would be impervious to bullets while destroying the hunters at Adobe Walls. Only white eyes would die. The medicine man's name should have evoked doubt, or at least an investigation as to whether there's anything in a name: Isa-tai is the equivalent of "coyote droppings." Nevertheless, Quanah accepted the novice's wisdom and persuaded hundreds from various tribes to join his band for sure and safe victory at Adobe Walls. Perhaps Quanah was emboldened by Kit Carson's defeat at Adobe Walls in November, 1864. Carson's punitive expedition was routed by superior numbers of the enemy.

Very early on June 27, 1874, a ridge pole cracked, awakening hunters. By the time they shored up the roof, it was too near dawn to return to sleep; therefore, they were not surprised as Quanah planned.

Billy Dixon was tending his horse when he saw the line of warriors coming. He dashed inside and warned his comrades, one of whom was youthful Bat Masterson.

Two brothers and their dog were sleeping in a wagon. Quanah killed them and scalped all three. But something was wrong: Indian bodies didn't deflect bullets! The hunters, armed with powerful, long-range rifles expertly unsaddled attackers; nevertheless, raiders were soon battering doors and chopping through roofs. At such close quarters, only pistols and light rifles were practical. The raiders withdrew to reconsider. Four Anglos had died—the brothers in the wagon, Billy Tyler and Bill Olds. Olds, the cook, died when his wife accidentally shot him through his head while handing him a reloaded rifle. Fifteen savage corpses lay near the walls.

The following day, a committee of more than a dozen Indians gathered on a knoll almost a mile from the fort to look over the terrain and assess their prospects; after Billy Dixon shot one off his horse, they decided prospects weren't favorable and went home. About two weeks afterward, General Nelson Miles' surveyors established the distance at 1,538 yards–nine-tenths of a mile! Though Dixon shrugged it off as a lucky shot, the feat was famed across the frontier.

Only three months after the battle, Dixon, another scout and two soldiers hunkered in a buffalo wallow and fought off a band of Indians all day. Cold rain during the night convinced the savages to withdraw. One soldier was killed and the others wounded. All four were awarded the Medal of Honor, but Dixon and the other scout were civilians and had to return theirs. History records the event as the Battle of Buffalo Wallow.

Dixon died in the spring of 1913, and was buried at Texline. On June 27, 1929, exactly fifty-five years after the Battle of Adobe Walls, he was buried at that site.

In the spring of 1875, Quanah accepted reality. With the buffalo gone, there were no hides for tipis and clothing, no meat to eat; they would freeze and starve; besides, McKenzie ordered that all Comanche who didn't enter the reservation be killed. The Quahadi, the last free band, had no choice but to accept white men's terms. Several weeks later, Quanah led four hundred men, women and children and more than thirteen hundred horses into Fort Sill.

Curtis Davis stated in the interview July 7, 2001, that his great grandfather promptly changed from a hater of white people to an adherent of their ways and did so with zeal. He prompted his people to embrace white culture, to build themselves wooden houses, plant crops and raise cattle. He promoted the building of schools on the reservation, and negotiated grazing fees from prominent ranchers. Quanah, however, continued to fight for their rights; nevertheless, they didn't get all of the land promised. He traveled several times to Washington, D. C. in behalf of his people. He and President Theodore Roosevelt became good friends. The president came to Oklahoma to be treated to a wolf hunt by Quanah.

Immediately upon entering Fort Sill, Quanah inquired about his mother. He hadn't seen her since Captain Ross caught her fifteen years before. McKenzie, now friends with Quanah, wrote a letter for the chief; the letter passed through the hands of several people, finally resulting in information in a Dallas newspaper; in this roundabout way, Quanah learned that Cynthia had died five years previously.

Quanah asked McKenzie to write to Isaac Parker and ask whether he would be welcomed in the homes of his mother's people. No member of the family responded.

The federal government chose Quanah to be chief of all the Comanche. Though this was without precedent or legal authority, the Indians wisely accepted him. He prevented efforts of some to repudiate the white man's ways, but some old traditions remained with his blessing. He became a tribal judge and supported the organizing of the Comanche police force. Wealth came his way from grazing fees and investing in the Quanah, Acme and Pacific Railway. Ranchers Burke Burnett and Charles Goodnight were numbered among his many friends. Quanah built a comfortable home and painted several huge white stars on the roof. The "Star House" is at Cache, Oklahoma. It's interesting to wonder whether he learned that Goodnight cut the trail that led to the Pease River massacre and his mother's capture.

The white man's hunger for land resulted in reservations being opened for settlement. Quanah's ranch, however, remained intact and profitable. His people named him deputy sheriff of Lawton in 1902.

Years after arriving at the reservation, Quanah yearned for a picture of his mother. He placed ads in newspapers. A. F. Corning, who had made the famous photo of her and suckling Topsanna more than twenty years before, sent him a copy. Indian agent P. Hunt wrote to Cynthia's relatives requesting information. Quanah learned, by 1880, of the Texas Legislature's grant of land and pension to her in 1861. Agent Hunt's efforts to locate those grants were unsuccessful.

Quanah asked Texas Gov. Thomas Campbell to help him receive the largess voted for his mother. He strove to learn more about Cynthia: Where was she buried? His son-in-law, Aubrey Birdsong, found her grave south of Poyner in Nov., 1910. With 800 dollars authorized by Congress, Quanah had her remains moved to Post Oak Mission cemetery, which was a few miles from his home in Cache, Oklahoma.

Efforts to locate his mother's land and pension had availed nothing.

A few weeks after the funeral, Quanah asked his friend, Charles Goodnight, to contact his legislator for assistance in the hunt.

Pneumonia claimed the great old chief in February, 1911. He was laid beside his mother. Neither land nor pension was ever found.

The army artillery school needed the Post Oak Mission cemetery for a proving ground. Seven hundred Comanche remains were removed to Fort Sill. Out of respect for Quanah's prominence, he and his mother were buried on Aug. 9, 1957, with military honors. Topsannah's remains were brought to Fort Sill in 1965. The trio, long separated by fate and years, were once again together. Father and husband, Chief Peta Nocona, lay somewhere far away, probably beneath prairie grass or brush.

Quanah's incredible history is one of rising from a primitive, greasy culture to civilization, wealth, and prominence among dignitaries, including the president of the United States and positions of honor among his fellow tribesmen.

Conclusion

A fluke of circumstance resulted in my getting an interview with Curtis Davis. I routinely get my haircut before leaving for a trip, even a short one; however, I failed to do so before attending a family reunion in July, 2001, in Altus, Oklahoma. Donald Cheek, my brother-in-law, works at the Ford dealership. He called Curtis, his barber of 25 years. Curtis said for me to come on over. Curtis's shop is titled "The Razor's Edge." Curtis and wife Kathy have three sons and a daughter. Two sons and the daughter are barbers, all in Altus. Only one son works with Curtis.

After a bit of friendly jawing while getting my hair cut, wife Kathy came in and we had a brief but pleasant visit. Only after returning to the Ford dealer down the alley, did Donald tell me that Curtis is the great grandson of Quanah Parker! Of course, I absolutely, positively had to talk with Curtis at length–well, as long as he would tolerate me! Don arranged for an interview for the next morning, a Saturday. Don drove me to the Davis home in Olustee. Curtis showed me books and pictures of his ancestor with President Theodore Roosevelt and the wolf hunt, and others—including Quanah's wives and children. We made several photos and bid him farewell.

Though lifting hair remains a family tradition, they leave the scalp. Thanks for that, and a fine job, Curtis; it was as satisfactory as I got in Millford's in Nacogdoches and Harvey's in San Antonio; it also passed muster at the reunion.

12
Yellowstone Streaker: John Colter's run for life

Collegiate streakers would envy mountain man John Colter's speed; his sprint across campus would be but a blur. But Colter had incentive that no student can imagine: hundreds of savages determined to lift his hair! And hair was his only covering during his flight. Strangely, Colter's miraculous escape proved invaluable to the United States. President Thomas Jefferson determined to acquire the land west of the Mississippi, known as Upper Louisiana. He dispatched James Monroe to Paris to join America's minister to France, Robert Livingston, in offering to buy that territory. To their surprise–and Jefferson's–Napoleon agreed to sell. For $15,000,000, America could gain more than 800,000 square miles.

Jefferson had secretly persuaded Congress to budget $2,500 for an exploratory expedition even before the purchase. Jefferson envisioned an overland route to the Pacific Ocean. The purchase was completed in 1803. The president chose Meriwether Lewis to lead the expedition.

Lewis and Jefferson were friends and neighbors in Virginia. Upon his election as president in 1801, Jefferson appointed the 27-year old Lewis as his private secretary. Lewis lived in the White House and served ably in numerous matters of state. Lewis requested that his friend, William Clark, be co-leader of the expedition. Captains Lewis and Clark would prove to be an ideal team.

Clark was also a Virginian. His older brother, George Rogers Clark, had been an officer of militia fighting Indians. His service in the American Revolution earned him the reputation as the Revolution's hero, second only to George Washington.

On October 15, 1803, Captain Clark recruited 29-year-old John Colter of Maysville, Kentucky. That city would, 125 years later, produce another destined to become famous–singer/actress Rosemary Clooney.

Eight more Kentucky men joined Colter. The Corps of Discovery– also known as the Lewis and Clark Expedition--consisted of 43 men assembled at Camp Dubois near the junction of the Missouri and Mississippi Rivers. The plan was for 12 men to return at a certain point. In February, 1804, while Captain Lewis was in St. Louis attending the ceremony transferring Upper Louisiana to the United States, Colter and three companions disobeyed orders and imbibed at a nearby tavern. Lewis restricted them to the camp for ten days. On May 14, 1804, the expedition headed up the Missouri River in three boats and rain. Lewis was 29 years of age, Clark 32.

At a Mandan village, Toussaint Charbonneau and his pregnant teenage wife, Sacagawea, joined the expedition, April 7, 1805. Toussaint, originally from Canada, signed on as interpreter. Sacagawea gave birth at another Mandan village and, with infant on her back, continued with the party.

Clark and Colter went ahead to search for a route through the Rockies. Clark saw his route could be traversed by horseback, but would be impossible for wagons. While he checked the North Fork of the Salmon River for possible navigation, he sent Colter to tell Lewis to follow the advice of Shoshone guide Old Toby to take the steep inter-tribal trail. They did.

Upon reaching the Columbia River estuary, they established their winter camp "Station Camp" on Chinook Point. Colter was one of nine who accompanied Clark about ten miles to the Pacific. Clark wrote "Ocian in view," November 7, 1805. The little group then proceeded nine miles north along what is now the coast of Washington.

The Lewis and Clark Expedition had traveled from the head of the Missouri River to the Columbia River. They helped establish claim to the Oregon country. John Jacob Astor's agents strengthened that claim by building a fur trading post at the head of the Columbia River in 1811.

At Point Chinook, the group subsisted on elk until a whale and a hundred pounds of blubber washed ashore. Sacagawea and her husband were flabbergasted at a creature resembling a fish that gave milk.

When the returning group reached the Big Horn River country in what is now Montana, Private John Colter received early discharge to trap beaver; that was in 1806. The others, eager for comforts of civilization and the company of the fairer sex, must have thought him daft. He joined trappers Forrest Hancock and Joseph Dickson of Illinois. The trio returned to the three forks of the Upper Missouri. Following a disagreement, Colter continued alone. In 1807, he helped establish Ft. Manuel Lisa, a trading post on the Little Big Horn River. Eventually, John Potts, a former member of the Expedition, returned and joined him.

To avoid the vicious Blackfeet Indians, they collected from their traps during early mornings and hid during daylight. One morning, they found themselves facing many hundreds of savages on the river bank. Colter recalled a former skirmish, and Captain Lewis killing two of them trying to steal horses. Colter never doubted the certainty of horrible death. They paddled to the bank. Colter got out of the canoe. A brave snatched Potts's rifle. Colter grabbed it returning it to Potts. Foolishly, Potts shot an Indian. He was, in Colter's words, "riddled" with arrows.

The Indians determined to make sport of killing Colter. Colter knew some Crow language, with which he conversed after a fashion. The chief asked whether he was a swift runner. Colter told him he was a poor sprinter. He was stripped naked and given about 500 yards start before the screaming horde thundered after him with spears. The land was covered with stones, prickly pears and thorns. Colter zipped through them as though they weren't there. He knew he was about six miles to the Jefferson Branch of the Missouri. The tributary was named for the president; another branch was named for James Madison. Six miles to his only hope for survival. His pursuers must have been livid to find their prey to be very swift, for he outdistanced them by far–except for one fleet warrior.

The mountain man's nose gushed blood upon his chest. The savage closed. Colter whirled, flung arms wide, and probably yelled. The Blackfoot, exhausted and startled, stumbled as he threw his spear. The weapon broke upon hitting the ground. Colter grabbed the section with the point and pinned the Indian to the earth. Colter gained a few precious yards as the pursuers paused over their fallen comrade. He was perhaps three miles from the river. With the enemy close and screaming for his blood, he dashed among the trees and dove into the water. A drift of logs lodged against the upper end of an island. Colter swam beneath them and found room to raise his head between logs. As the Indians dashed wildly over the drift looking for him, he submerged then surfaced to breathe after they moved away. They abandoned the search at dark and left.

John swam downstream, then gained the bank. Being a seasoned mountain man, he knew which berries and bark and such were edible. In order to avoid a pass, where he feared his enemies lay in wait, he climbed a virtually impossible cliff. About a week after escaping, he stumbled into Ft. Manuel Lisa. He scarcely resembled a human.

In September, 1806, the Corps of Discovery arrived in St. Louis. Much jubilation welcomed them. They had been gone two years and four months and feared lost or killed. Miraculously, Sgt. Charles Floyd was the only casualty; he became ill and died only a few months into the trip.

The party left for Washington in November, 1806. Lewis resigned from the army. President Jefferson appointed him governor of the new Territory of Louisiana. In 1809, Governor Lewis left for Washington on government business. While staying overnight at an inn, he died from two bullet wounds–one to the head, the other to his chest. The mystery was never solved. The Meriwether National Monument near Hohenwald, Lewis County, Tennessee, marks his grave.

In 1813, William Clark was appointed governor of the Northwest Territory and superintendent of Indian affairs, offices he held until Missouri became a state in 1820. In 1822, he was again appointed Superintendent of Indian Affairs. He died in St. Louis on September 1,

1838 at age 68.

After John Colter recovered, he and another former member of the Lewis and Clark Expedition joined the Andrew Henry company for another foray into Blackfoot country. At this time, Clark was preparing a map to be published with his journals in 1814. Finally, Colter gave up trapping and headed for St. Louis.

John Bradbury wrote in *Travels in the Interior of America* that he met and talked with Colter upon the latter's arrival in St. Louis on May 10, 1810. Colter traveled in a small canoe 3,000 miles in 30 days from the Upper Missouri. He told Bradbury of his adventures, mentioning that the trapper, Dickson, with whom he had allied, had traveled alone from St. Louis to the Missouri headwaters.

Colter related his adventures to Clark. Colter's exploration of territory far removed from that covered by the Expedition helped Clark to improve his maps. Colter's description of the Wind River area was especially helpful. He was undoubtedly the first white man to visit what is now Yellowstone National Park. His account of boiling mud geysers and such were met with skepticism, and called "Colter's Hell."

Colter married young Nancy Hooker and settled down a short distance west of St. Louis. John died May 7, 1810, at age 36. Some say he died of jaundice. One must wonder whether the ordeal of his strenuous escape sapped his physical constitution. Nancy buried him with his rawhide leather case and left the area. In 1926, road builders unearthed his remains. Papers in the leather case identified Colter.

Doctor Seeck delivered the eldest son of Michael Colter of Washington, Missouri. The infant was named John. The doctor asked whether they knew about the explorer and trapper, John Colter. They named him John because they loved the Yellowstone area and were familiar with the mountain man's name. Dr. Seeck told them that John was buried on her property near Washington, Missouri.

But as is often the case with historical events, there is controversy as to the location of Colter's grave. Early biographer Burton Harris (who believes Colter died of jaundice) writes that Colter was buried at Dundee, which eventually became the site of a railroad tunnel; it was called "Tunnel Hill." A descendant of Colter, Ruth Frick, believes she found the grave near New Haven during the 1980s. A small bunch of men calling themselves the "Tavern Bluff Party" erected a marker there in 1998. It states that Colter served with Nathan Boone's Mounted Rangers in the War of 1812. Dates of service are given as "Mar. 3, 1812 to May 6, 1812."

Controversy aside, John Colter ran himself into history records. One wonders if Olympic champions called the fastest humans alive attained speeds approaching that of mountain man John Colter.

13
Joe R. Lansdale's Funny House

Not his present home, but the one he occupied when he was a young student at Stephen F. Austin State University in Nacogdoches, Texas. Nor is "funny" exactly appropriate. Most would call it "haunted." Up front, be it known that Joe Lansdale doesn't believe in ghosts, not even on a route on which people traveled and died for centuries.

The El Camino Real (The King's Highway) connected Mexico City with Natchitoches, Louisiana–the capital of Spanish Texas. The route ran through the ancient Indian village that became Nacogdoches. For centuries, the road was tramped by Indians, soldiers, soldiers of fortune, adventurers, politicians, revolutionaries, smugglers and missionaries. Franciscan Antonio Margil de Jesus founded Mission Nuestro Señora de Guadalupe on the future site of Nacogdoches in 1716. The thoroughfare led the New Orleans Greys and David Crockett and his band to the Alamo and glory in 1836. It is known today as Texas State Highway 21.

Many people settled in East Texas following independence from Mexico in 1836. A few dogtrot cabins survive those years. Homes were often built with a breezeway separating two sets of rooms. This passage, called a dogtrot, created a draft that cooled the rooms. In addition to dogs and children–of which families were certain to have several of each–calves, goats, chickens and other livestock often raced through the passage. Family cemeteries were then common on homesteads.

It was on this historic route that Joe and two other students rented an ancient and primitive farm house west of Nacogdoches. A cemetery was just across a fence adjacent to the house. Two graves were those of a young woman and a baby. The area around the house, Joe said, was the darkest place at night that he had ever seen.

Phenomena included objects flying off the mantel, invisible force sweeping bowls from the table, and voices barely discernible, as if coming from a radio at minimum volume. Footsteps on the rear porch, accompanied by whistling and a load of wood being dropped on the porch. Doors opening and slamming shut. Footsteps in the dogtrot were not those of four legged creatures.

A student was there alone, while Joe and the others were in class. When they returned, their buddy was gone. A note pinned to the door informed them that he had decided to attend Tyler Junior College!

Joe's mother came for a visit. He didn't tell her about the strange occurrences. She was there alone one day. When Joe returned, she told him about the footsteps, whistling and wood dropped on the porch. He calmly explained their resident "ghost."

Joe and his friend slept on the floor on opposite sides of the dogtrot. One night, Joe's cover was yanked off. He jumped up and learned that the same thing happened to his friend, simultaneously. Joe is fearless; he owns a black belt in Karate earned from practice beginning when he was thirteen. They determined to put an end to the mischief. Together, they thoroughly searched the property and found nothing.

Joe's friend was alone there one night, with a fire in the fireplace; he slept with his back to it. He suddenly woke with a chill, and turned over. Never mind the cliche of ghost stories featuring a wispy young woman in a flowing white dress and long black hair–that is exactly the image he described. The trespasser was transparent, the flames clearly visible through her. Then she faded into nothing.

No apparition ever appeared to Joe. He attributes the strange phenomena to some kind of energy. Though extremely rare, science has indeed proved that movement totally unrelated to inanimate objects can cause them to move; for instance, an oil pump's action.

One day an elderly man asked Joe's permission to visit the cemetery. Joe helped him through the fence and stood by. The fellow stared long and silently at a grave, obviously deep in thought. Joe assisted him back over the fence. The gentleman thanked him and left to be seen no more.

In the barn, Joe accidentally discovered, in a concealed nook, evidence of an illicit love affair of long ago.

With the powerful imagination of the fine novelist that he is, Joe looked with awe across the fields and envisioned pioneers plowing. Perhaps he saw a plodding donkey carrying Father Margil de Jesus–whose feet barely cleared the ground. Senator Robert Potter riding up the road after a session in Austin to sup with Nacogdoches postmaster Adolphus Sterne before continuing to his home on Ferry Lake (Caddo) and his death? Sam Houston riding toward his home in Nacogdoches? His mind's eye might have seen a woman in a long dress, apron and bonnet–all homemade—drawing water. Barefoot boys dashed through the dogtrot, opening and slamming doors on each side. Their father whistling as he dropped firewood on the rear porch. Did he see the adulteress in the barn? The transparent lady from across the fence warming at the fireplace on a cold night?

Joe bluffed the strange happenings and stayed until unrelated and normal circumstances dictated that he move. A family then occupied the house–briefly!

Eventually, the spooky occurrences ceased, leaving the old home to weather in peace, and sparing inhabitants bumps in the night.

14
Clarence E. Sasser, Medal of Honor Recipient

He earned it on January 10, 1968, in Ding Tuoung Province, Republic of Vietnam. Clarence Eugene Sasser was a medical aid with one chevron denoting his rank in Co. A, 3rd Battalion, 60th Infantry, 9th Infantry Div.

The unit landed by helicopter and was immediately pounded by fire from three sides. Rifle, machine gun and rocket fire resulted in more than thirty casualties within minutes. Specialist Fifth Class Sasser received a shoulder wound, but kept on tending others. He dashed through a hail of bullets to reach the wounded, until taking hits in both legs; then he crawled to do his duty. He led his group to a safer spot and continued to tend to them for five hours. President Nixon gave him the Medal of Honor the following year. The Texas Legislature held a joint session in his honor. His state representative, Neil Caldwell of Alvin, sketched a portrait of Sasser, which is displayed in the House.

Sasser and his family live at Rosharon, Texas. In an interview for *Touchstone Literary Quarterly* 1976, he proved to be modest and rational. He allowed that spit and polish in basic is okay but silly in Vietnam. Everyone in combat knew what to do and did it as a matter of course. He had no opinion about beer in the barracks. How about long hair and whiskers? He grinned and felt his beard. Long hair isn't relative to performance, he said, adding that some are biased against anything that differs from their concept of correctness, mostly from ignorance. For instance, white people aren't aware that black men's whiskers are ingrown, and that mere pillow pressure irritates.

He neither supports nor condemns draft-dodgers, reasoning that had the Vietnam War been of the nature of WW II, most dissenters would have volunteered in the American tradition. He believes young people should make a career of what they like, and parents should support them.

No, he acknowledges with a smile, all politicians aren't crooks.

He had problems adjusting to civilian life. He had missed something and sought to compensate for it. Veterans are responsible for adjusting, he said. He was studying toward becoming a doctor at the University of Houston when he was drafted. After service, he studied at Texas A & M on a scholarship until outside conflicts interfered. He worked for Amoco for several years before becoming a counselor for the VA in Houston.

Sasser was the first Texas African-American to receive the Medal of Honor, but he doesn't lean on that fact; nor does he talk about the battle that gave birth to it. He remains a sensible and productive veteran and does what he can to improve life for others.

15
Nacogdoches History

Nacogdoches is known as the oldest city in Texas. Its roots reach into antiquity. An Indian village older than anyone can determine nestled on a peninsula that separates LaNana and Banita Creeks. The streams once joined immediately below the hill, but time moved them farther south. This village became the thriving city of Nacogdoches.

A loose confederation of related tribes called the Hasinai occupied northeast Texas, northwestern Arkansas and southeastern Oklahoma. They included the Adaies, Anadarkos, Neches, Nasoni, Natchitoches and the Nacogdoches. Eventually, they were lumped together as Caddos.

The Caddos grew corn, squash, beans, pumpkin and tobacco. A large number of natives joined in an annual buffalo hunt west of the Trinity River. Huge mounds were built over the graves of the elite. Food and utensils were interred with them. Mound Street in Nacogdoches got its name from burial sites that once lined both sides.

Cabeza de Vaca met the natives in 1535. Coronado visited them five years later. In 1541, DeSoto's successor–Luis de Moscoso—happened onto natives at the bend of the Red River. A 1718 French map puts de Moscoso in the general area of Nacogdoches; it also shows paths of Luis St. Denis's forays across Texas in 1713 and 1716. Only three settlements are noted on this highly-esteemed map: Nacogdoches, Ft. St. Louis on Matagorda Bay and San Juan Bautista on the Rio Grande; East Texas missions received supplies from the latter. The Indians greeted the strange men with "Tejas," meaning friendship, thereby giving Texas its name. Nacogdoches was the gateway for many explorers and adventurers from various countries and eastern states looking for empire and fortune in this land. Disregarding the fact that Spain claimed this land, entrepreneurs used Nacogdoches for their base for expansion.

Spain, tired of trying to contain French adventurers, ceded Louisiana to France; nevertheless, Frenchmen probed across the Sabine River. To counter the French, Spain sent soldiers and missionaries from Mexico to establish forts and missions in East Texas. Fray Damain Massanet established a mission at present day Alto in 1690. Franciscan Antonio Margil de Jesus founded Mission Nuestro Senora De Guadalupe in Nacogdoches in 1716; it was a short distance north of the present town square and on the southwest corner of present day Highway 59 (North Street), at Muller Street. For centuries, this old route connected Nacogdoches with tribes to the north.

Drought devastated the area the following year. Father Margil is credited with creating the miracle of two springs on the LaNana Creek banks, thus relieving the dry spell. The springs are known as "The eyes of Father Margil." French incursion forced Mission Guadalupe to close shortly after the "miracle," but Marquis of Aguayo restored it in 1721. The lot of the missions was difficult from the beginning. The natives accepted neither the white men's religion, nor their soldiers molesting their women; additionally, sporadic French incursion and the long and tenuous supply route caused the missions to be withdrawn to San Antonio in 1773. Two soldiers deserted and lived among the natives. Their descendants in the area must be legion.

Among settlers withdrawing was Don Gil Y'Barbo, born in Nacogdoches County in 1729. His group did not favor San Antonio. After an effort to settle on the Trinity River failed, he led several hundred of his people back to Nacogdoches in 1779. Twenty-six counties were eventually whittled from the province of Nacogdoches, which reached very close to present day Dallas. Y'Barbo immediately began transforming the shabby settlement into a permanent village. He laid out the civic and church squares on the south of El Camino Real—The King's Highway, later known as Old San Antonio Road and Highway 21. This was originally an ancient Indian thoroughfare taken over by adventurers, traders, immigrants and smugglers; it reached from Natchez, Mississippi to San Antonio, and ultimately to Mexico City.

* * *

The Stone House: Y'Barbo built a stone house on the north side of El Camino Real, facing upon the civic plaza. The structure was two storey and long. A covered balcony spanned the length, and was reached by outside stairs. As chief of both military affairs and civil government, Y'Barbo, established law and penalties and ruled from the Stone House. Serious crimes were punishable by hanging, then drawing and quartering. The "Old Stone Fort," as it is often called, hosted more history than any other building in Texas, including the Alamo.

Philip Nolan survived several controversial expeditions into Texas to gather mustangs for the Louisiana militia; but he was suspected of activities to separate Texas from Spanish rule. During a trip in 1801, troops from Nacogdoches killed him. Also in 1801, future Nacogdoches politician, Robert Potter, was one year old in Granville County, North Carolina; Gail Borden, Jr. was born in Norwich, New York; the British drove the last of Napoleon's troops from Egypt; and Nolan associate, Peter Ellis Bean, was imprisoned in the Stone House.

Mission Guadalupe closed in 1802 when the Parish church, Nuestra Señora de Pilar de Nacogdoches. was opened at the west end of Pilar

Street, where the current courthouse stands.

Don Gil Y'Barbo sold the Stone House in 1805. Traders Barr and Davenport occupied it the next year; at the time, numerous Spanish soldiers occupied the civic plaza, because war with the United States appeared imminent; fortunately, a treaty put that to rest.

Mexico rebelled against Spain in 1810. Manuel de Saucedo, governor of the Eastern Province of Spain, officiated from the Stone Fort for several months.

A vague account has a transient anglo boy of seventeen recording in his journal about spending a cold night beneath a buffalo robe in the upper storey of the Stone House. He looked upon Spanish soldiers huddled around numerous fires in the plaza.

Nine flags flew over the Stone House: In chronological order they were those of France, Spain, Magee-Guitierrez, Dr. James Long, Mexico, Fredonia Rebellion, the Republic of Texas, the United States, the Confederacy, and the United States. The Magee-Guitierrez, Long and Fredonia Rebellion movements were all headquartered in the Stone House.

The first scheme to take Texas from Spain was hatched by former U. S. Army officer Augustus Magee and Bernardo Guitierrez in 1812. For propaganda purposes, they published "Gaceto de Tejas," Texas's first newspaper–published in the Stone House. If the conspirators thought Mexico's struggle for independence from Spain would weaken Mexico's opposition, they were soon disappointed. After several spirited battles, the rebels were vanquished.

The second attempt to wrest Texas from Mexico was engineered by Dr. James Long of Natchez, Mississippi, in 1819. Leaving his pregnant wife, Jane Wilkerson Long, in poor circumstances on Bolivar Island, he rode to Nacogdoches and made the Stone House his base of operations. While Long was at Galveston trying in vain to secure pirate Jean LaFitte's help, his force was killed. A second effort also failed.

The third effort to make Texas independent occurred in 1826. This was the ill-fated Fredonia Rebellion, brainchild of Haden Edwards, Adolphus Sterne and associates. Edwards fled to Louisiana, but eventually returned to Nacogdoches. His huge home fronted East Main, but was moved to the rear and is now the Haden Edwards Inn.

Mexico won independence in 1821. Moses Austin forged an agreement to bring colonists to Mexico. Upon his death, his son, Stephen Fuller Austin assumed charge. Santa Anna became dictator and abolished democracy and forbade further immigration. Friction between Mexico and immigrants increased. In 1832, Colonel Piedras and troops occupied Nacogdoches. The colonel's residence was at the northeast corner of South Street and Pilar. Troops were housed in barracks on the same site and in the Stone House. With help from Adolphus Sterne and volunteers, they were driven out of town and captured near the John Durst home on the Angelina River west of town.

* * *

Sam Houston: Sam was born March 2, 1793, in Virginia's scenic Shenandoah Valley. The date–March 2–would prove to be of historic significance for much of his life. He was thirteen when his father, Major Sam Houston died. The following year, Elizabeth Paxton Houston moved with her nine children to Blount County, Tennessee. Young Sam exchanged farming and tending a store for life with the Cherokees. It would not be the last time he sought solace with that race. Though he had little formal education, he established a school and earned enough to pay a creditor.

Sam followed his father's example and enlisted in the army. He was twenty. In less than a year, he had progressed from a private to a junior officer. He suffered two wounds in the War of 1812. General Andrew Jackson was impressed with his bravery; thus began a lifelong association that would affect history, especially that of Texas. Sam was soon promoted again.

At age 23, Houston became a minor agent for Indians. Two years later, he was a First Lieutenant. He and his Cherokee charges went to the nation's capital and met with President James Monroe and Secretary of War John Calhoun. Calhoun chastised Sam for wearing Indian clothing. Nor would this be the last time Sam was criticized for Indian dress. Robert Potter and other enemies in the Texas Revolution ridiculed him for favoring Indians and wearing Indian apparel. Within months of the Washington D. C. visit, Houston resigned from the army after being wrongfully accused of slave dealing.

In those days, one could read law in an attorney's office and become a lawyer. Sam studied with Judge James Trimble in Nashville for six months, then passed the bar. Almost immediately, he became Adjutant General of Tennessee, and was back in the military as a colonel. The next year, he was elected Attorney General of the Nashville District. Not bad progress for a fellow of 26 years.

A couple of years later, Sam resigned to enter private practice. He also became Major General in the state militia. In 1823–probably through Andrew Jackson's influence–Sam was elected to the nation's House of Representatives. His next public office would be as governor of Tennessee. He was only 34 years of age.

In addition to Sam's affinity for things Indian was his penchant for women much younger than himself. While preparing to campaign for reelection–he was almost 36—he married 18-year-old Eliza Allen. In less than three months, they separated. Heart-broken, Sam resigned the governorship and again fled to his Cherokee friends. The Chief, John Jolly, welcomed the man he had named "The Raven" during his first sojourn with that tribe as a teenager. The summer of his return, Sam met and soon married tribal member, thirty-year-old Tiana Rogers, in the summer of 1830. Humorist/actor Will Rogers was Tiana's nephew several times removed. Though Chief John Jolly was considered Sam's Indian father, Sam officially became a Cherokee citizen.

Sam maintained contact with Andrew Jackson and was strongly suspected of political intrigue to bring Texas into the Union years before Houston's victory at San Jacinto. Jackson's "Manifest Destiny" was no secret.

After conferring with Jackson in Nashville, Sam went to the Army post, Cantonment Gibson. Gibson was a forbidding fort and steamboat port on the Arkansas and Three Forks Rivers. Sam and Tiana settled in a cabin on the Neosho River just above the fort. The Houstons' home was known as Wigwam Neosho. Sam established trade with Indians and also catered to soldiers and adventurers. On an earlier steamboat trip to Tennessee, he met Alexis de Tocqueville. At Fort Gibson, he enjoyed the company of Washington Irving. The fort was a pest hole of heat and a sweltering stockade that regularly hosted a sizable population of drunken soldiers. Sam's love of Indian culture, old whiskey and young women continued unabated; however, it was here that his reputation for drink escalated to the extreme.

It came about like this:

Controversy arose as to whether Sam was required under United States law to obtain a trader's license. Sam countered that he, being a citizen of the Cherokee Nation, needed no permit. Among trade goods ordered by Sam were nine barrels of liquor, which a steamer delivered to the Fort Gibson dock. Though introducing liquor into Indian country was illegal, the government agreed to let Houston take all of the liquor home for his personal use! These were five barrels of whiskey, and one each of cognac, wine, rum and gin. Those who knew his appetite for spirits probably figured nine barrels a normal ration for a brief period; however, Sam said that applying for a license would be an affront to Cherokee sovereignty.

The issue went to the Supreme Court. The case was pre-empted by a ruling that the Cherokee Nation in Georgia was still dependent on the state, and subject to its laws. It is not clear whether Sam applied for a license or was allowed to take the liquor to Wigwam Neosho. The marathon binge he embarked upon suggest that he not only kept the nine barrels of spirits, but eagerly and swiftly depleted them. Irrational ideas and behavior emanated from Wigwam Neosho and Cantonment Gibson. Friends suffered violence and embarrassment. He challenged an employee to a duel, which ended harmlessly, the weapons not being properly loaded. Much of 1831 passed in an alcoholic haze that probably surpassed even that of the most notorious alcoholic soldier, earning Sam the dubious distinction of being called Big Drunk.

In August-September, Sam went to his dying mother's side in Tennessee. This was the period in which Nat Turner led the slave revolt in Virginia. North Carolina Congressman Robert Potter, future Sam Houston nemesis, castrated two of his wife's cousins.

In 1832, Sam went to Washington to confer with Andrew Jackson. Ohio representative William Stanbery published an article accusing Houston of fraud; for that, Sam beat him with a cane on Pennsylvania Avenue. Though Sam engaged Francis Scott Key to represent him before Congress, Sam personally gave his story to that body and left with a reprimand.

Sam returned to Wigwam Neosho and resumed efforts to drink the Nation dry. Whether Tiana tired of her husband's continual alcoholic stupefaction and invited him to leave or he volunteered in a moment of sobriety to improve local society, is a matter of conjecture. Perhaps he thought it timely to bring to fruition visions of grandeur in another clime. He left Tiana with Wigwam Neosho—divorce in the Cherokee tradition--and headed for Texas. Tiana, who remained on the property with a couple of slaves, probably got the best end of the split. The former governor left with hat, cloak and probably a hangover on a sorry mount that he empathized with and was embarrassed to ride–a tailless pony named Jack. Poor Jack–minus the fundamental ability to even swat flies--bore the destiny of Texas and the nation.

From Fort Towson on the north bank of Red River, Sam crossed into Texas the first week of December, 1832. Fewer than half a dozen cabins marked the trail between the river and Nacogdoches.

Neither palm fronds nor dogwood branches were strewn before Jack, welcoming the savior of Texas to town. Nor was there a welcoming committee. Wastrels in Brown's tavern on the plaza were likely the first to welcome the thirsty immigrant from the Cherokee Nation. Tailless Jack stood humbled between whole mounts at the hitching rail.

Only recently, Colonel Jose Piedras and his troops had been driven from the Stone House and Nacogdoches. Sam applied for land under Stephen F. Austin's colonization agreement with Mexico and, in the spring of the next year, established a law practice in the Stone House. He kept Andrew Jackson informed about Texas and joined the movement to secure independence for that coveted land. He also fell in love–again.

* * *

Anna Raguet: Sam Houston and John Durst met Henry Raguet in New Orleans–perhaps in Bank's Arcade--in February, 1933, and persuaded him to go with them to Nacogdoches. Henry was pleased with the place and returned north to bring his daughter, Anna–a product of Pennsylvania, by way of Ohio—came to Nacogdoches in March. While going for his daughter, Henry convinced Bill Logan of Vicksburg, Mississippi, to join him in the mercantile business in Nacogdoches.

Nacogdoches was a crude community of log cabins and Mexican jacals*. One visitor–obviously seeking an icon of base culture—lamented that the pitiful settlement had not a tavern worthy of the name, thus denigrating Brown's saloon and the Hotel Cantina del Monte.

Of course, the population was small. Alcalde Adolphus Sterne's census of 1833 listed 1,272 citizens–including Sam Houston; therefore, it was inevitable that Anna and Sam soon met; and Sam was soon smitten by the teenaged girl. Sam was forty, considerably more than twice her age! Nevertheless, he courted the girl and wished to marry her. Sam's marriage to Tiana and divorce was simply moving in and moving out–a perfectly acceptable Cherokee tradition; but he had not obtained a divorce from Eliza Allen; his effort to this end was blunted by Mexican law, which forbade divorce. Even so, he continued to woo the comely adolescent.

At some point, Sam wrote about a time with the Cherokees, when he meandered along a watercourse with one Indian girl or another and Homer's *Iliad*, alternately romancing and reading; it is not reported which emerged from the woods less worn–Sam, Homer, or the girls. Without casting aspersion on the Raguet maiden, it is easy to imagine Sam strolling along LaNana Creek with Anna and the *Iliad*. Perhaps she played the harmonica alternately with his quoting passages from Homer. After all, it is safe to assume that the tall, ruggedly handsome former Tennessee governor and Homer's classic did not seduce every female of his acquaintance. Nor is it inappropriate to assume that Adolphus Sterne sauntered from his home at the corner of LaNana and Pilar Streets to Sam's home on the southwest corner of the Plaza–or to his office in the Stone House—to plan rebellion and share drinks. A surviving ledger sheet, probably from Barr and Davenport's trading post, charged Sam with six grogs and Adolphus with a couple of whiskeys.

---

* *jacal: huts of upright poles or sticks chinked and plastered with clay or mud with thatched roofs.*

* * *

Adolphus Sterne: Sterne was a Jew from Germany. He was condemned to death for supporting the disastrous Fredonia Rebellion; but his Masonic association won him parole. Nevertheless, late in 1835, he organized two companies of volunteers in New Orleans in–where else?– Bank's Arcade. One company went by boat to Brazoria, then overland to San Antonio. The other company went through Nacogdoches, enjoying a feast of wild game across the street from the Sterne home. Both companies–totaling approximately 120 men—joined the Texas Army in San Antonio. The unit participated in seven major battles, including the Alamo and San Jacinto. William Cooke, original captain of the company that went by sea, was the only surviving senior officer; he and half a dozen other Greys fought at San Jacinto. Most of the New Orleans volunteers perished, many in the Alamo and the Goliad Massacre.

* * *

Robert Irion: Born in Tennessee in 1804, Irion became a physician in Kentucky. He practiced in Vicksburg, Mississippi, San Augustine and Nacogdoches, Texas. As did others, he desired land. He became a member of the Nacogdoches Committee for Safety and Vigilance in the fall of 1835. Five months later, he was Commander of Nacogdoches. He was also a senator in the republic's first congress.

Following independence won at San Jacinto on April 21, 1836, Houston became first president of The Republic of Texas. He appointed Irion secretary of state in 1837. Irion traveled widely in that capacity.

The Republic's first capital was the very new and very raw city on Buffalo Bayou named for Houston. The war and all its complications hadn't diminished Sam's affection for Miss Anna. Dr. Irion carried letters from the president to Anna, but brought none in return.

Sam's Cherokee wife, Tiana Rogers, lived quietly and alone until her death by pneumonia in 1838.

Sam Houston was to Robert Irion as Miles Standish was to John Alden. Anna Raguet was Priscilla Mullins. Both Sam and Miles were much older than the objects of their affection. Both sent others with words of love. Both were shunned. Priscilla married John. Anna married Robert–but not for a while. Sam had not given up. Subverting the proper duty of congress, Sam decreed that a judge privately consider his petition for a divorce from Eliza Allen. The divorce was eventually allowed; but Anna was among others not pleased by the murky procedure, and spurned the president.

As Senator of the new Republic of Texas, Robert Potter also schemed to obtain a divorce for Harriet Page.

Sam fell in love with Margaret Lea while on a trading trip to Alabama. A friend begged him to forego marriage, to spare the poor lady his deplorable lifestyle. Anna and Robert married about the end of March, 1840. Anna was 24, Robert 36. Sam and Margaret married several weeks later. He was 47, she 21. The Irions had five children; they named their first son Sam Houston Irion. Surely Sam preferred the boy to be his own flesh and blood, but was probably pleased with next best; besides, his attention was obviously focused on Margaret, for she bore eight offspring–four sons and four daughters.

Houston's career included two terms as President of the Republic of Texas, three terms as U. S. senator, one as governor. Two days after Houston's 68th birthday, Texas seceded from the Union. Sam refused to swear allegiance to the Confederacy. Two weeks later, he left the office of governor.

He died in the "Steamboat" house in Huntsville of the same malady that had taken Tiana's life. The date was July 26, 1863. He was 70. His last words were those of the loves of his life, "Texas" and "Margaret."

There are numerous memorials and accolades to the legendary Sam Houston, but not one to tailless Jack who carried him to Nacogdoches and everlasting fame.

* * *

Thomas Jefferson Rusk: Rusk, a native of South Carolina, practiced law in Georgia's gold region. In 1834, embezzlers fled westward with Rusk's investment in that industry. Tom slammed his office door, leaped into the saddle and pursued the crooks to Nacogdoches. He never apprehended the crooks nor recovered his funds, but he found fame and honor. The opportunity to recoup his losses induced him to stay and apply for land in David Burnet's colony. Early in 1835, he sent for his family.

Rusk soon became involved with the movement for independence from Mexico and the dictator, Santa Anna. Sam Houston was active in the cause, when not in pursuit of winsome Anna Raguet. The two men would prove to have much in common, both serving in numerous high offices in the Texas provisional government, the Republic of Texas, the state of Texas and the United States.

Mexican troops demanded the return of the cannon they had furnished to the settlement of Gonzales for protection against Indians. Defenders fashioned a flag that dared the Mexicans: Its message was "Come and get it! " Thanks to their resolve and Rusk and the volunteers he recruited in Nacogdoches, they didn't get it. In December, 1835, the provisional government appointed Rusk to the office of inspector general of the military in the District of Nacogdoches.

After signing the Declaration of Independence at Washington-on-the Brazos, March 17, 1836, that body of men named David Burnet president and Rusk secretary of war. But the Alamo fell while the convention was in session, and the new government was rapidly relocated to Harrisburg.

Rusk led and fought bravely in the Battle of San Jacinto on April 21, 1836. With General Houston suffering a shattered ankle, Rusk became commander in chief.

Rusk and company gathered the pitiful remains of Colonel James Fannin and his men murdered in the Goliad Massacre, and Rusk conducted a tearful funeral. Sam Houston was elected President of the Republic of Texas; he named Rusk secretary of war. While serving in the new capital of the Republic, Tom taught a church Sunday class. He soon resigned his government office for personal reasons. He was elected to the Texas Congress in 1837. A Freemason, he joined Lodge No. 40 in Nacogdoches in 1837 and, later that year, became a charter member of the Grand Lodge of Texas.

The immensely popular Rusk declined several times to become a presidential candidate. Congress elected him major general of the militia. In that position, summer of 1838, he stopped the Cordova Rebellion, a joint movement by Cherokees and Mexicans to reclaim Texas. At issue was the unratified Cherokee Treaty of 1836 that would give Cherokees title to land they had always occupied in East Texas. Rusk illegally entered United States territory and brought Indians back into the charge of their agent in Shreveport. Eventually, with President Mirabeau Lamar's blessing, Rusk helped to drive the natives into Oklahoma.

Near the end of 1838, Rusk became chief justice of the Republic of Texas Supreme Court. Early in 1841, he joined J. Pinckney Henderson in law practice. In 1842, Rusk successfully defended his friend, William Rose and nine others charged with the murder of Senator Robert Potter. Tom's brother, David, was Nacogdoches County sheriff, 1840-46.

Tom had a long on and off affair with the militia, being named major general in January, 1843. He resigned six months later, because President Houston objected to his call for war with Mexico. Rusk was content to retire to his family in Nacogdoches. One account claims he donated land across the road from his home for the University of Nacogdoches chartered in 1845–the year of annexation; another source says the Republic of Texas deeded the property to the school. Rusk was vice president, then president of the institution the following year.

It is hard to conceive of others than Thomas Rusk and Sam Houston being the first U. S. Senators from the State of Texas. The dynamic duo's efforts and accomplishments for the Republic and then the State fill volumes. Postal service and postal roads were improved by Rusk's oversight of the appropriate committee. Senator Rusk and President James Polk wanted war with Mexico, and the acquisition of California.

The Gadsden treaty and railroads owe Senator Rusk for his support.

As he had in regard to the Republic of Texas, Rusk declined consideration for the presidency of the United States; however, the Senate elected him President pro-tem in 1857. But the fire had burned out in Senator Thomas Rusk. His wife's death early the previous year left him devastated and empty. That trauma and his declining health prompted him to shoot himself at his home, reportedly in a slave cabin. That was July 29, 1857. The brave and illustrious warrior and statesman lies in Oak Grove Cemetery on LaNana Street in Nacogdoches. Numerous of his contemporaries share that historic soil.

The year following Rusk's death, the University of Nacogdoches building was erected. It became a Confederate hospital before becoming headquarters for federal forces. It is a museum and a popular place for weddings and other special events. And of course, its successor is the very fine Stephen F. Austin State University.

Rusk's home and slave cabins are long gone. Lumberman Eugene Blount built a huge, brick home on the site decades ago. That beautiful building is the current home of the Nacogdoches Chamber of Commerce. And therein lies another story–perhaps Rusk's legacy: It is haunted. Commerce employees have separately reported weird phenomena. Occasionally an employee working late at night hears footsteps, doors opening and closing and toilets flushing. But perhaps it is merely errant plumbing and the wind sweeping boughs against windows. Then again, maybe Tom visits the lovely wooded site. Who can blame him?

* * *

Louis (Moses) Rose: After escaping the Alamo just before its fall, Rose, a Frenchman, became known as "the coward of the Alamo." Most accusers were ignorant of Rose's bravery while serving for at least eight years in Napoleon's Army. He joined in 1806 and worked up to lieutenant. Areas of service included Russia, Spain, Portugal and Naples, Italy. He was an aide-de-camp to General Jacques de Montfort for which he was named to the French Legion of Honor in 1814.

The next account we have is of him in Nacogdoches, participating in the Fredonia Rebellion in 1826. Undoubtedly, the intervening years were filled with adventure. A man such as Rose doesn't lie fallow. Frost Thorn and John Durst employed him in their sawmill. Rose's war experience extended with his participation in the Battle of Nacogdoches in 1832 and the Battle of Bexar in December, 1835. Louis Rose and James Bowie became friends and went together to the latter battle.

The following March, Rose chalked up ten more days of combat in the Alamo. It was here that he was nicknamed "Moses" because of his age of 51. Some took advantage of Santa Anna's offer of safe passage to those who would leave the engagement. Moses stayed on until the night before the fatal end. He was credited with bravery throughout his time there. It is said that a window was opened for him and he slipped out and through the Mexican lines; however, the Alamo was a ruin with the roof long caved in, and there wasn't likely a window to raise. After a grueling and dangerous trek, he found refuge at the Zuber home in Grimes County.

The Zubers' son, William P., was one of about 200, including Solomon Page, who guarded the army's sick and baggage while Sam Houston and company defeated Santa Anna at San Jacinto. Zuber outlived every veteran of that battle, and repeated Rose's story of Travis drawing the line in the sand and inviting all who would die with him to step across. Louis was the only dissenter. If Rose actually told the story, it rings true; he never made excuses other than openly admitting that he simply wasn't ready to die. And what of those who accepted Santa Anna's armistice? Their names seem to be lost to history and free of the charge of cowardice. Perhaps some of them joined General Houston and fought at San Jacinto. After all, Colonel Travis defied Houston's order to abandon the Alamo.

But history wasn't through with Louis Rose. He operated a butcher shop across the street behind present day Cason-Monk Hardware on Nacogdoches' Main Street. Rose vouched for many Alamo dead in order for their survivors to receive land grants from the new Republic of Texas.

Six years after the Alamo's fall. Rose moved to the Aaron Ferguson farm near Logansport, Louisiana, and lived there until his death in 1851.

The De Soto Parish Historical Society, eventually established Rose's grave site a little more than six miles northeast of Logansport, Louisiana, near Castor Creek. Yuccas marked the grave; the plants being indigenous to Texas convinced them to designate the grave a historical site and erect a marker. Ironically, one of Rose's guns made it back to the Alamo.

Rose was a life-long bachelor, but one of his brother Isaac's sons donated one of his uncle Louis's guns to the Alamo Museum.

* * *

William Goyens: Goyens, the son of a white woman and a free mulatto, came from his birthplace in South Carolina to Nacogdoches, Texas, about 1820. As did many others, he seemed to have left no tracks, simply arrived and stayed. He was 26 and free. Skilled as a wagon maker and blacksmith, he began building a future.

He operated an inn in conjunction with his home, which was on the south side of El Camino Real (Highway 21) between present day North Street (Highway 59) and Banita Creek. Very probably–as was common— the "inn" was merely a room or two added onto his residence and guests served at his table. Traders, soldiers, and adventurers from the east passed directly past his home. Guests could stroll a few yards to confession at Nuestra Señora de Pilar, or to Brown's tavern on the civic plaza. Goyens' hotel enterprise supplemented his other businesses, one of which was freighting goods to Nacogdoches that arrived by way of New Orleans, Red River, and Natchitoches. In 1832, the year that Spanish troops were driven from Nacogdoches, Goyens took Mary Sibley–a white woman–to wife. In addition to gaining a reputation as an astute businessman, William earned the trust of both whites and Indians for his diplomacy.

After the revolution, fresh opportunities opened for settlers, but not necessarily for Negroes. The Constitution of the Republic of Texas forbade black people to own land. William Goyens' personal constitution proved superior, for he forthwith bought property on Moral Creek several miles west of Nacogdoches. Further disregarding the possible consequences of illegalities, he built a gristmill and a sawmill. Strict enforcement of the Constitution could have stripped him of his total investment. That situation was ideal for the unscrupulous to manipulate and gain his property. Goyens had already learned that he was especially vulnerable. More than once, white men claimed him as their property. Having a white wife further encouraged the bigoted to find fault. Though Rusk was largely responsible for founding the Republic and knew full well the laws thereof, he and Charles Taylor protected Goyens and his property. Ironically, Goyens owned slaves!

William Goyens' fortitude and industry carried him from a penniless pioneer to wealth and respect. He survived his wife only a short time, dying in the summer of 1856. This was when Adah Isaacs Menken was reading Shakespeare and writing a newspaper column in Liberty, Texas, and perhaps entertaining in Nacogdoches. In 1936, the Texas Centennial Commission erected a marker at the graves of William and Mary near the fork of Moral and Alitos Creeks.

There is much speculation as to what became of the Goyens' gold; perhaps it rests beneath the soil of Goyens' Hill.

On May 29, 1984, William Goyens, Sister Josephine and Karle Wilson Baker were inducted into Nacogdoches' Heritage Festival Hall of Fame.

* * *

Sister Josephine (Renee Ernestine Francois Potard): During Reconstruction, the federal government's aggrievement of Texans was bad enough, but ignorant and mean men overran the state. Depredations by Civil War deserters and regular outlaws rendered travelers and rural folk susceptible to rape and pillage. The scurviest of these villains would not hesitate to ravage sisters of the cloth–would especially delight in doing so. Who could question the courage and integrity of Sister Josephine, who forsook the wealth into which she was born to become a nun and bring her nursing skills to Texas and Nacogdoches?

Renee Potard entered life in France, 1822. At age 22, she became a novitiate in the Sisters of the Holy Cross. In that capacity, she went to Indiana and became a nurse. Her expertise got her promoted to the staff. Upon taking perputual vows on August 6, 1857, she became Sister Joseph; this was exactly eight days after Thomas Rusk committed suicide in Nacogdoches.

Nacogdoches University, having served as a Confederate hospital during the war and as headquarters for Federal troops afterward, stood empty–a mockery to the noble cause established by Thomas Rusk and other men of vision. The Sisters of the Holy Cross accepted an invitation to revive the University in the spring of 1871. Sister Joseph came from Notre Dame to teach. When the convent moved to Clarksville, three years later, the nun chose to remain and work alone; and she did until her death at age 71 in1893. But there was much work to do before giving up the ghost, and there are those who are convinced that she tried to do it all! When the convent moved, management of the University fell to the Masons; they accommodated her as much as possible, but she eventually bought property and taught from there.

Sister Joseph had changed her name to Sister Josephine about 1874. After briefly teaching from her home, she moved to the Moral community west of town, the former domain of William Goyens. Goyens had been dead for 24 years when Sister arrived, but one can't help but believe that he smiled from his grave, pleased that a great benefactor had come to nurse and love his neighbors as he had.

Ill health eventually moved the nun to Houston's St. Joseph's Infirmary, where she passed into eternity on April 27. 1893. The president of St. Edward's College in Austin, the Reverend P. J. Hurth, C. S. C., who inherited her home in Nacogdoches, had her buried at St. Edward's College.

As formerly mentioned, Sister Josephine joined William Goyen and Karle Wilson Baker in the Nacogdoches Heritage Festival Hall of Fame on May 29, 1984.

16
Nacogdoches authors and other personages

Given Nacogdoches' rich intellectual history, noting all authors and artists would require space beyond the scope of this work; therefore, most of the subjects listed here are those with whom the author associated during his sixteen years in this beautiful and charming city. Apologies to all other writers and artists.

* * *

Karle Wilson Baker (1878-1960): Mrs. Baker was one of the first Texas writers to win national literary recognition. Born in Little Rock, Ark., she attended Little Rock Academy, Ouachita Baptist College and the University of Chicago, and taught in Little Rock and Bristol, Virginia. In 1901, when she joined her parents, Kate Floy and William Thomas Wilson, who had recently moved to Nacogdoches, Texas, she was already launched upon a promising literary career, publishing poetry, short stories, essays and articles in such national magazines as *Yale Review*, *Scribners*, *Harpers*, *Atlantic Monthly*, *Cosmopolitan* and *Redbook*.

Her daughter writes, "In the natural beauties and dramatic history of East Texas, she found fresh inspiration for her writing, and in 1907 she married Thomas Ellis Baker, a Nacogdoches banker and civic leader who shared and encouraged these interests.

"Their homeplace, 'Tanglewood,' was a wooded area abounding in plant and bird life. Mrs. Baker's enthusiastic study of birds led to a book of essays, *Birds of Tanglewood*.

"Two fanciful story books, *The Garden of the Plynck*, 1920, and *The Reindeer's Shoe*, 1938, were read, chapter by chapter, to her children, Thomas Wilson and Charlotte, when they came each day from school.

"Two school books for children, *The Texas Flag Primer*, and *Two Little Texans*, combine the author's interest in nature and history. Publications of her poems in *Blue Smoke*, 1922, and *Dreamers on Horseback*, 1931, further established Mrs. Baker's reputation as a poet.

"Her two novels with historical themes are *Family Style*, 1937, concerned with family life during the East Texas oil boom during the Depression, and 'Star of the Wilderness,' dealing with Dr. James Grant's fatal Matamoros expedition during the Texas Revolution.

"She was an inspiring teacher, and as a professor at Stephen F. Austin State University (then Teachers College) she contributed immeasurably to the cultural life of the community, bringing such distinguished guest lecturers as Robert Frost and Vachel Lindsey. Her extensive contacts included fellow writers Theodore Dreiser, Willa

Cather and Dorothy Scarborough.

"She was the first woman elected a Fellow by the Texas Institute of Letters, of which she was a charter member, and the Poetry Society of America. She was a member of The Philosophical Society of Texas and The Authors' League of America. She received an honorary Litt D. from SMU."

* * *

Francis Edward Abernethy is Distinguished Regents Professor Emeritus of English at Stephen F. Austin State University, the Executive Secretary and Editor of the Texas Folklore Society, the Curator of Exhibits for the East Texas Historical Association, and a member of the Texas Institute of Letters. Dr. Abernethy attended Stephen F. Austin State University and Louisiana State University, where he received his doctorate in Renaissance Literature. He has taught at Woodville High School, Louisiana State University, Lamar State University, and Stephen F. Austin State University. He is the editor of *Tales From the Big Thicket*, *Built in Texas*, *Legendary Ladies of Texas*, *Folk Art in Texas*, *Texas Toys and Games*, *Juneteenth Texas*, and fourteen other volumes for the Texas Folklore Society. He has published poetry, short stories, a folk music book entitled *Singin' Texas*, a book of legends entitled *Legends of Texas' Heroic Age*, and a history of the Texas Folklore Society in three volumes. He has lectured widely, both popularly and academically. He is a World War II veteran, he worked in the caves of Mexico and the Yucatan for over twenty years, he is a world traveler, a scuba diver, and he plays the bass fiddle in the East Texas String Ensemble of Nacogdoches.

He was born in Altus, OK, Dec. 3, 1925, grew up in the Panhandle and East Texas, has been married to Hazel Shelton Abernethy since 1948, and has five children and six grandchildren, whom he loves dearly.

* * *

Charlotte Baker Montgomery is the author of nineteen published books. Her latest, *The Trail North*, published by Eakin Press, traces in fictional form the ebb and flow of life along North street in Nacogdoches, Texas, from prehistoric times to the present.

Her first publication was a paragraph in the *Nacogdoches Daily Sentinel* during World War 1, urging the public to buy Thrift Stamps. A few years later during a visit with her mother, Karle Wilson Baker, to the Yale University Press, her ambition to be a writer was acknowledged by a gift book, inscribed by the editor, "To Charlotte Baker, with all good wishes for her future literary career."

Born in Nacogdoches, TX, in 1910, Charlotte Baker Montgomery received academic degrees from Mills College and the University of California at Berkeley. Her subsequent career included teaching, commercial art, museum docent and Acting Director. In 1942 she married Roger Montgomery, then a captain in the Army. After the war they lived in a houseboat on the Willamette River, (the inspiration for her book for children, *The House on the River,*) until their return to Nacogdoches to make their permanent home.

Magic for Mary M, and *The Best of Friends* received awards from the Texas Institute of Letters. *Cockleburr Quarters.* received The Lewis Carroll Shelf Award, First Prize Book World Children's Spring Book Festival, and a Newberry Nomination.

With Mrs. Winifred Hall, who shared their concern for animals, Roger and Charlotte Montgomery founded the Humane Society of Nacogdoches County in 1960, which in turn inspired other humane societies in the East Texas area. In 1983 Mrs. Montgomery was awarded the Humane Society of the United States Joseph Wood Krutch Medal 'for significant contribution toward improvement of life and environment.'

Roger Montgomery died in 1981. Their homeplace, part of the historic Thomas J. Rusk plantation, has been designated the Banita Creek Nature Preserve by the Natural Areas Preservation Association.

Her column, "Noah's Notebook," about animals from a humane standpoint was published weekly by the *Nacogdoches Daily Sentinel* for 37 years.

The Montgomery Fellowship in Humane Education has been established at Stephen F. Austin State University to encourage the teaching of humane concepts in the schools through teacher education.

In 1996, Mrs. Montgomery was inducted into the first annual Nacogdoches Women's Hall of Fame.

* * *

Ardath Mayhar used to write a column, "View From Orbit," for the *Nacodoches Daily Sentine*l. Many columns bared a writer's life and travails, including examples of common naivete as to a writer's routine and abuse of same. Ardath asks why–given the uncertainties, misunderstanding, greed, and stupendous ignorance that victimizes a writer–anyone would take pen in hand. The following quote from the *Nacogdoches Daily Sentinel,* July 5, 1981, is a prime example:

"A chemist with his own home lab can go into his sanctum and nobody dares to interrupt his esoteric rituals. A writer can retire to his study (or, in my case, the corner of a bedroom) to earn his daily bread, and nobody thinks anything at all about barging in amid a crucial battle, love-scene, or whatever, and saying, 'I know you don't work . . .' (Read that, 'you don't leave for work in the morning and return in the evening, the way my husband does) . . . 'So I thought you wouldn't mind. . . (Insert here 'getting my cat out f the transformer at the corner,' 'unstopping my toilet,' or 'babysitting little Oliver while I go to my bridge club.') We have no social respect."

Rodney Dangerfield would have understood.

Ardath continues: "If we write fiction, it's ten times worse. The putting of factual material on paper (no matter how inexpertly) seems, by definition, more respectable than 'making things up.' Sigh! ! ! And when one is introduced to a total stranger as a science fiction writer, the scene itself is often worthy of recording. The initial blankness of shock is replaced, very quickly, by an expression that says as plainly as words, 'Should I lay aside all dignity and run right now, or is it safe to stand my ground?' I have a writer friend in Ohio who actually had somebody run, without saying a word."

Ardath's career is undergirded by gutsy perseverance. She is best portrayed by her own words:

"Author of sixty novels, forty of them published by standard print publishers, Ardath Mayhar began her career in the early eighties with science fiction novels from Doubleday and TSR. Atheneum published several of her Y/A and children's novels. Changing focus, she wrote westerns (as Frank Cannon) and mountain man novels (as John Killdeer). Four prehistoric Indian books under her own name came out from Berkley.

"Her earlier life as a dairy farmer, bookstore owner, postal clerk, editorial proofreader, and grower of broiler chickens has given her a rich mix of backgrounds upon which to draw in her fiction. Rearing sons, gardening, raising beef cattle, wood-cutting, and surviving political activism have added their own elements.

"Over the years she has taught writing classes at Chemeketa Community College in Salem, Oregon; Texas Women's University, Denton, Texas; Stephen F. Austin University, Nacogdoches. She has appeared at many writers conferences, including Golden Triangle Writers' Guild in Beaumont, TX and Pineywoods Writers' Conference, SFA in Nacogdoches.

"Recently she has been working with on-line and on-demand publishers. A number of her published and unpublished novels are now available through several such sources.

"Now more than seventy years old, Mayhar has recently been widowed, after forty-one years of marriage, and has closed the bookshop she ran with her husband for fifteen years. A car wreck lamed her for a time, but she recovered quickly, as tough old ladies do, and is forging a new life. She now works in her home office, teaching writing, doing book doctoring professionally, and continuing to write. She can be reached via e-mail at ardathm@netdot.com."

* * *

Marylois Dunn graduated from Nacogdoches High School with Ardath Mayhar. Marylois graduated from Stephen F. Austin State University, then took her Master's in library science at LSU in Baton Rouge, Louisiana. During the late sixties, McGraw Hill published her first book, *Man in the Box*, which won the Sequoyah Award in Oklahoma. Steven Spielberg took a movie option on the book. In 1983, Harper and Row published *The Absolutely Perfect Horse*, which Marylois wrote and Ardath rewrote; it was a finalist for the Bluebonnet Award in Texas in 1984. *Timber Pirates*, which Marylois and Ardath wrote together, was published by Blue Lantern Publishing in 1997.

Complications from diabetes ended Marylois's writing career years ago; also, macular degeneration rendered her unable to read. Special Collections at SFA University archived her papers.

Marylois and Ardath remain fast friends.

* * *

Joe R. Lansdale was born in Gladewater, TX, and grew up there and in every library in every other place he lived–even read every book in the Mt. Enterprise library. Even a small town library has enough material to keep most of us busy for years of steady reading. Joe reads fast, writes fast and fights fast. At age 13, he began martial arts to protect himself against abuse at school. He is in the International Martial Arts Hall of Fame as is his teaching method. Ideas bang into his keen mind at supersonic speed and find themselves on paper quicker than Sherlock Holmes can fetch his magnifying glass and assure Watson that it's all elementary.

When Joe was in college, each student was assigned to write a story. The teacher told Joe after reading his story that he would never become a writer! A manuscript was returned to aspiring novelist Victoria Holt with a note on it written in red warning her to not consider a career in writing! She cried for a "fortnight." Who's crying now? Yeah, as they say, all the way to.... Well, you know. Many who felt their dignity and intelligence assaulted by writers have eaten their bitter words while contemplating the considerable fortunes that rejected writers generated for their competitors.

Joe grew up with his mechanic father, housekeeping mother and an older brother. Joe wrote while working various jobs, including farming, janitor work and back-braking labor in the renowned Tyler rose fields. He continued to write while attending Tyler Junior College and Stephen F. Austin State University, and found publishers for some of his first works.

Joe and Karen married and tried the back-to-the-earth life. Plowing with a mule and making lye soap left little energy and time for writing; therefore, adjustments were made.

Eventually, he wrote the suspense novel, *Act of Love*, which was rejected thirty times! Perseverance and Karen's unwavering support paid, and is still paying.

In 1981, Joe chose to become a full-time writer and has practiced his craft ever since. He is the author of over 200 short stories, articles and essays, as well as 20 novels, and several short story collections. He has also edited or co-edited seven anthologies—five fiction, two non-fiction.

He is well known for his series of crime/suspense adventures featuring Hap Collins and Leonard Pine. *The Two Bear Mambo, Cold In July, Savage Season, Bad Chill, Rumble Tumble, The Boar* and *Freezer Burn*. Several of them had been optioned for film. Among them, *Mucho Mojo*, a *New York Times* Notable Book, has recently been scripted for film by Oscar winner Ted Tally.

His better known short story collections are *By Bizarre Hands, Writer of the Purple Rage, Electric Gumbo, The Lansdale Reader, High Cotton, Selected Stories by Joe R. Lansdale*, and a unique graphic story collection of his work titled *Atomic Chili, The Illustrated Joe R. Lansdale*.

Besides editing anthologies like the ground-breaking *Razored Saddles* and *Dark at Heart* (Co-edited with Karen) which contained many "Best of Nominees," including Lansdale's own award winning novella, *Events Concerning A Nude Fold-Out Found In A Harlequin Romance*.

He has scripted teleplays for the Emmy winning, animated Batman series, sold numerous options and screenplays to film.

His novella *Bubba Ho-Tep* recently filmed, was directed by Don Coscarelli of *Phantasm* and *Beast Master* fame, starring Bruce Campbell and Ossie Davis. It appeared in the fall of 2002 and made its premier at the Cinevegas Film Festival in June of 2002.

He has written for comics, including the award winning *D. C. Comics* Jonah Hex series, *Two Gun Mojo, Riders of the Worm and Such*, and *Shadow's West*. He also scripted *It Crawls*, the comic that revived the Lone Ranger, for *Topps*. He had his own comic series at *Dark Horse*, featuring adaptations of his short stories and the novel, *Dead in the West*.

He is a member of the Texas Institute of Letters and has won numerous awards for his work: *The Bottoms* (2000) earned the Edgar Award for Best Novel, and was designated "Notable Book" by the *New York Times*—the second such honor for Joe. Additional honors include six Bram Stokers, the British Fantasy Award, the American Mystery Award, the Horror Critics Award, The Shot in The Dark International Crime Writer's Award, The Booklist Editor's Award, The Critic's Choice Award, The Inkpot Award, and others.

Children Keith and Kasey, ages thirteen and nine, respectively, in 1985, wrote with their father's guidance, "The Companion," which was published in the collection, *Great Writers & Kids Write Spooky Stories.*

Edgar Rice Burroughs died leaving an unfinished manuscript; Joe had the honor of being chosen to finish it. No insignificant occasion, that!

Joe continues to write, as good writers do, and enjoys success forged in the fiery furnace of the writing/publishing business.

* * *

L. K. Feaster is a connoisseur of the American West. His *Banditry with Panache* is an excellent account of "Black Bart, the Poet," who robbed stages in the California gold country. Also, "Charles Goodnight, Monarch of the Staked Plains," and "John B. Stetson's 'Boss of the Plains'." All three pieces were published in the anthology, *The West That Was*, by Wings Books, a Random House Company, edited by Thomas W. Knowles and Joe R. Lansdale. Feaster is at work on a children's fantasy.

* * *

Carol J. Scamman, a librarian at Stephen F. Austin State University, also contributed several pieces to *The West That Was:* "Road Tests of Covered Wagons," The Dirty Dozen of Wagon Packing, or do Leave Home Without Them," "How to Spot a Conestoga," and "Sassparilly."

* * *

Dr. Alfred S. Shivers, research scholar, recently retired from more than three decades of teaching in the Department of English at Stephen F. Austin State University. Born in Lakeland, Florida, he came from a family of non-readers. His father, terribly wounded during WW1, and too ill to hold a steady job when he left the service, confessed that he had spent only one day in public school and could barely write his name. Alfred alone in the family got any formal education beyond high school– thanks largely to the GI Bill "and to his wife's money."

He enlisted in the Army in 1948, attended a military pharmacy school, and spent most of his service in Alaska (considered overseas in those days). Upon discharge he attended the University of Florida, received a B.A. in English three years later, and, having run out of money while working on the masters degree, obtained a direct commission in the Navy (a feat almost unheard of in peacetime, fellow officers told him). Marriage followed in 1959. In 1962 he received a Ph.D. from Florida State University and began a career of teaching, genteel poverty, and bibliography at a succession of universities, ending with Stephen F. Austin State, where he rose to the rank of professor after a year.

Shivers penned several novels, including *The Spectral Mozart*, a ghost story for young people; *Enoch Diamond*, an adventure story about the American Revolutionary War; and *The Angel and the Heir*, a fantasy.

The novels are currently making the rounds of the publishers.

His scholarly works include: *Jessamyn West* (1972), *Maxwell Anderson* (1976), *Maxwell Anderson: An Annotated Bibliography of Primary and Secondary Works* (1985), and *The Life of Maxwell Anderson* (1983).

The Life of Maxwell Anderson (397 pp.) Represents the culmination of eleven years of research and writing. Along the way Shivers learned that much of what passes for biography contains a good deal of sloppy scholarship and factual error. In his own work he was fortunate to interview many of those who knew Anderson personally (very important!); this included his third wife, some of his brothers, a sister, all four of his children, and some of his neighbors and participants in the Playwrights Producing Company. He received valuable mail from some of the playwright's childhood friends and acquaintances (fortunate to reach these people before sunset put an end to all such records).

Theater legend Joshua Logan wrote a glowing review for *The Life of Maxwell Anderson*. (You may recall that Logan directed numerous films and plays including *Mr. Roberts* and *South Pacific*, as well as Anderson's own *Knickerbocker Holiday*.)

Shivers tells us that Anderson gave few interviews and discouraged anyone from writing a life of him–and for good reason. Among the curious things that Shivers learned was that Anderson was not actually married to the second woman that he lived with, Mab, known to the world as Mrs. Maxwell Anderson. Also that he published–under a pen name– a touching and nostalgic novel about adolescent sex called *Morning, Noon and Night*. The background is Atlantic, Pa., where he was born. Even today extremely few people know that he had written the book.

A special ceremony by the SFA Alumni Association celebrated the gift of *The Life of Maxwell Anderson* to the Ralph Steen Library, becoming their one-millionth book. It is also the definitive Anderson biograpy to this date (the same applies to the West books). The biography also won Shivers the Regency Professor Award which consisted of a bronze medal the size of a buckwheat pancake, $2,500 in cash, and temporary freedom from teaching freshman English.

Shivers is proud to say that he helped build the Lamp Lite Playhouse in Nacogdoches, and was lucky enough to act in a half-dozen plays produced there.

Dr. Shivers--soldier, pharmacist, sailor, professor, actor, amateur horticulturist, author–likes to think he is a credit to American literary scholarship and to the literary scene in Nacogdoches.

* * *

Garland Roark was one of the most prominent American authors, but, as is often the case for both writers and artists–Garland was both--the road was long and arduous; and the path from Groesbeck, Texas-- Roark's birthplace–to the Gulf of Mexico, the birthplace of his many sea novels, was fraught with perils of little less concern than those encountered on the road to Biblical Jericho. Rejection and frustration repeatedly battered the writer as would a hurricane. Fortunately, he was aided by a good Samaritan--his wife, Leola. As did author, Ardath Mayhar, Garland spells out in a newspaper column the hazards of writing and publishing a book. Friends look at the author in a new (and usually skewered) light. Columnists will praise you and scour you. You will be one reviewer's Shakespeare, another's Bulwer-Lytton.

Garland's lawyer father died when he was only four. His mother taught school; however, Garland was far from being the teacher's pet! When the class misbehaved, she paddled her son as an example! Sharon describes a photo of her father as a small boy wearing knee pants and a deep frown; perhaps he had just been made an example!

As a child, he took a mail order course in cartooning, reportedly costing 25 cents. Garland was ambidextrous; he drew pictures with both hands simultaneously, depicting his subjects in various poses and situations. His instructors scarcely knew what to make of them–or him!

Leola and Garland finished reading a novel, only to be disappointed by its ending. He said he could write a better story than that. At first, he rejected his wife's suggestion that he do exactly that, allowing that nobody would read it; however, he wrote one, which failed to find a publisher. The next three also failed. It all took a long time, for he wrote longhand in spiral notebooks. He regarded typewriters as annoying contraptions.

Leola wore many caps–those of critic, editor, monitor of his calendar and communicator to his publisher. She proofed his copy and sent it out for typing. This was the routine for twenty-six published books. His fifth book, and the first one published, *Wake of the Red Witch*, published by Doubleday, brought forth a new and exciting realm. It brought international acclaim and a movie. It brought John Wayne into the Roarks' life and home. Wayne and the Roarks became fast friends. The actor said that was his favorite role, and he named his own movie company Batjak Ltd. from the novel. The best seller, 1946, was selected by the Literary Guild. It brought a new career.

In Houston Garland was advertising manager for Walgreens. With the success of "*Witch*," the Roarks purchased a home on South McGregor in Houston. The dwelling afforded a spacious study for the author. Daughter Sharon was approximately seven years of age. John Wayne visited. Sharon, her sister and boy cousin put on a show influenced by

Wayne's fight with the octopus in the movie. They came into the room with a balloon that was shaped like an octopus and commenced stabbing it with pins. John roared with laughter and asked Sharon if she would like to be in movies. Her mother gave an immediate and resounding, "No! " Therefore, the world was deprived of a talented actress before she could hop a plane for Tinseltown! As guests arrived for the party, Sharon and her sister turned on the lawn sprinklers, wetting the guests! Sharon admits that they got into big trouble for that bit of mischief!

Sharon is very successful in the arts, and gives much credit to her persevering and talented father. He instilled in her to be what you want to be. She is a concert-quality pianist.

Fame brought by *Wake of the Red Witch* elevated Garland to the status of VIP. In addition to being a member of the Heart Board with Dr. Michael DeBakey, he was a one-man welcoming committee for celebrities arriving in Houston. Personages such as Clint Walker and Gene Autry were overnight guests of the Roarks. The famous Shamrock Hotel was often their hostelry of choice. One morning about 2:30, Garland received a call from the Shamrock. Would he please come get John Wayne and Gene Autry? They had gotten into a drunken fight, one being knocked through the shower door! The hotel certainly didn't want the police or attending publicity!

Sharon recalls being in a restaurant when John Wayne paged her father.

General Douglas MacArthur and his young son, Arthur, met the Roark family in the Shamrock Hotel. They went to the penthouse. Sharon remembers the general as huge, polite and a fine conversationalist. He and Garland discussed world affairs. Garland was a polished conversationalist and gentleman who could hold his own with any intellectual. He and Dr. Ralph Steen of the University of Stephen F. Austin in Nacogdoches often discussed history. Sharon played the piano and got acquainted with Arthur. The boy's hobby was collecting postcards. He and Sharon exchanged cards for years afterward.

A banquet was planned for Brownies and their fathers. Each scout was to introduce her father and tell his occupation. This caused Sharon considerable anxiety for her father didn't go to work as did others. Instead of leaving with a briefcase every morning, he merely stayed at home and wrote!

The Roarks were good friends with Congressman Albert Thomas and wife, Lera. The couples were on the steps of the capitol in Washington when they met Lyndon Johnson wearing a Stetson. Garland also wore a Stetson. Naturally, they posed together for photos. Leola busily snapped the shutter. They parted proud that she had gotten the famous men on film for posterity. When she opened the camera, there was no film!

Once during a party, Sharon's father said, "Little Doll, what are you going to do the next few minutes?"

"Anything you want."

"Good. I have a getaway car outside; let's get in and take off."

"Where are we going?"

"To get something for your mother."

The car braked at a magnolia tree. They got out and he told her, "Little Doll, climb up there and pick the largest blossom you can find."

"But what will people think?"

"Just tell them that you're hunting bugs."

Success and fame can have negative effects. Sharon relates that shortly after *Witch* became a movie, her family was on a train between Houston and Dallas. A man entered the dining car and with mysterious emphasis asked if anyone knew who was on the train. "Joan Crawford! " he triumphantly announced.

"Well," Leola responded, "so is Garland Roark."

Within minutes, a man approached and said that Joan wished fifteen minutes with Mr. Roark. Very well. As Garland got up, his wife checked her watch. The man showed Garland into Joan's compartment, shut the door and stood outside. Crawford requested a part in Roark's next film. He tried to assure her that he had no control over that. Convinced that her persuasive method was superior to Hollywood powers, she put it into action.

Leola's watch told her that her husband was overdue. She went to Joan's compartment. The guardian told her that Miss Crawford was tending to business and she couldn't be disturbed. There was scuffling against the door. Mrs. Roark reached around him and shoved open the door, which Garland was struggling to open. Joan was undressing! "That's my husband! " Leola shouted, pulling Garland out.

Joan's companion casually said, "That's Miss Crawford's way of doing business."

From "A 12-Part Series by Garland Roark" reprinted by *The Houston Chronicle,* and this author's interview with Sharon Roark Zillmer, we learn of a fantastic series of circumstances that gave Texans a precious record of Texas' struggle for independence. The good fortune began when Leola developed shingles from their five-year-old daughter's measles in 1946. Further, Dr. Charles R. Reece tended to Leola and, knowing her fondness for antique furniture, mentioned the estate sale of the late Mrs. S. E. Murrelle. Mrs. Roark hastened to 1416 Rosalie Street in Houston only to learn that most of the furnishings were gone. A yellowed bundle of letters bound by a faded ribbon caught her attention; they were among attic trash fated for burning. The lady supervising the sale told Leola she could have them.

They were letters from William P. Zuber! Zuber was the last survivor of Sam Houston's San Jacinto army. Actually, Zuber was one of about 200 of those ill and the guards keeping the army's baggage at Harrisburg during the battle. The letters began on August, 24, 1891, to Miss Mary Gillaspie of Huntsville, daughter of Zuber's captain during the Texas Revolution. Zuber eventually corresponded with Mrs. S. E. Murrelle (the former Sue Gillaspie). The letters served as a journal, noting movements of the Texas Army throughout the Revolution, including the battle at San Jacinto and beyond.

Within a few years, the Roarks moved to 1323 North Fredonia St. in Nacogdoches. The solitude and beauty of the locale provedto be ideal for a writer. Garland and Leola knew that a few blocks away, fellow writers Karle Wilson Baker and her daughter, Charlotte Baker Montgomery were recording the magic of flora and fauna on paper. Generations would benefit from the works of all four writers. The gracious and lovable mother of attorney/humorist Bob Murphey lived a short distance from the Roarks. Mr. Roark was inducted into the prestigious Texas Institute of Letters. For relaxation, Garland painted in oils. Two subjects were Sam Houston and the Old Stone Fort. He made a book of sketches and poems, a treasure that remains in the family.

Garland indeed had an indelible connection to the sea; he was onboard a yacht battling through a hurricane to Velasco. The Texas Navy inspired several of his novels. In addition to *Wake of the Red Witch* were *Star in the Rigging, The Lady and the Deep Blue Sea, Fair Wind to Java, Slant of theWild Wind, Should the Wind Be Fair, Outlawed Banner,* and *The Wreck of the Running Gale.* Also, *The Coin of Contraband; The True Story of United States Custom Investigator Al Sharff.* Garland wrote newspaper articles about Texas historical figures.

Though Garland preferred writing to making speeches, he often addressed groups. Roark chronicled Al Sharff's experiences in *Coin of Contraband,* one of which was being hired in Arizona by the F. B. I. to stop a German radio station in Mexico in 1917,which he did. After the book was published, Garland and Al and their wives attended events in San Antonio related to the men. American Broadcasting Company sent a crew from New York to film the function. Garland and Al were honored with certificates designating them alcaldes of San Antonio.

The original manuscript of *Witch,* composed of more than a dozen notebooks, was put in an old freezer for safekeeping. The manuscript was eventually lost, probably when the appliance was disposed of–a heart-breaking incident, but at least inadvertent. Perhaps equally rendering is the story of Woodrow Wilson Rawls.

Rawls, though uneducated, always wanted to write. He told a conference of English teachers that he wrote a manuscript on scraps of paper and brown grocery sacks. He met an educated woman while repairing her roof, and they became engaged. He was ashamed for her to see evidence of his ignorance and, on the night prior to their wedding, burned the manuscript in his rear yard. His wife liked his dog stories and encouraged him to write. He reconstructed the burned story. After numerous rejections (of course!) the story was published as the famous and incredibly successful *Where the Red Fern Grows.* The audience was horrified that he had destroyed the original. This story is courtesy of retired English professor, Jerry G. Nye--a fellow citizen of my hometown and friend of Woodrow Rawls–published in The Lindsay (Oklahoma) News, March 28, 2002.

Roark, who during his youth, worked in the oil fields around Mexia, Texas, wrote a novel, *Drill A Crooked Hole.* It was inspired by the crooked hole scandal of Northeast Texas during the early 1960s. Of course, he was roundly criticized by those who were convinced that he wrote about them. Nasty letters and threats were common.

The Roarks owned a place in Boulder, Colorado. General Spaulding, retired, lived across the street. A party of about 125 guests celebrated his 80th birthday. General Dwight Eisenhower was present. The Roarks observed from their yard. Spaulding invited them over to meet "Ike." Guests brought something that Spaulding had given to them. Garland hired a blue grass band to play Texas music. General Spaulding was very alert and appreciative.

Garland enjoyed a long and successful career. One wonders how many pencils/pens expired in his hands! While visiting his daughter in Colorado, he contracted pneumonia. Shortly after being flown by private plane to Nacogdoches, he died in February, 1985.

Sharon told the funeral director to bring his body home. She began making a room ready. She said her mother and sister "threw a fit." But Sharon insisted that it only proper that he be at home the night before his funeral. Sharon looked outside and said, "Well, here he comes." She said she would sleep in a sleeping bag beside the casket. Silence reigned supreme.

The following morning, Lera Thomas and Mary Bates, wife of Bill Bates, whose name was given to the University of Houston Law School, came to pay their respects. Leola, Wanda and Sharon received them. Leola and Wanda were still not speaking to Sharon.

Lera told Leola that she was so proud of her for having Garland's body at home as was customary in years past.

Mrs. Roark beamed and replied, "Thank you. Wanda and I thought it a wonderful idea."

The funeral was held February 11, in the Rock Springs Presbyterian Church northwest of Nacogdoches. A blue norther howled across that hilltop and flailed the trees guarding the ancient church. Garland told Sharon long ago, "Little Doll, say something at my funeral, even if you have to stand on your head to do it."

Fortunately, she stood on her feet and read the prelude to *Wake of the Red Witch*. She read that Sam Rosen had a story to tell. Sam warned that his varied and incredible adventures might wrench readers. He had learned much from Mayrant Sidneye and Ralls about shipping and greed in the tropics. Garland Roark tells it expertly in that great, classic novel. Sharon finished reading, turned to the casket and said, "Good night, Daddy," and took her seat beside her mother and sister. More than a few tears stained the floor of the church. The warmth of Sharon's reading, the sermon and anecdotes rendered the frigid air of less consequence.

The great architect Frank Lloyd Wright designed the Johnson Wax plant. When the building was finished, he was asked about a sign. He replied that the building itself was the company's signature. Garland's grave marker simply gives his name and the dates--all that is needed to know him. His work and memory live in perpetuity. But when you see a Walgreens sign, salute it for it is a replica of Garland's writing.

(A steeple was installed on the Rock Springs Presbyterian Church on December 26, 1985, courtesy of Adlai T. Mast, Jr. and son, John.)

* * *

Pearland, Texas
October 11, 1979

Mr. Roark:

I enjoyed the article about you in The Sunday *Sentinel,* July 22, 1979. Recently, I had the pleasure of seeing *The Wake of the Red Witch* for the first time since it first came out.

I note that you wrote four novels before publishing "Red Witch." Did you eventually sell any of those four?

I wish you success with your new book. I would enjoy hearing from you.

> Best wishes,
> Roy Fish

* * *

Garland Roark
1323 North Fredonia

Nacogdoches, Texas 75961

Mr. Roy Fish
Pearland, Texas

Thanks for yours of Oct. 11th. John Wayne was really young when making *Wake of the Red Witch*. It was his first big hit movie and we became great friends. A great guy–

Yes, I wrote 4 novels before that. No sales, but experience, which I certainly needed! ! And how!

Nice of you to write me. I appreciate it very much.

All the best to you–

Sincerely,
Garland Roark

* * *

Nacogdoches, Texas
October 28, 1980

Mr. Roark–

I have just finished reading *Wake of the Red Witch*, and enjoyed it as much as the movie I saw first as a teen-ager. A friend in Houston played "hookey" from school for her first and last time to see the film when it first came out.

Your writing, in my opinion, is better in that first novel than that of many, if not most, prominent authors I've read.

John Wayne was a natural for the role of Ralls.

P. S. According to the library card, "Witch" is still very popular. Also, looks like Nell Harris* might sell her book soon.

Regards,
Roy Fish

*The late Nell Harris, a mutual friend, founded Hedgecroft Hospital in Houston in the 1940s for the treatment of polio victims and wrote a fictionalized account in her novel, The Castle Makers.

* * *

Nacogdoches, Texas
February 11, 1985

Mrs. Garland Roark
1323 N. Fredonia
Nacogdoches, Texas 75961

Dear Mrs. Roark,

Decades ago, when *Wake of the Red Witch* came to our Oklahoma theater, I certainly had no thought of being touched by its creator. Eventually that fine man and novelist had the occasion to encourage this struggling writer and to wish me well. I am aware that you strongly supported Garland and helped him to be successful. Thanks to both of you for enriching mankind's lot, especially mine.

I was at Rock Springs today to say farewell to Garland–a man I regret not knowing better.

Warm regards and best wishes to you and yours.

Roy L. Fish
1824 Heather
Nacogdoches, TX 75961

* * *

Wayne Davis: An adage among writers is that to be successful is to write what you like. Wayne has done exactly that, thanks to encouragement from both his Carlsbad, New Mexico, high school English teacher, Miss Hazel Melaas, and author Joe Lansdale of Nacogdoches, Texas.

Wayne was born in Richmond, Virginia, to a mechanical engineer, who moved his family to a house and a spread south of Carlsbad to be near his employment with potash mines. Wayne was little more than a decade old. Eventually, he married and worked in the mines–a job he disliked. What he liked was horses and gathering cattle. He kept a horse and occasionally assisted rancher friends; but mining overshadowed the good and he checked out to build Carlsbad's first fitness gym. He eventually managed gyms in San Angelo and Abilene, then started one in Nacogdoches. Joe Lansdale, member of Western Writers of America and physical fitness practitioner, signed up with the new gym. Joe and Wayne talked books. Wayne attended WWA conferences, beginning in 1986.

Wayne's love of the West became evident in *John Stone and the Choctaw Kid*, who rode between hard covers at M. Evans & Company in 1992 and into fame the following year. The WWA gave it the Medicine Pipe Award for the Best First Western, and it was runner-up for the Golden Spur Award for Best Western Novel. Berkeley obtained the paperback contract. G.K. Hall published it in large print in 1999. Among those praising the novel are Elmer Kelton, Richard S. Wheeler, Joe R. Lansdale, Gary McCarthy and *New Mexico Magazine*. Two more novels followed: *Reklaw*, and *Silverthorne*.

Wayne and wife, Joan, live on acreage near Nacogdoches. Horses are still an important part of his life. And Wayne–gentleman and Westerner— remains important in our lives.

* * *

Archie Philip McDonald, PhD, historian, tells us about Texas through numerous publications, disciplines, offices and associations. He received his BS from Lamar University, Beaumont, TX, in 1958. He was Research Assistant at Rice University, 1958-1960, during which he earned an MA. His PhD came from Louisiana State University at Baton Rouge.

From 1960-1963, he served LSU as Graduate Assistant, Coordinator of Assistants and Teaching Assistant. Murray State University employed him as Assistant Professor, 1963-1964. Except for a stint as Visiting Professor, Winter and Spring, 1970, at Central Washington State College at Ellensburg, Washington, he has been at Stephen F. Austin State University from 1964 to the present (Assistant Professor, 1964-1967, Associate Professor, 1967-1972, Professor of History, 1972 to present).

Professor McDonald has been Executive Director of the East Texas Historical Association since 1971; also editor of the *East Texas Historical Journal*, published twice annually, since 1971. He was President of the Nacogdoches County Historical Survey Committee, 1976. He served as a member of the Texas Committee for the Humanities from 1979-1983, at which time he became Chair. The Executive Council of the Texas State Historical Association benefitted from his services for two terms. He was Chair of the Program Committee, member of the Nominating Committee, Chair of the Long-Range Planning Committee, and President, 1985-1986.

He was on the Board of Directors for the Texas County Records Inventory Project, and Counselor to the Texas Folklore Society. The Texas State Library disseminates information throughout the state; this very responsible function is served well by the Editorial Board, of which Dr. McDonald was a member.

Dr. McDonald was Editor of *Encyclopedia U. S. A.,* 1982-1989. He was Chair of the State Board of Review for the National Register, 1985-1987; and Chair of the Old San Antonio Road Preservation Commission, 1989-1993. He was Book Review Editor for the *Journal of Confederate History*, 1990, and *Civil War Regiments*, 1992 to 2000. He served on the Texas Sesquicentennial of Statehood Commission, 1994-1995. The professor was Advisory Editor of the Texas State Historical Association, *The New Handbook of Texas*, 1996. He was Editor of the quarterly *Nacogdoches Sampler,* 1988-1996. He began his Red River Weekly Commentary in 2001, and continues to present.

McDonald has served Friends of the Texas Historical Commission from 1998 to the present as Trustee, and as an Antiquities Advisory Board member since 2000. He was Researcher and Evaluator, Texas

Parks and Wildlife Department/Texas Historical Commission Historical Survey, 1998-1999.

Books authored by Dr. McDonald bisect and chronicle Texas history; among them are *By Early Candlelight, The Story of Old Milam; Travis; Texas: A Sesquicentennial Presentation; Texas: All Hail The Mighty State* (Eakin Press: Austin, 1983: revised edition, Eakin, 1991); *America to 1877 Study Guide; Texas: Yesterday and Today.* Fourth Grade Text, with Gary S. Elbow, Mary Garcia Metzger, and Rudolfo Rocha, 1988. Co-author. Revised 1996; *Where the Corn Grows Tall*, Eakin Press, Austin, 1991; *Texas: What Do You Know About The Lone Star State?; Nacogdoches*, with James G. Partin, and Joe and Carolyn Ericson; *Nacogdoches, Texas–A Pictorial History*, with R. G. and Ouida Whitaker Dean; *Historic Texas: An Illustrated Chronicle of Texas' Past; "Uncommon Valor . . . Common Virtue:" A Tribute to Bennett P. Blake, U. S. Marine on Iwo Jima*, compiled by Roy M. Blake and Archie P. McDonald.

Books As Editor

Make Me a Map of the Valley: The Journal of Jedediah Hotchkis, 1862-1865. Southern Methodist University Press: Dallas, 1974 listed in Civil War Illustrated in 1980 as one of the One Hundred Best Books on the Civil War, in Richard Harwell, *InTall Cotton, The 200 Most Important Confederate Books for the Reader, Researcher, and Collector* (Austin, 1978), and again *Civil War, The Magazine of the Civil War Society* (January,1995) as one of the 100 Best Books in the Civil War.

Hurrah for Texas! The Diary of Adolphus Sterne. Listed in John H. Jenkins/ *Basic Texas Books* (Austin, 1983), as one of the 269 essential works for a research library in Texas history; *The Mexican War: Crisis for American Democracy; Fighting Men, The Western Military Heritage; Recollections of a Long Life; First United Methodist Church, San Augustine, Texas, 1837-1976; Eastern Texas History; Nacogdoches: Wilderness Outpost to Modern City, 1779-1979; The Texas Experience; Notable East Texans; Encyclopedia USA*, an open ended encyclopedia published at the rate of 2-3 per year, for Academic International Press, Volumes 4-12; *Shooting Stars: Heroes and Heroines of Western Film; Helpful Hints for House-Husbands of Uppity Women*, 1988, Second Edition, 1997; *On This Day of New Beginnings: Selected Inaugural Addresses of Texas Governors.* Texas State Library, Austin, 1979; *The Texas Heritage.* With Ben H. Procter. Forum Press: St. Louis, 1980, Harlan Davidson, 3rd ed., 1997; *A Nation of Sovereign States: Secession & War in the Confederacy; Dare-Devils All: Texas Mier Expedition, 1842-1844.* J. M. Nance. *To Live and Die in Dixie": How The South Formed A Nation.* Journal of Confederate History Series, Vol. XX.

Southern Heritage Press, Murfreesboro, 1999. Reprint.

Monographs

The Old Stone Fort. Texas State Historical Association: Austin, 1981; *The Texas Republic*. American Book Company: Boston, 1981; *The Trail to San Jacinto*. Listed as one of the ten most helpful books by novelist James A. Michener in preparation of his novel, *Texas; Travis: One Chief Rol'd Among the Rest; Americans Elect Their President from Washington to Reagan or Mondale?* Published serially in the *Nacogdoches Sunday Sentinel*, September 2-November 11, 1984.

Newspaper Columns

"Not So Long Ago," weekly column in *Nacogdoches Daily Sentinel,* February 1991-present. "Special Days" in *Nacogdoches Daily Sentinel,* February 1994-1996, 1999-present. "All Things Historical," with Bob Bowman, appears in 30 newspapers in East Texas.

* * *

Joe Ellis Ericson, PhD was born June 9, 1925, at North Camp, Throckmorton Division, of the SMS Ranch in Throckmorton County, Texas, to Lester Y. and Lena A. (Ellis) Ericson. In 1927 the family moved to Spur, Dickens County, where his father entered the grocery business and where his younger brother Lester Lane was born. He attended public school in Spur, graduating in 1942, having been awarded varsity letters in football and basketball, beome first chair of the saxophone section of the band, and having participated in speech and drama activities. He was also active in the Boy Scouts, earning the rank of Eagle Scout in 1941.

In 1943, Joe attended classes at the University of Texas, transferring to Texas Technological Collete in 1944 where he received a BS degree in 1946 with majors in secondary education, government and history. He earned the MA degree at the same school in 1948 with a major in government and minor in history. Thereaftter, he entered the graduate school at the University of Texas at Austin, but transferred in 1955 to Texas Tech, where he earned a PhD in 1957 specializing in American government, American history, and American literature.

In 1955, he married Carolyn Reeves (Easter) in Lubbock, and the couple went to Arlington, where he was an instructor in the Social Sciences Department. They moved in 1957 to Nacogdoches, where he received an apointment as Assistant Professor of History and Government at Stephen F. Austin State University. During his career, he also taught at the University of Texas, Texas Tech, West Texas State University, and Arlington State University. He was promoted to Associate Professor of Government, SFASU, in 1965 and to Professor in 1967. In the meantime, he was chosen to head the newly created

Department of Political Science in 1965 and served in that capacity until his partial retirement in 1987. He continued to teach on a part-time basis until 1997 and became Professor Emeritus in 1998.

During his academic career he was elected to three honor societies: Pi Sigma Alpha (political science), Phi Alpha Theta (history) and Alpha Chi (national honor). He received a Certificate of Achievement for his teaching in 1969 and in 1975. The SFA Alumni Association voted him their Distinguished Professor Award in 1973. He also held memberships in the American Studies Assn., American Political Science Assn., Southwestern Political Science Assn., and Texas Association of College Teachers, serving as president of the American Studies Assn. of Texas and president of Region Ii, Alpha Chi. For more than two years he was co-sponsor of the SFA chapter of Alpha Chi.

For eight years Ericson was SFA's representative on the governing board of the Lone Star Athletic Conference, serving as its president for two years. He holds membership in: Sons of the Republic of Texas, Knights of San Jacinto, Jamestowne Society, Magna Charta Barons, Descendants of Ancient Planters, and Descendants of World War I Veterans. He has been President General, First Vice President General and Historian General of the SRT, Knight Commander and Knight Chaplin of Knights of San Jacinto, Regent and Vice Regent of the East Texas Colony and State Herald of the Magna Charta Dames and Barons.

During his academic years Ericson co-authored a widely adopted college-level textbook, *Practicing Texas Politics*, that attained some ten editions, and its companion, *Practicing Texas Politics: A Brief Survey*, six editions (both Houghton Mifflin, Boston) His articles dealing with Texas government appeared in *Southwestern Social Science Quarterly*, and articles relating to Texas history appeared in *West Texas Historical Association Yearbook, Southwestern Historical Quarterly* and *East Texas Historical Journal.*

Beginning in 1989, he began researching and publishing books and articles on prominent figures in Texas history, among them *Spoiling for a Fight: John S. Roberts and Early Nacogdoches* (1989), *Personalities on the East Texas Frontier* (1998) and *Martin Palmer—The Man and the Legend* (1999). He has authored or co-authored three books relating to East Texas history: *Nacogdoches: The Oldest Town in Texas* (1995), *Nacogdoshes, An Informal History* (2000) and *Early East Texas* (2002).

Other works include *Judges of the Republic of Texas* (1980), *A Guide to Texas Research* (1993, co-author), *Banks and Bankers in Early Texas 1835-1875* (1976). Articles on a variety of genealogical topics have appeared in *Stirpes, Texas State Genealogical Quarterly, Selected Papers of the Seventh Grand Reunion of the Descendants of the*

Founders of Natchitoches, the *Nacogdoches Sampler, Reflections,* and *Yesterdays.*

Seventeen articles prepared by Ericson are included in the six-volume *The New Handbook of Texas* (Texas State Historical Assn., 1996). Book reviews by Ericson appeared in the *American Quarterly, Southwestern Social Science Quarterly* and the *East Texas Historical Journal.*

Joe E. and Carolyn R. Ericson have three children: Linda Ericson Devereaus, Joseph Reeves Ericson, and John Ellis Ericson. All three are graduates of Stephen F. Austin State University.

Tim James, JD, attorney: Many professionals begin at or near the bottom and work up. Dishwashers become restaurant owners. Brick tenders become masonry contractors. Mechanics helpers and porters eventually own repair shops. Rookie policemen become detectives or chiefs. Mr. James became an attorney, then a patrolman! In no way does that signify failure; to the contrary, only a person of wise and remarkable character would arrange his career in that order. To learn the nuts and bolts of life, one must tread trenches with those who do it routinely. Mr. James truly learned and served Texas and the United States in numerous and various capacities. To his further credit, he didn't trade on his famous parents' reputations. Trumpeter and band leader Harry James gained fame during the heyday of the Big Band era. Betty Grable became his step-mother when he was very young. Mr. James did for law what his father and step-mother did for entertainment–strove for and obtained excellence.

Tim earned a Bachelor of Arts degree from Texas Christian University in 1963. While attending the George Washington University School of Law, 1963-1965, he was special assistant to Senator Carl Hayden (Democrat, Arizona). Tim received his Doctor of Jurisprudence from the University of Houston in 1967. Immediately, he served the Texas Attorney General's staff as trial lawyer.

In 1968, Mr. James joined the Houston Police Department, and was named "Rookie of the Year." He served as a policeman and practiced law for ten years, 1968-72; 1980-85. He was responsible for all police litigation and applying Civil Law to the Department's procedure. Numerous awards from both the Police Department and civic organizations were bestowed upon him during that period.

In 1973, he served in the Texas Attorney General's organized crime division. Also, he worked with Mexican and international officials regarding narcotics and contraband. Mr. James was elected by the 250 graduates of the F. B. I. Academy, 109th Session, 1977, to give the graduation address. The Texas Supreme Court appointed him to its Board of Disciplinary Appeals.

The United States' participation in the war in Kosovo, Yugoslavia, effected numerous complicated legal issues. International and European laws were relative to war crimes, human rights and constructing judicial procedures—no easy task in a divided nation. Mr. James had the honor of assisting in working through the situation.

Mr. James sank roots in Nacogdoches, Texas, and became Assistant District Attorney for the145[th] Judicial District in 1985. He then established a solo practice. He served two terms as District Attorney for the same District, before resuming private practice. His office is conveniently located across Pilar Street from the Nacogdoches County Courthouse, and one block from the site of Sam Houston's home on the plaza. Incidentally, the civic plaza occupies the former church plaza.

Mr. James proved worthy of following historical attorneys Thomas J. Rusk, Charles S. Taylor and Sam Houston in Nacogdoches. In 1996, he was appropriately honored with the designation of Master Peace Officer.

* * *

Bob Murphey, attorney/humorist: Numerous folk throughout the United States, including the United States Supreme Court, Canada and Mexico, agree that Mr. Murphey was the ideal Goodwill Ambassador of Nacogdoches and East Texas. It is appropriate that he received, September, 2000, the first Best of East Texas Award. Bob and Doris Bowman, owners of The Best of East Texas Publishers in Lufkin, instituted the award. Mr. Bowman, member of the East Texas Historical Association, authored more than twenty books about East Texas. He shared the love of the area with Mr. Murphey.

Mr. Murphey wasn't quite a teenager when he lost his left arm in an incident with a horse; but fortitude drove him to graduate from SFASU in 1942 and, after serving in the Merchant Marine during W. W. II, earned a law degree from the University of Texas. After several years in Austin as the Sergeant-at-Arms of the Texas House of Representatives, he returned to Nacogdoches and became District Attorney for six years, during which time he undoubtedly made miscreants unhappy.

He enjoyed a distinguished career in law, but later mostly occupied himself making people laugh. For decades, he had been guest speaker at SFA's Distinguished Alumnus Banquet. In 2002, he was named to the SFASU Hall of Fame. He became a member in 1972, 30 years after his graduation. The International Platform Association bestowed its Mark Twain Award on him in 1994. He was also a member of the National Speakers Association Hall of Fame. He had been a guest on many programs, including Ralph Emery's "Nashville Now" and "Hee Haw."

But for all of that and more, Murphey remained modest and reserved. He was the nephew of the late former Governor Coke Stevenson, but like his colleague Tim James, he didn't invoke his prominent kin's name. Bob wasn't exactly fond of name-droppers.

Bob traveled extensively, speaking at conventions and numerous other gatherings. Seasoned and wise fellow that he was, he knew that laughter mends damaged spirits. He was responsible for belly laughs across a large piece of our planet. He has spoken in 44 states, Canada, and Mexico. He recorded albums, broadcast, and traveled telling about mules running away with a wagon and spilling kids who don't know the way home. Though modest, he wasn't beyond correcting dictionaries and thesauruses. For instance, a level-headed East Texas woman is one who has snuff juice running from both corners of her mouth! Don't look for that in the SFASU Library—not even in Special Collections. His stories convert our despair into hope, makes the good in us better. Like fellow attorney Tim James, his work is a credit to Nacogdoches and Texas and beyond. Mirth recognizes no boundaries.

* * *

Gene and James Milford's Barber Shop: For many years, Ocie Milford and sons James and Gene operated their shop at 119 West Main, just off the northwest corner of the Nacogdoches town square. A picture on the wall is of the shop located there in 1926. No one knows how long it was there before that. Another picture depicts an angry Geronimo. There is a very early television with a screen that looks like a ship's porthole, and a hairball as large as a softball. A rare lever-action shotgun and other reminders of the past lend an old-time ambience to the place. Both men and women love it!

The brothers continued to barber at that location for years following their father's death. James's daughter joined them. Eventually, they moved to 110 North Church Street, when Jack Ward gave it up for retirement. It is appropriate that it is located across the street from the former opera house where the Marx Brothers developed their famous routine. Laughter echoing from Milford's could be mistaken for that of the funny brothers across the street many decades past.

O. H. "Bobby" York is responsible for much of the merriment; aside from serious accounts as a member of the 7th Infantry Division in Korea, he is a spinner of tales and jokes.

Bob Murphey regularly drops in at Milford's. Others of note that one sees there are attorney Tim James, and authors Joe Lansdale and Larry Feaster. Wilford Ray Jones "Crazy Ray," famed mascot of the Dallas Cowboys, used to drop in occasionally and entertain. Entertainment at Milford's might not weigh heavily against Groucho, Harpo, Chico and

Gummo, but it's worth the trip, even if you drive from Timpson, Bobo or Blair. Incidentally, you can get a good haircut while having fun.

* * *

Wilford "Crazy Ray" Jones, a native of Nacogdoches, was a showman in his youth long before moving to Dallas. The late Mrs. Ella Mae Fleet Sheffield was Ray's elementary school teacher. While directing tours through her museum on South Street, she described her unique student. The boy wasn't a strong student, she said with a smile, but he followed her about the classroom and willingly performed any chore she assigned to him. A man admiring Mrs. Sheffield's memorabilia said he worked with Ray at Nibco, the local valve factory. He opined that Ray's chief contribution was in entertaining fellow employees.

Barber Gene Milford tells that Ray stood on the corner of Church and Main Streets and "threw" his voice into a trash receptacle. That voice was likened unto that of a dog barking and whining. Naturally, a man strolling past determined to rescue the poor creature. The only thing he found that needed help was the trash to be hauled away. He shook his head in bewilderment and sauntered away.

Gene also relates that Ray shined shoes in the Milford shop. Merchants and courthouse personnel occasionally dropped in for a spot of news or simply to visit–perhaps to hear a Bobby York joke. Noble Shaw owned and operated the old-time department store next door to Milford's for decades. Noble practically wore a path from his entry to that of the shop. One day, Mrs. Shaw had occasion to be in the shop.

Mrs. Shaw suddenly became concerned that a dog had been shut inside a drawer in the shine stand. That "dog" was very vocal about it! Ray and the barbers, struggling to keep straight faces, nonchalantly went about their business. Mrs. Shaw returned to the store and told her husband about the abused pooch. Of course, Noble investigated. Shucks, Mr. Noble, that was just Wilbur Ray honing his skills and having fun. Fun is what Ray is about–for himself and multitudes. Ray would never mistreat a dog. In fact, he earned money from dogs.

Wilbur Ray left Nacogdoches for Dallas in 1953, at age twenty-two, and began to regularly entertain at the State Fair. Neil Fletcher, Sr. hired him to perform antics near his corn dog stand.

Seven years after arriving in Dallas, Ray and his famous stick horse began entertaining Dallas Cowboys fans. For decades, he and his steed raced back and forth before the crowds, seemingly competing with the players for yardage. Eventually, health problems slowed him. Heart surgery came in 1995. Two years later, at age 66, his right foot was removed because of diabetes complications. But he is game to keep on entertaining, especially children. Mattie, his spouse, takes him about.

17
Ezekiel Airship

Burrell Cannon's seventy-four years were filled with creativity and accomplishments. Before he was twenty years of age, he was a blacksmith, mechanic and an ordained Baptist minister. He spoke several foreign languages, was a missionary, sawmill operator, and inventor. One source gives his birthplace as Coffeeville, Mississippi; another says Jackson, Mississippi. Both agree that he was born April 16, 1848, and attended college at Clinton, Mississippi. We do not know when he arrived in Texas.

The minister might have first settled in Upshur County. The Cotton Belt passenger schedule as published in the *Lafayette Iron Record*, November 3, 1893, lists Cannon Station and Pine, Texas, as being the same stop. He lived at Pine and preached in a one-room school. Pine's Baptist church was organized in 1905.

Mr. W. H. Fowler of Gilmer visited the Cannon home at Pine and noticed "strange contraptions" on the rear porch. Others had seen the preacher doing something with weird mechanical devices in a pasture near his home.

Burrell bought a wooded tract, established a sawmill and built a home from the first cutting before harvesting the rest. He then repeated that procedure in other areas.

P. W. Thorsell of Pittsburg, Texas, built the Pittsburg Foundry & Machine Shop at 131 West Fulton on the Cotton Belt railroad several years prior to the turn of the century. It undoubtedly serviced many of the twenty-six cotton gins and numerous cane mills in the county. Most probably Burrell had his sawmill equipment repaired there. The Reverend moved his family to 227 Lafayette Street in Pittsburg.

The minister had long believed that the secret of building a flying machine lay in the first and tenth chapters of Ezekiel. While among the captives at the River Chebar, Ezekiel saw a vision, which included wings and a wheel within a wheel. The Reverend Cannon studied the Scriptures, drew plans and made models for about twenty years before presenting his idea to P. W. Thorsell. Mr. Thorsell was interested.

During the summer of 1901, Burrell Cannon, P. W. Thorsell and others met in Pittsburg's Camp County Court House and decided to form a company. Days later, they assembled in the Carnegie Library and elected officers for the Ezekiel Airship Mfg. Company. They were President J.J. Tapp; Vice-President P.W. Thorsell; Secretary W.C.

Hargrove; Treasurer A.J. Askew. Directors were B. Cannon, R.W. Heath, P.W. Tapp, J.C. Bailey, R. G. Lewis, S. D. Snodgrass and C. A. Dickson. Capital was $20,000 with shares at $25 each as needed. The picture on the certificates reminds one of a large insect. A canvas wing arcs over the framework. Several wings protrude from each side. Two wheels on each side. No engine is shown. Decades later, Mr. Charles Winkle donated an original stock certificate to the Camp County Historical Commission. Work was under way on the upper floor of the Pittsburg Foundry & Machine Shop in August, 1901. In that month, Cannon appealed in a letter in the *Pittsburg Gazette* for the curious to confine their visits to 2 p.m., 25 cents admission, because crowds interfered with his work.

In 1975, the Camp County Historical Commission launched an effort to secure a Historical Marker to commemorate the Airship event. Lacy L. Davis accepted the daunting task to prove to the Texas Historical Committee in Austin that the Ezekiel Airship actually flew. Davis interviewed descendants of Cannon and others associated in some way with the development of the Airship.

Local historians told Davis that Rowe Lockett, a machine shop employee, worked full time on the project; Morris Thorsell, P. W.'s son, confirmed that. Haskel Smith, eventual owner of the shop, and Davis went onto the upper floor. Smith lent Davis three cardboard boxes of soaked papers and about thirty work orders. After drying the work sheets, Davis determined that employees who worked on the Airship entered their hours worked. The sheets were signed by Bill Roark, J. B. Stamps, Gus Stamps, D. E. Allread and F. B. Abbott. The dates ranged from March–October, 1902. After photographing some of the work sheets, Davis returned them to the shop. Weeks later, he asked Smith to give them to Cannon's family, which he graciously did. Davis said that Smith and his employee, Mr. Gober, were both willing to aid the research as much as possible. Smith, however, said business would not allow the expense of maintaining the building in good shape as required by the Texas Historical Committee to qualify for a plaque on the structure.

Mrs. C. F. Gordon, the Reverend Cannon's stepdaughter, said that it was impossible to remove the Airship by the stairway or doors, therefore, a door was cut in the south wall allowing the craft to be lowered. Morris Thorsell doubted the story. One worksheet, however, dated November, 1902, is marked "Door."

Speculation is that the machine was finished in the winter of 1902-1903. A newspaper article states that Cannon returned from Washington on July 4, where he obtained patents. The Airship was said to be almost finished. Shortly after completion, it was put on a flatcar destined for the

St Louis Fair when a storm wrecked it near Texarkana. Cannon said that God didn't intend for it to fly, and left it where it lay.

Mrs. Lenita Tacea, The Reverend Cannon's granddaughter, furnished Davis with newspaper articles published as early as 1901. One article is from the *Dallas News*, November,1923; it reiterates articles from that paper published in "1900 or 1901." The Reverend Mr. Cannon describes his Airship in that paper:

"The Airship is twenty-one feet wide and twenty-six feet long, has four wheels, each with an inner wheel. Power is by gasoline engine and sprocket chain transmission. Each inner wheel has a fan of four blades."

With one revolution forward of the outer wheels, the inner wheels reversed half a turn. The fans could propel air up to 180 miles per hour. The force could be reversed while the propeller continued turning. In flight, the inner wheels could be angled to act as rudders. Cannon planned to manufacture ship propellers employing that principle. Further descriptions have the small wings directed by chains, operated in pairs to lower, raise, or make the machine fly backwards.

The engine was built in the machine shop. Four cylinders made of eight inch pipes were hammered together at one end and drilled for spark plugs. It was estimated at 80 horsepower.

Kilgore resident, E. A. Stracener, quoted his father, who worked on the aircraft, said the Wright brothers came to Pittsburg to see Cannon's machine, and quickly saw that the engine was too heavy. Their first successful flight employed a 12 horsepower engine that weighed 179 pounds.

During the 1920s, a Mr. Stamps of Gilmer visited the machine shop and discussed the Airship with shop owner, Morris Thorsell. Stamps said he worked on the Airship and was the pilot. Two men named Stamps signed worksheets, and Thorsell did not know which one he talked with. According to Mr. Stamps, the craft was taken to P. W. Thorsell's pasture across Fulton Street from the shop. Stamps got in the ship, the engine was started, then the craft lurched forward for a few feet before rising. It rose but a few feet; it vibrated and drifted. Alarmed, he shut off the engine and the craft settled to earth. He explained that the wheels were driven by a chain powered by the engine. There was no money for a quality chain. A vastly inferior chain had been substituted–a dust chain used to remove dust in a sawmill. The engine was too heavy; it had been built in the shop and designed to run on kerosene; that is contrary to other sources which specify a gasoline engine.

In 1939, Rowe Lockett–who helped build the machine–said that Cannon's engineering was correct, but the engine was too heavy.

Mrs. Nina Berry, who furnished Davis with much information,

added that she talked with a long-time friend of her family, a Mr. Aubrey Swaim. Swaim was president of the State Bank in Pittsburg. When he was small, he heard a date had been set for the Airship's maiden flight and went to watch. The Airship rose and drifted over a wooden fence. Several boys sitting there scrambled to get out of the way.

Mrs. Carl Tacea, daughter of Margie Burrellina Prothro–Cannon's eldest daughter–extensively researched the story of her grandfather and his Airship. Her mother told her many times that the Airship actually flew in Pittsburg. It flew about one hundred and sixty feet, and no more than twelve feet off the ground. It hit a fence and tipped over it.

H. Ray Coley's mother grew up in Pittsburg. She was nine years of age when the test flight was made. She said a man was evidently tangled in a rope and lifted off the ground by the Airship.

Media publicity aroused much interest in the Reverend Cannon's invention. In an interview of J. W. Smith of Tyler, he said he saw the Airship in 1902. Mr. Smith was 96 and vigorous at the time of the interview.

Mrs. Victor Locke's mother–Lizzie Warrick–saw the Airship in flight. She and other girls were playing when they heard a noise. They looked up and saw the machine briefly in the air.

Roy Lockett said he was present when Mr. Stamps told Morris Thorsell about piloting the Airship. According to Lockett, employees took the machine out of the shop on a Sunday while Cannon was away preaching. After the flight, they agreed to not tell anyone for fear of getting in trouble. This contradicts Nina Berry's account that Aubrey Swaim attended the flight on a prescribed date.

Cannon was reportedly afraid of German and French spies. Unproven is the claim that the government of Germany offered $100,000 for Cannon's patents.

The Pittsburg Gazette reported on May 17 that Ezekiel Airship Mfg. Company stock soared like Beaumont oil stock, going as high as $1,000 per share. Cannon became a popular speaker.

Even after aviation was established and advanced, Cannon made another attempt to build the Ezekiel Airship. In 1913, he and a Captain Wilder built one in Chicago. Wilder flew it into a telephone pole, ripping out the bottom.

Cannon served a Longview congregation 1914-1922. Shortly before his death, he wrote to a daughter, expressing confidence that he could build a successful aircraft if he lived long enough. He was also working on a cotton picker and boll weevil eradicator. One source has him dying at a relative's home in Longview, August 9, 1922; another says he died at his son Lawrence's home in Marshall on August 9, 1923.

The Reverend Burrell Cannon was described as fat, having three daughters and one son by his third wife.

The Texas Historical Commission erected a Historical Marker in the pasture where the Ezekiel Airship flew. It states:

"Baptist minister and inventor Burrell Cannon (1848-1922) led some Pittsburg investors to establish the Ezekiel Airship Company and build a craft described in the Biblical Book of Ezekiel. The ship had large, fabric-covered wings powered by an engine that turned four sets of paddles. It was built in a nearby machine shop and briefly airborne at this site late in 1902, a year before the Wright brothers first flew. Enroute to the St Louis World's Fair in 1904, the Airship was destroyed by a storm. In 1913 a second model crashed, and the Rev. Cannon gave up the project." (1976)

The state legislature credited Pittsburg's Ezekiel Airship with being the first self-powered aircraft in Texas.

* * *

Author's comments: During the Texas Sesquicentennial, I stepped outside for some forgotten reason and had entered my home to catch about the last five seconds of a "Sesquicentennial Minute." Those seconds exploded in my mind as the speaker mentioned the Ezekiel Airship flying in Pittsburg, Texas, a year before the Wright brothers flew at Kittly Hawk, N. Carolina.

That revelation has burned in my mind ever since. I found the account in *The Road to Kitty Hawk,* Time-Life Books, 1980, at the Nacogdoches, Texas, City Library.

In 1987, My wife and I drove to Pittsburg to learn more and to visit the Pittsburg Foundry & Machine Shop at 131 West Fulton Street. We had never been to that city. Having no idea of Fulton Street, I angled off of Highway 271 and very soon faced the birthplace of the Ezekiel Airship.

Fortunately, the day was bright and clear. I photographed all four sides of the building. We visited Bunny's Gift Shop on Jefferson, the main thoroughfare. Bunny was very helpful. Pittsburg owes its Main Street program largely to her efforts. Jefferson Street had been brightened considerably: Formerly empty stores were rehabilitated and occupied. A painter was restoring the Coca-Cola sign that occupied the full wall of a building. Beautiful! We visited again on Pioneer Days and enjoyed an antique car parade, street entertainment and the "Spirit of Pittsburg" play.

Warrick's restaurant, one block north of the machine shop, hyped the Ezekiel Airship. A stage had been built in the southwest corner of the dining room to receive the replica. An employee led me several doors down to an empty store where the replica was under construction.

Through the opening between worn and chained doors, I saw the frame. Later that year, the completed project was put in place. And it was beautiful with a bright white wing and polished wood.

* * *

My comments on the Ezekiel Airship: Having gown up in a mechanic's household and having assisted Dad more than a little, I question some aspects of the Airship's development.

While engines can be rebuilt and radically modified, manufacturing an engine in a machine shop–especially at that date—is extremely unlikely and certainly impractical. Forming cylinders of piping is beyond imagination. And eight-inch piping? Good grief! That makes for tremendous displacement! It is stated that one end of each pipe (cylinder) was "Hammered together" and holes drilled for spark plugs. Cylinders alone do not an engine make, and hammering cylinders together is caveman technology. There are essentials such as an engine block, crankshaft, valves, timing gear or chain, fly wheel and a distributor–all of which require precision manufacturing. Given that the Airship was obviously heavier and of radical design compared to the Wright brothers' airplane, surely a more powerful engine was required than any manufactured at the time. Automobiles sported two cylinders, perhaps four. If the engine was somehow made in the shop, and fueled by kerosene as pilot Stamps said, the Airship would have indeed vibrated. Ford Model Ts could run on kerosene. I knew a 1946, eight-cylinder Ford that ran– if one could call it that—on kerosene. It laid down a smoke screen that could have camouflaged a naval flotilla. Of course, modern technology brought efficient fuels such as diesel and jet fuel.

My profession was brick mason. Morris Thorsell doubted that the Airship was let down from a door cut into the south wall. I carefully examined the whole wall and couldn't visualize such a thing. I agree with researcher Lacy L. Davis that if the story is true, a bricklayer did a marvelous job of restoring. Our trade has a saying that "a patch is a patch is a patch." Even allowing that decades caused newer mortar to blend with the old, I question that it would have cured that well.

The Reverend Cannon's stepdaughter, Mrs. C. F. Gordon, was absolutely correct in saying that the finished aircraft could not be removed by the stairs or existing doors. Sounds like the old thing about building a boat in a basement. Building a ship in a bottle is one thing, but getting a ship out of a basement poses a problem.

Obviously, given huge machinery (some of which was in place when I visited), there did not appear to be room on the ground level to service regular trade and construct an object as large as the Airship. But building it on the upper floor would have been even more impractical; parts would have been toted upstairs and assembled, then disassembled, carried downstairs, then reassembled! Lowering it through an opening in the south wall would have required much of the same procedure; this fact had to be realized in the beginning. Obvious, also, was that the upper floor was suitable only for offices, parts storage, or possibly living quarters. The lower southeast corner room was apparently an office.

Imagine that employees lowered and flew the Airship on a Sunday while Cannon other company officials were absent, and planned to keep it secret! There are few secrets in large cities and absolutely none in small towns! Keeping the world's first flight secret? Need this be considered further?

At least four people supposedly saw the Airship in flight. Some of Cannon's family say it never flew prior to being blown off the railcar–which might have been its maiden flight as well as its final one. With age, some of us swear seeing things we didn't. Decades can flim-flam us into remembering wrongly. I have exceeded the Biblical allowance of three score and ten years. A boyhood friend seriously told tales of no basis about me at family reunions.

I am a hopeless romantic. I love history. Nothing would thrill me as much as someone building an Ezekiel Airship and flying it. Bill Gates, are you reading this?

Panther Creek Press published my suspense novel (*Iceman*) in October, 2000. The setting is Pittsburg, with the upper floor of the Pittsburg Foundry & Machine Shop being my protagonist's apartment. The novel's cover features my photo of the frontal view of the shop. I made the photo strictly for historical interest. Despite having the uncontested claim of ranking extremely high among the planet's two worst photographers (my wife jealously claims the top notch), I admit to making a perfect shot, which is beyond my comprehension–as is the mystery of the Ezekiel Airship.

–Roy L. Fish

18
Wiley Post, aviation and space pioneer

Like Henry Ford, Wiley Hardeman Post was a genius with scant book learning. Ford was a Cadillac engineer before earning fame for himself. Post took a course in auto mechanics, a discipline which helped in a general way to understand airplanes and set aviation records. Oklahoma has a general claim to both the famed aviator and Gene Autry, but both were natives of Texas.

Wiley was born on his family's quarter-section farm near Grand Saline on November 22. 1898. William Francis and Mae Quinlan Post and their three sons had recently returned in a covered wagon after a brief and unsuccessful stint of farming in Indian Territory. On their way home, they spent the summer at the Hardeman place near Denison. In 1902, they moved near Abilene. The next move, in 1907, took them west of Rush Springs, Oklahoma. Three yeas later, they moved several miles south.

In 1913, Wiley saw his first air show and automobile at the county fair in Lawton, and his fate was sealed. He finagled a ride in the car. He later haunted the Army air field at Fort Sill.

The family bought a farm at Alex in 1918, then, two year later, they bought a farm two miles north of Maysville.

The oil industry paid better than following a mule. One didn't have to wait until the crops were in to pocket cash; therefore, Wiley became an oil-field "roughneck." Besides, he hated school and farming. He was mechanically inclined. The proceeds from a few acres of cotton afforded his tuition at an auto school in Kansas City. Times were rough, though, and he occasionally returned to the oil fields.

The oil patch gave Wiley an eye patch: an injury took his left eye. With time and determination, his right eye became trained and strong, giving better than normal vision. He read signs that his friends with normal vision could not read–one friend being James Doolittle. With a settlement of less than $2,000, he bought an airplane for $200 and spent more than $300 for repairs. Fred Slaughter owned a station and store on a curve on Highway 77 between Purcell and Noble. The community is on the map as Slaughterville. Numerous fatalities on that flat curve prompted people to attribute the name erroneously to those deaths. Fred allowed Wiley to use the field behind his establishment. The field was about 25 miles by air from Maysville, making it a convenient landing strip. Wiley sharpened his skills flying that circuit. Shortly thereafter,

Post and Will Rogers met. Post flew the humorist to an engagement, and they became friends to the end–which was too soon.

Soon after becoming fascinated with airplanes, Post barnstormed, parachuted and eventually took the controls. He made almost 200 jumps in two years. A planned stunt over Maysville was thwarted when William Post hid his son's parachute! Wiley later jumped with a borrowed chute. He had an exceptional aptitude for piloting. His license, issued in 1926, was signed by Orville Wright. He now returned to aerial exhibits and won an exceptional prize in Sweetwater, Texas: seventeen-year-old Mae Laine, the daughter of local ranchers. The Laines had known the Post family at Grand Saline; Mae was born there long after the Posts left. Given Wiley's profession–and perhaps considering the age difference— they frowned on the romance; therefore, she eloped with him in his plane to Oklahoma. His plane developed engine trouble, forcing a landing at Graham, Oklahoma. That was convenient enough, so they found a local minister and were married; that was in 1927, the year of Lindberg's flight to Paris.

Oilmen F. C. Hall and Powell Briscoe needed an airplane to compete in the oil business. Briscoe knew the Posts from years back when he had a store in Marlow. Wiley practically lived in Hall's outer office before getting a hearing. Hall finally hired Wiley to fly him about in Hall's biplane and to chauffeur for about $200 per month. It was later that Post received a license. Hall bought a Lockheed Vega, then, in 1930, bought an improved model 5-C. Both crafts bore the name of Hall's daughter, Winnie Mae.

The Lockheed Vega was a superb plane. Famous aviatrix Amelia Earhart favored it, but the Lockheed in which she and navigator Fred Noonan sank into the Pacific was a twin-engine Lockheed. Hall generously allowed Wiley to use the Winnie Mae as his own. Post had crashed his own craft. He set a record for a flight from Los Angeles to Chicago, winning more than $7,000. Hall sponsored Harold Gatty and Wiley's plan to fly around the world.

Gatty, an Australian, was an expert navigator, having studied ship navigation for years at the Royal Australian Naval College. He eventually established a school in California and taught Anne Morrow Lindbergh to fly. Hall, whose headquarters were in Chickasha, Oklahoma, wanted the flight to begin and end there; however, circumstances mandated that Roosevelt Field in New York be the point of departure. Harold and Wiley flew around the world in June23,1931–July 1, in less than nine days. The flyers were much worn and disheveled, in need of rest. Wiley had conditioned himself to get by with little sleep, and indeed, he had, sleeping only 15 hours during the trip. But fatigue and rough Russian beds with attendant bugs had taken a toll.

They were treated to a Broadway parade, a visit with President Franklin D. Roosevelt in the White House and other celebrations.

However, Post and Gatty made Chickasha their first Oklahoma landing, flying nonstop from Columbus, Ohio. A rousing crowd, including Governor "Alfalfa" Bill Murray, welcomed them. As soon as practical, Wiley and Mae set out for the quiet countryside of Maysville in their 1929 Ford coupe.

Maysville News editor, W. Showen, always eager to promote his town and Post, editorialized that Maysville had joined Berlin, New York, and other cities along the aviators' route as an equally important city. He put Gatty and Post in the category with Magellan, Lindbergh and Columbus.   Two years following the global flight, several recent technical improvements helped Post to circle the world alone, shaving almost a full day from his previous flight. He declined to wear his glass eye, for it got cold during the 1931 flight, causing headaches. Approximately 50,000 watched him land at Floyd Bennett Field only minutes before midnight on July 23, 1933. Hundreds of police tried to restrain the admirers. Wiley was the first to fly twice around the world and the first to do it alone. This last accomplishment placed him in the distinguished company of James Doolittle, Igo Sikorsky and Charles Lindbergh as winners of the Harmon International Trophy.

Guards were placed around the Winnie Mae to protect it from souvenir hunters. Editor Showen again heralded Post's achievement and Maysville as the hero's home town. The record stood until Howard Hughes and crew broke it in 1938. Given the equipment and numerous other factors, Wiley's feat stood above all. Hughes gave Wiley credit for the most important feat in aviation history. In 1934, Post was awarded the Gold Medal of the Federation Aeronautique Internationale; Lindbergh received it in 1927. Post also received the Harmon International Trophy. Wiley gained title to the Winnie Mae and continued to set records.

In 1934, Phillips Petroleum Company owner, Frank Phillips, financed Post's quest for high altitude flight. James Doolittle referred Post to the B. F. Goodrich Company for help to develop a pressure suit that would enable him to fly at extreme altitudes and discover the jet stream. The stream, the pressure suit and a supercharger enabled the Winnie Mae to add 100 mph to its normal speed of 179 mph and to soar more than nine miles above the earth. Sometimes, the Winnie Mae sped at 340 miles per hour ground speed!

Wiley became president of a company in Oklahoma City that manufactured two-seater biplanes utilizing modified 40 horsepower Model A Ford engines. They produced only about a dozen.

Post contracted to deliver air mail for TWA. He made a movie with Ralph Bellamy, Columbia's "Air Hawks."

James Doolittle pioneered instrument flying. Post and Billy Parker earned that rating early in 1935.

Airlines financed Post's endeavor to establish a regular air route between the West Coast and Russia. His mechanical skills and thorough knowledge of aircraft came into play. Airplane broker, Charles Babb, joined an Orion Model 9E fuselage and a Lockheed Explorer Model 7 wing–to build a hybrid monoplane. Though the fuselages of the Orion, the Explorer and Vega were the same length at twenty-seven and one-half feet, the Explorer wing was more than six feet longer. Lockheed did not approve; nevertheless, Post bought it and installed some instruments from the Winnie Mae. He and Mae planned a trip to Alaska, inviting Will Rogers. Rogers was undecided, stayed behind while the couple flew to Seattle. The pontoons to have been delivered there hadn't arrived. Wiley bought too large pontoons that were for a large Fokker plane. Rogers arrived, and Mae decided to forego the trip. Wiley was aware when he bought the airplane that its big engine made the nose heavy, and that the huge pontoons and large fuel capacity made flight even more dangerous. He calculated that shifting Rogers toward the rear would counter-balance sufficiently. Post knew the craft wouldn't pass inspection, so, with Roger's impatience and absolute confidence in Wiley's skills, they lifted off on August 6. At Fairbanks, Pacific-Alaskan Airway's main pilot, Joe Crosson–citing the dangerous plane—urged Wiley to alter it before leaving; but Post decided to take a chance.

They got lost in the notoriously wicked Alaska weather. They put down in shallow water less than twenty miles from Point Barrow. They received directions from a sealing camp operator and lifted off. The engine quit. The craft plunged, crashed, then toppled onto its back. Both famous men died instantly. Wiley was jammed against the engine, Will thrown into the water. The camp operator ran several miles to report the accident to authorities. That tragedy occurred on August 15, exactly five months after the Winnie Mae's incredibly swift stratosphere flight from Burbank, California, to Cleveland, Ohio.

Wiley had experienced several potentially fatal events through the years. He made three forced landings. Gasoline had been stolen from the Winnie Mae's tank. Another time, someone put several gallons of water in the tank. Emory shavings were put in the intake, ruining the engine. Then there was the time he and Mae eloped and were forced down by a failed rotor. Ironically, after soaring into the frontier of space, a short plunge took his life.

Charles Lindbergh prevailed upon Pacific-Alaskan Airways to bring the bodies home. Joe Crosson flew the bodies to Seattle by way of Fairbanks. Bill Winston flew them to Oakland. Rogers' body was taken to Los Angeles. He had served as mayor of Beverly Hills after declining a nomination for governor of Oklahoma. Post's remains went to Oklahoma City municipal airport, where many thousands awaited. Post 's body lay in state in the Oklahoma State Capitol Building, as twenty thousand paid their respects. Post's aviator friends and military flyers flew over and dropped flowers.

Services were held at the First Baptist Church in Oklahoma City and at Maysville's Landmark Baptist Church. Pallbearers included Leslie Fain, who had married Winnie Mae Hall; Ernest Shultz, prominent mechanic who worked on Wiley's aircraft; and Joe Crosson, who had warned Wiley and flew his body to Seattle. Ironically, Wiley's father, who had hidden his parachute to forestall Wiley's jump over Maysville, had helped to build the Landmark Church. Naturally, Editor Showen made much of the event. He gave the front page of the *Maysville News* to Wiley on August 22, 1935. To inform newcomers to the area, The *Maysville News* published a Commemorative Edition on June 13, 2002.

Also ironic is the fact that the Winnie Mae's license expired the date that he did. Mrs. Post sold the Winnie Mae (the second Winnie Mae, in which he accomplished all of his achievements between 1930-1935) to the Smithsonian for $25,000, and bought land at Ralls, Texas. Mr. Garber from the Smithsonian came to Bartlesville, Oklahoma, dismantled the plane and put it into a boxcar. He rode in the car to safeguard it. The Winnie Mae was, within a few months, ready for display. A revolving airway beacon was installed on the New York side of the George Washington Bridge as a memorial to both Post and Rogers.

Wiley won the 1930 National Air Race in Hall's second Winnie Mae, while Art Goebel--who Harold Gatty taught to fly–came in second in the original Winnie Mae. Post's friend, James Doolittle, advanced aviation in numerous ways, and led the first raid on Tokyo on April 18, 1942.

Congress arranged for Post to be buried in Arlington National Cemetery, but his family chose Memorial Park Cemetery on Memorial Road, on the north side of Oklahoma City.

Laura Ingalls came into ownership of the original Winnie Mae and flew it from 1936 to 1941, when she crashed it at Albuquerque, New Mexico. Relatively unknown details of Post's life emerged after his death: He took several baths per day. He collected watches. Fortunately he liked black cars, because during his time, there were few others to choose from. He liked kids, but had none; he enjoyed them crowding about him and his Winnie Mae. It is obvious from the numerous photos that he preferred to fly in business suits–except for wearing the pressure suit. None of those fancy scarfs, riding britches and boots for him, not even a hat with his suits. Nor did he lounge about talking shop with other pilots. Somewhat conservative, a loner was Wiley. He did his flying in aircraft, not in hangars or in bars.

Aviation in general and the United States Space program owe much to pioneer Wiley Hardeman Post.

It is ironic that two women and two planes bore the name "Mae." Perhaps if the pontoon plane carried the lucky name . . .

A sign in Maysville informs travelers of the proud heritage that Wiley left them. The high school auditorium is named Wiley Post Memorial Auditorium; the Wiley Post Music Contest is held there as part of the Wiley Post Festival. The Elliot-Lasater Library is commonly known as the Maysville Public Library, which has plans for a library-Wiley Post Museum on the southwest corner of Highway 19 at Williams Street downtown. In addition, there is "The Wiley Post Lake," and "The Wiley Post Monument" at the Kiwanis Walking Trail. While the Will Rogers World Airport in Oklahoma City bears the name of his companion in death, a smaller field on Oklahoma City's north side is simply Wiley Post Airport.

Wiley's boyhood home remains on the west side of Highway 74 about two and one-quarter miles north of Maysville, exactly nine-tenths of a mile north of the Washita River in which he liked to fish. The home is a simple, rectangular frame structure, which is occupied and appears to be in good repair. A covered front porch reaches the width of the house. Numerous trees shade the property; however, there is no marker. The author grew up in Lindsay, eleven miles west of Maysville, and has driven past the house all of his long life. I salute it every time.

The site of the Landmark Baptist Church, at the intersection of Highway 19 and Highway 74, is now host to a Sinclair station.

Part of the movie "Twister," featuring Helen Hunt, was filmed in Maysville.

19
David Lee "Tex" Hill, Flying Tiger legend of San Antonio

The Japanese invaded China in 1937. Japanese warfare included killing and imprisoning civilians. Although China had millions of potential warriors, they had little equipment, especially airplanes. The behemoth needed help; they got it, strangely enough, from a Louisiana rice farmer. Claire Lee Chennault had been a flight instructor and acrobatic pilot for the Army Air Corps. His face, lined and burnished by farming and flying in open cockpits, gave birth to his nickname, "Old Leatherface." At the time of Japan's invasion, Chennault was a rice farmer at tiny Waterproof, ironically located hard on the Mississippi River. Although his parents were born and lived in Louisiana all their lives, Claire managed to be born in Commerce, Texas. Given his strong personality, perhaps he insisted upon that.

Realizing that the war would eventually spread to the U.S., he joined the Chinese air force as a colonel and strategist. Not only did the farmer instruct Chinese pilots, he downed 40 enemy planes while piloting his Curtiss Hawk 75; not bad for a man of 44 years–double the ideal age for pilots; and that despite a double-whammy received as a young man:

LSU enrolled Chennault as a cadet. The Regular Army officer superintending the program caustically denigrated the freshman before the company, yelling that cadet Chennault didn't have what it takes to become a soldier. Nor did he have basic qualifications to become an aviator, according to the rejection of his application when the U.S. joined the war against Germany in 1917. He became an infantry officer.

Chennault's tally in China equaled P-38 pilot Major Richard Bong, top U.S. ace of all time. The former record was Eddie Rickenbaker's 26 kills during WWI. But by 1940, China's situation was perilous.

In October, Generalissimo Chiang Kai-Shek dispatched Chennault to Washington, D.C. to seek help. The colonel went immediately to the Generalissimo's brother-in-law, Dr. T. V. Soong; Banker Soong's job was wrangling aid from the U.S. Government, the difficulty of which he impressed upon his guest. Washington concentrated upon the war raging in Europe, and favored Britain with supplies and equipment. British authorities in Burma concurred, sure that the Japanese had no designs on Burma. The War Department simply did not take the Japanese seriously.

Pliant ears were difficult to find in the capital. Chennault described the new and very agile Japanese airplane known as the "Zero" to experts in the War Department. The incredible machine, introduced into combat in China three months previously, was far superior to the P-40. Chennault stressed that it could be defeated by properly training pilots to take advantage of the Zero's weaknesses. He was not believed and was dismissed as a nut or worse. Many high ranking Air Corps officers thought him pompous. They refused his plan and took special offense at his confidence plainly spoken. There is controversy as to whether a significant number of Zeros were in China during the era of the American Volunteer Group. Some believe that Nakajima KI-43s were the most prevalent planes encountered. However, Zeros are commonly referred to in most accounts by the people involved.

How long had it been since upstart Billy Mitchell dared to argue with his superiors that planes where superior to ships and could sink them with bombs? Battleships were all-important; bombers and pursuit planes weren't needed, thank you. Hitler favored bombers, but had little use for fighter planes. Numerous Army and Navy officers vigorously opposed Mitchell's proposed revolution in aerial warfare, Secretary of the Navy Josephus Daniels being perhaps the most vocal. Eventually Mitchell was allowed to prove his theory by bombing captured German ships. President Harding told Mitchell that if he sank the vessels, he would build a powerful air force. Dignitaries, including President G. Harding and General John Pershing witnessed Mitchell and company demolish the vessels. The president reneged. The commander of US naval forces in Europe during WWI was convinced of the superiority of planes over ships. Admiral W.S. Sims, head of the Naval War College, also became an advocate. But numerous diehards refused to accept proven facts.

Mitchell and his radical ideas had to be banished; he was sent to Hawaii. Ironically, he returned from exile with a report that scalded his superiors even more. He warned that Japan would likely invade the Philippine Islands and attack Hawaii by air—on a Sunday morning and without declaring war! Hawaii's defenses were poor. Further, Germany was militaristic and could–probably would—attack England. Mitchell's strong condemnation of authorities brought a court-martial, courtesy of anti-aviation President Calvin Coolidge. General Douglas MacArthur, Mitchell's long-time friend, was the only dissenter of three judges. Ironically, Clayton Bissell was on Mitchell's defense team. Bissell would eventually cause Chennault much pain. Mitchell was found guilty on all charges. He refused a moderation of sentence offered by the president and resigned early in 1926.

Fourteen years after Mitchell's ordeal, Colonel Chennault struggled against the same obstinate attitudes in the high echelons of government. Unlike President Harding's Secretary of the Navy, F. D. Roosevelt's Secretary of Navy Frank Knox, Treasury Secretary Henry Morgenthau and several others eventually persuaded the president to approve Chennault's plan. Chennault now had authority to recruit officers and enlisted men from the Army, Navy and Marines–and he got them– several hundred, because the pay was good: Pilots were to receive $600 per month; flight leaders, $675; Squadron leaders, $750. Bonuses of $500 per plane shot down were to be paid to pilots. Eventually, the Generalissimo, in a moment of exuberance at a banquet, declared that the bonus would also be paid for each plane destroyed on the ground. Recruits signed one-year contracts.

Commanding officers vigorously wailed objections, some of which were delivered in person to the White House. But the president's order was ironclad. One hundred P-40s, 100 pilots and about 250 crewmen were pulled together to form the American Volunteer Group (AVG). Marine Major Gregory Boyington's domestic problems had him deeply in debt; the prospect of money was irresistible. Two Navy dive bomber pilots were recruited off the USS Ranger–Ensigns Ed Rector and David Lee "Tex" Hill; as gung-ho as they were, Ed and Tex realized that the war would soon envelope the United States. They weren't about to skip the opportunity to deliver early punches for Uncle Sam.

Ironically, Tex Hill was born to missionary parents in Japanese-occupied Korea in 1915. His first airplane ride, which set him back one dollar, addicted him to aviation. After college he served in the Navy until the AVG offered excitement and getting acquainted with the Far East.

Chennault organized three squadrons: First Squadron was "The Adams and Eves," mostly Army fliers. Second was "The Panda Bears," Navy pilots predominating. A mixed bunch of Navy, Army and three Marines made up the third known as "Hell's Angels." There was neither rank nor uniforms. A great variety of casual wear abounded on AVG posts. Tex wore cowboy boots with his flight suit–you might say a cowboy riding herd on the Japanese.

Joseph Alsop went to Manila and contacted Washington, pleaded for the solenoids necessary for the P-40s' .50-caliber machine guns. Undersecretary of War for air Bob Lovett assured him of delivery. The Pearl Harbor was attacked. Alsop also had a taxi driver catch the last commercial flight from Manila as it taxied down the runway. The plane flew to Hong Kong. The last plane from there left him, because the last seat was taken by a Chinese banker's wife's dog. The Japanese imprisoned Alsop in a concentration camp.

Neil Martin was the first Flying Tiger to lose his life. Over Rangoon, he and three buddies attacked a large formation of bombers. Martin's plane was hit many times by turret fire.

Even after the AVG's spectacular success, Chennault would

eventually be stymied by iconoclastic U S Army General Joseph Stilwell. Stilwell wanted equipment for his soldiers; Chennault wanted more air power. "Vinegar Joe" Stilwell, overall commander of the China/Burma area–including the Chinese Air Force-- considered ground troops the totality of warfare. Never mind that swamps, impenetrable jungle, rain, snakes and the lack of supplies bogged Stilwell's troops, while the AVG flew overhead to devastate the enemy.

The Royal Air Force in Africa had P-40s with shark teeth and eyes painted on them. Several of the AVG saw a picture of them in a magazine and opted for the same. Fortunately, pilot Allen Christman—former artist for the Associated Press—added the fierce shark features to Chennault's planes. Appropriately, the AVG tore into flights of Japanese planes as sharks rip schools of fish, and with the same deadly results. Zeroes and bombers became minnows for the sharks. Chennault's unorthodox tactics, which Washington brass scoffed at, were successful. The P-40, at 6,200 lbs. empty, was 2, 500 lbs heavier than the Zero. While the Zero was highly maneuverable, the Tomahawk dived from above, its weight carrying it too fast for the enemy to evade or catch. The Tomahawk's firepower ripped the thin-skinned Zeros to shreds. Japanese pilots had no protective armor, no self-sealing gas tanks; their craft were engineered to be expendable, rather than repaired–apparently the same applied to the pilots–and the AVG rapidly expended both.

Chinese peasants throughout the country warned of enemy formations. A flight of Tomahawks attacked Zeroes escorting bombers, then broke away. Just ahead, another flight of P-40s pounced. The Zeros had no fuel to battle. They and the bombers were massacred; such was Chennault's "ridiculous" strategy!

Auxiliary gas tanks for the P-40s were made from bamboo and fish glue. The Tomahawk was basically very tough. Some survived with much of their fuselage shot away. Spare parts were scarce. Where possible, crashed planes were salvaged. Rags were stuffed into the openings where tail wheels were missing. Ground crewmen worked tirelessly with considerable ingenuity. There were never as many as 20 P-40s in the air at one time, yet they consistently won over vastly superior numbers of the enemy. Tex Hill wasted no time running up a tally.

The Chinese built airstrips in the hinterlands and stocked gasoline. Chennault shifted the planes about. The Japanese couldn't find them. The AVG were often stationed with the Royal Air Force. The British didn't always notify the Tigers when Japanese planes approached.

A raid devastated the AVG base at Magwe, leaving only seven flyable planes. Japanese radio announced that the AVG was utterly destroyed--dead; but they didn't know that all AVG craft were never in the same location. Chennault put together a flight of ten, with Jack Newkirk and Bob Neale scheduled to lead the retaliatory raid on Chiengmai, Thailand, which the colonel figured to be the place that launched the attack on Magwe. Newkirk had a premonition of death, and told Hill. He declined Hill's suggestion not to go, and told Tex he wanted him to take over the Panda Bears should he die, a wish that Newkirk put in a note to the colonel. It all came to pass.

Harvey Greenlaw was Chennault's chief of staff. He had the rare privilege of having his wife with him. Olga Greenlaw wrote in her book, *The Lady and the Tigers*, that English authorities in the area were absolutely confident that the Japanese would not occupy Burma. To the growing consternation of Chennault and company, the British continued their lackadaisical way of life–the tea and party society of privileged rank. The British were initially contemptible of the AVG for their uncouth ways—rowdy drinking and taking violent exception to being excluded from certain diners. Newspapers called them trash and allowed as to how the British could very well do without them. But the Tigers' success soon convinced the English that American trash was quite acceptable; nevertheless, British colonels gave priority to their "How about a spot o' tea and a bit o' cricket, old chap?" routine. And the Japanese crept closer.

Tex Hill and Frank Lawlor thwarted a clever Japanese tactic and fought off a large flight of aircraft that almost caught a flight of reinforcement planes for the R.A. F. landing short of fuel. The Tigers shot down several attackers during about a quarter hour duel, before the British joined the melee.

Tex notched up his score over Rangoon, Mingaladon, and other places. He and others broke up enemy formations before they reached their intended targets. Christman, the artist who gave the P-40s, their fearful countenance, had to bail out, and was killed in his parachute. Angry Tigers assailed the Japanese with awesome vengeance, exacting a high toll. The Generalissimo decided that low-flying Tigers would boost the morale of his infantry.

Such dangerous strategy added to battle fatigue and other hardships sent Tiger morale plummeting; that, coupled with an order to accompany slow Blenheim bombers to Chiengmai, Thailand, brought revolt. Tex urged them to fly; he said he would lead. Ed Rector, Tom Jones, Pete Wright and Frank Schiel went with Tex. The British bombers failed to show. Tex and fellows strafed a convoy. But more than 20 pilots resigned. Chennault, who resented having to issue the order, appealed to Chiang Kai-Shek, explaining the necessity of keeping the unit functioning as a pursuit organization. Unfortunately for the Japanese, Chiang agreed.

Immediately, fifteen Tigers, Hill and Olson out front, went hunting. They soon encountered twenty-seven bombers and a swarm of escorting Zeros. The Tigers feasted well, killing more than twenty Zeros without losing one Tiger.

In Olga Greenlaw's *The Lady and the Tigers*, she writes that Tex went with her and Harvey by train to Delhi. Tex was to ferry a plane back. He told her about the raid on Hanoi that Tom Jones led. He said they had caught the enemy with their pants down. In addition to other havoc, they damaged and destroyed at least 40 planes. Only Donovan was lost. Tex told Olga that none of the other planes had a single hole. He mentioned the gold chain with cross that Olga let Tom wear for good luck, and asked her for one. She told him he was so mean he didn't need one. She warned him, though, to not get careless. He strongly stressed his confidence that he would survive and ride horses on his father's Texas ranch. Olga asked whether he would stay on if the AVG were inducted into the Army Air Corps, and would he want a commission? Of course, he would stay and fight anywhere his country sent him; and, yes, he would like a commission; It was that simple. He said he wouldn't even take leave home, because he might lose his comfortable and effective gait.

She delighted in reminding him of his bet with R. C. Moss that she had to be cold-blooded to live in that country, nearly always in primitive conditions. He admitted he was wrong. Actually, Olga and the Tigers were close, as the title of her book implies.

Harvey, Olga and Tex finally found space in the Cecil Hotel in Old Delhi. A cot was put in for Tex. Tex and the Greenlaws shopped and enjoyed the hotel pool. She described him as a little over six feet tall, with long blond strands overlaying his thinning top. Blue eyes. He spoke border-town Spanish. A delightful conversationalist. But he was soon ferrying a P-40 to Kunming.

Olga was particularly fond of Greg Boyington. "Pappy" Boyington had acquitted himself well, but by his own admission in *Black Sheep One* had a natural affinity for liquor. He sometimes flew inebriated, veered off the runway at least once. Chennault wrote that Greg had potential, but was a problem. Greg told Olga the others were ganging up on him, and he resigned and received a dishonorable discharge. Of course, his great fame and the Medal of Honor came through his Marine Black Sheep Squadron.

And the American Volunteer Group continued to hit hard; nevertheless, the Japanese swarmed into Rangoon, the main port of supply. The British began to get focused. Tea and cricket became secondary. The AVG had operated from Mingaladon, Toungoo, Magwe, Mandalay, Lashio, Loi-wing and now Kunming. The first week in May, the Japanese entered deserted Loi-wing; all they got was smoke in their eyes and lungs from the more than twenty damaged planes that had been burned on orders from Chennault.

A day after the occupation of Loi-wing, a Flying Tiger saw a large force moving north on the Burma Road; it was the elite Red Dragon Armored Division; two days later, it reached the Salween River. Engineers began constructing a pontoon crossing to replace the destroyed bridge. British and Chinese troops had been squashed. China was open to invasion. General Stilwell sent some of his staff to India to establish a new headquarters, while he chose to walk out with his soldiers. Only the tiny AVG remained to counter the horde. David Lee "Tex" Hill was about to lead the most important campaign of the Burma/ China Theater.

Much has been written about Generalissimo Chiang Kai-Shek's corruption and divided attention–fighting Communists more than he fought Japanese-- but his spouse was an unwavering supporter of the AVG and sometimes persuaded her husband to do Colonel Chennault's bidding. Madam Chiang, a daughter of T. V. Soong's, was a sophisticated graduate of Wellesley College and spoke English fluently. Furthermore, she was a Lt. Colonel in the Chinese Air Force and, in effect, in charge of the AVG. It was to Madam Chiang at Chunking that Chennault's radio request was sent. Madam replied that the Generalissimo agreed that he must hit the Japanese between the Salween River and Lungling City near the east bank. Fleeing soldiers and civilians would surely be sacrificed, but such are hard decisions of war.

The Japanese armor was trapped like a giant snake between a high rock wall and a sheer precipice. The snake's head was at the river, its tail many curves to the rear. The reptile was about to bleed profusely upon that section of the Burma Road.

The P-40 Kittyhawk E, an improved craft, hosted six wing-mounted .50-caliber machine guns and 1,500 lbs. of external ordnance. Eight of those deadly machines headed for the Salween River. Four planes, led by Arvid Olson, provided cover for the others, led by Tex. Hill, Rector, Jones and Lawlor put their demolition bombs on target, causing landslides to largely block retreat. Next, they bombed and strafed the trucks and tanks until all their ordnance was gone. Olson and company then attacked. Chinese troops on both sides of the river rallied to pour fire into the panicked Japanese. Fire and smoke was everywhere. Troops, with nowhere to hide, died either directly from enemy fire or by their own exploding fuel and ammunition.

All eight planes safely returned. Tex's four planes were armed again and returned to attack the terrorized enemy again. Only three pilots were replaced for that run, because Tom Jones's fierce argument persuaded Chennault to let him go again. Again, the results were outstanding. Pilot Chuck Baisdon wrote in his *Flying Tiger to Air Commando* that each P-40E carried six fragmentation bombs weighing about thirty pounds each. They were made by Chinese and were detonated by .38 caliber blanks. Very effective against the armored division at the Salween River.

Every plane at Chennault's disposal, including old Russian bombers, were hurled at the Salween crossing for several days. About a week after the first attempted crossing, the Japanese finally gave up.

But the AVG was hurting, with about half of their planes out of commission. In addition to damage from enemy fire, humidity rusted bearings and other vital parts. There was never enough of anything. It was make do or do without almost from the beginning. Besides a shortage of planes, the number of pilots was too few. Many ground crewmen resigned. Chennault's request that his pilots be given leave was refused by General Stilwell's aviation officer, Clayton Bissell. Chennault strongly stressed his beliefs to *New York Times* reporter, Harrison Forman. One tenet was that his airmen deserved home leave. General Clayton Bissell, General Stilwell's aviation officer, killed that story; therefore, the Tigers didn't know for years that Chennault had fought hard and bitterly for their benefit. Morale was at a new low, but the few who remained improvised with their few aircraft to deal much damage.

The Army desired all of the AVG brought into the regular Army Air Corps. Chennault joined with the rank of brigadier general, but he vigorously argued for the Tigers to remain independent. To break up the unit would thrill the Japanese. Under protest, he talked to the Tigers about joining. Some were offered high rank. But the AVG had little respect for Bissell. All declined, including the ground crewmen.

But Tex, who had ferried a plane from Chungking, brought a plea from the Generalissimo for some to stay and initiate replacements. Tex and buddy, Ed Rector, chose to remain and join Chennault in the Army Air Corps. Hill convinced others of the staff and ground crew to follow suit. Chennault asked Hill to talk others to delay leave for two weeks. Almost twenty pilots and some ground crewmen agreed to stay.

On July 4, 1942, the AVG fought their last fight as an independent unit. Tex was somewhat depressed at the breakup of the group, and parting with friends. In little more than seven months of combat, the AVG had officially destroyed almost 300 planes, but most likely the score was twice that number. It is difficult to estimate the men killed, equipment demolished and goods shredded, burned or sunk. The AVG lost only 21 men, several to accidents. The Warhawk, a formidable weapon once mastered, was nevertheless cantankerous and treacherous.

Those who chose to enlist were now part of General Clayton Bissell's 10th US Air Force (the China Air Task Force). General Chennault, still in charge, still had too few planes and too few pilots; nevertheless, Tex Hill and company downed thirty planes in two days; that must have awakened the Japanese who thought the end of the AVG meant safety.

Hill, now a major, and four companions learned that about 70 enemy craft were in their vicinity. Hill improvised conversation that suggested they were many in number; the Japanese, picked up the message and struck for home. Four Tigers had bluffed seventy Japanese pilots.

Once, Tex, wearing only a loincloth, responded to a night raid. The following day, he fought a head-on duel with a leader; he downed the Oscar. The losing pilot, in honored ritual, dived into what appeared to be a row of P-40s; they were dummies made of bamboo. One wonders whether he realized that his grasp for glory was wasted. The truth lay among shredded and burning bamboo.

Tex received the Silver Star for a solo dive-bombing of planes at Hankow. Planes preparing to take off, never left the ground. During the next several days, Tex lost only two craft while the Japanese lost 21. New pilots quickly learned and the Japanese continued to pay a heavy price in men, planes and material. Tex was awarded another Silver Star when he and seven others drove away two dozen fighters attacking bombers. Chennault wanted the Distinguished Service Cross for Hill, but Generals Stilwell and Bissell objected. Actually, Stilwell and Bissell turned down three such recommendations for Hill–perhaps a record.

As with thousands who served in Asia, Rector and Hill suffered with malaria and dysentery. General Bissell remained obstinate about granting them leave. Perhaps Hill's dive-bombing a gunboat, winning the Silver Star, finally resulted in leave–that and General Chennault's constant battle in their behalf. Tex was terribly ill–much too ill to be flying. The pressure of a lurching and diving airplane on a body weak from malaria and loose bowels is incredible. Telling Olga Greenlaw that he wouldn't accept leave notwithstanding, time, fatigue and debilitating disease convinced him to the contrary; he and Ed Rector went home.

Chennault married then instructed pilots at Eglin Field, Florida. At Chennault's request, Pres. Roosevelt ordered Hill back to China. Hill's wife agreed with him that he should go. He had always wanted to return.

He became commander of a fighter group and deputy to Vincent Casey, Maj. Gen. Chennault's chief of staff. The 14th Air Force was about to rain ruin on the Japanese like they hadn't seen. New aircraft–P-38 Lightnings and North American P-51 Mustangs, far superior to the latest Japanese efforts–were at the 14th's disposal. Tex, wearing cowboy boots and charging with a 1,500 horse power Mustang, led the first attack on

Formosa, surprising a flight of bombers landing. The bombers and the few planes that got aloft were all destroyed--about 40. Bombers dropped deadly ordnance on the docks. In the days to come, many thousands of tons of shipping were sunk. Some twenty ships were sunk or damaged. More than 150 ships were located for submarines. December, 1944, 250 planes were ruined. Thirty-seven locomotives were demolished in one day. Appropriately, Claire's eldest son, Jack, now flew with the 14th.

January, 1945, more than 330 Japanese aircraft were destroyed. Three months later, only three enemy planes were seen flying. Phenomenal success, despite President Roosevelt's promises of plentiful supplies that always came up short.

Major General Chennault's fantastic success with the AVG and the Army's 14th Air Force made his enemies in Washington even more jealous and vindictive. How dare that outspoken rice farmer prove them wrong? They gathered forces and replaced Chennault with Lt. General G. E. Stratemeyer. Chennault accepted the Distinguished Flying Cross and retired. His job was done. The war was practically won.

But his detractors weren't finished with pettiness: Chennault was the only absentee among the prominent leaders in the Pacific Theater attending the Japanese surrender aboard the USS Missouri. Success needs no stamp of approval; Maj. Gen. Claire Lee Chennault accepted that truth with satisfaction, and didn't give a rotten grain of rice what anybody thought.

David Lee "Tex" Hill finished the war with eighteen and one-half planes shot down. It is very likely that he downed twice that number. He took home numerous awards, including three Silver Stars and three Distinguished Flying Crosses.

The National Guard never had a younger brigadier general than 31-year-old Tex Hill. He commanded various fighter groups, including an early jet outfit, and finished active duty in the Air Force reserves in 1958.

Sig Christenson of the *San Antonio Express-News* has written several articles about David Hill. In his account of April 21, 2002, Christenson writes that Tex received the Distinguished Service Cross almost 60 years after Stilwell and Bissell deemed Hill's extraordinary battle with two dozen fighters unworthy of the distinction. Thanks to friend Ollie Crawford, Sen. Phil Gramm and Rep. Lamar Smith, a board awarded the honor and ruled that Stilwell and Bissell improperly withheld it. Unfortunately, the dissenting generals weren't alive to hear it. Tex said he didn't fight for medals, but is proud to receive it.

Sig Christenson's article of Sunday, April 21, 2002, tells us that some former military pilots are returning to active duty. Tex said he would if he could be of use. And he is eighty-six!

Chapter 20
Michael Allen, R.A.F., and the "too old" Yankee pilot

Britain's Royal Air Force was formed during WW I and served well, but it gave new dimensions to dedication and courage during the struggle with Nazi Germany. Beginning with Archie McKellar's kill of a big Dornier bomber over the Firth of Forth, English airmen filled the era with uncommon valor. Perhaps the ghosts of Camelot were lurking over London exhorting the weary fighter pilots who often rallied several times a day. The RAF's boldness and tenacity won the world's respect, including that of Germany's aces and Adolph Hitler. While the Spitfires and Hurricanes hurled the "invincible" enemy air armadas back across the channel, England's industry raced non-stop producing heavy, long range bombers–something the Germans neglected to make. Halifaxes and Manchesters sped from assembly lines to be manned by airmen eager to return the war to the barbarians' homeland.

By late 1943, German territory had been ravaged extensively by the British and American bomber commands. Nearly two and one-half years had passed since the last Nazi plane had flown over London, and a glimmer of victory graced the British Isles. English resolve had held, but the war was far from won and losses were heavy.

Twenty-two operational Training Units were turning out more than 30 bomber crews every month, most of whom would man the Manchester bomber's successor, the Lancaster. Bomber crews flowed rapidly and smoothly into operational squadrons–except for the pilotless, "Hard Luck Crew" that languished at Lindholme while friends went to war.

The six demoralized flight sergeants were chafing from the loss of two pilots in succession. They had met in the 1656 Conversion Unit in November, 1943, where, according to the RAF's unique system, they had mingled with a throng where each man was free to join with whomever he pleased to form a crew. Stan Redshaw, an insurance agent from London, was the navigator. The wireless operator was Joe Williams, a Welshman fresh out of grammar school. Joe Pickering was the flight engineer. "Jock" Stephens, a fisherman from Blackpool, was the mid-upper gunner, and Ted Percival from London manned the rear turret. Another recent grammar school graduate, Michael Allen of Halifax, Yorkshire, was the bomb aimer. Pickering was the youngest at 17. Percival–the quiet, married one–was the eldest at 27.

After joining the RAF at 18, Allen was accepted for pilot training and sent to Cochrane Field at Macon, Georgia, in the detest program. From Macon he went to Lakeland, Florida, then back to Cochrane where he washed out. He went to Canada, trained as a bomb aimer, and returned to England. After leave, he trained in Wellington bombers for ten months, then joined the conversion unit at Lindholme.

Just prior to finishing the Lindholme phase and moving into operations, the pilot lost his nerve during a training flight. A flight line inspection was delayed for an hour while the crew pooled their talents to bring the craft down safely. The pilot said he wanted no part of bombing women and children, and became a conscientious objector. As their friends moved on to operational squadrons, the crew marked time, impatiently waiting for another pilot.

They got another skipper and once again were on the verge of being posted to an operational squadron when they decided their good fortune justified a celebration. Just before midnight, the commanding officer and his adjutant visited a party at the sergeants' mess; they left their caps and coats in their car. Mike and Jock, returning to the base from the local pub, noted the car and its contents, particularly the heavily-braided cap of the commanding officer. The door of the Hillman Minx was open and the key was in the switch–too tempting for the intoxicated duo.

The shortest route between the sergeants' and officers' mess lay directly across the parade ground and down a narrow footpath bordered with a picket fence. With Jock acting as the navigator they performed a series of figure eights on the parade ground before peeling off down the path toward the officers' mess. They put on the officers' clothing, staggered to the door, and bellowed for the officers to fall out for inspection. The imposters were recognized and shooed out with orders to return the car. Undaunted, they drove to the Women's Auxialary Air Force barracks and staged a bedside inspection. Within minutes the drowsy, half-clad women realized the farce, and again the airmen were shooed away–more forcefully this time.

The car had not been missed upon its return. Nearby was a tennis court marker which they pulled over a large area, leaving a trail of loops and zigzags lines that ended at their skipper's quarters. Mike pounded on the door; an unexpected female response sent the two into uncontrolled fits of laughter, heightened by the sight of their nude skipper padding down the hall from the bathroom. Entering the room where the WAAF struggled valiantly to cover herself, Jock locked the door and promptly passed out on the floor. Meanwhile, Mike, clutching his aching stomach with one hand, reached out for support with the other, missed, and tumbled head-first over the second-story railing onto the stairs below.

All were found out. The pilot was convicted and removed from active duty. Allen and Stephens were pending trial. For the second time, again on the eve of operations, the crew was minus a pilot. They considered themselves the "Hard Luck Crew."

The frustrated airmen had closed all the pubs in Doncaster and were staggering the ten miles to Lindholme in a pea-souper when a jeep came from behind and scattered them like chickens. First Lt. Lail K. Dawley of the USAAF, who had just arrived in England, ordered his WAAF driver to let them aboard.

Early the next morning, the commanding officer introduced Dawley to the hung-over crew as their new pilot. They stared incredulously at the short, stocky American. He looked much older than any pilot they had seen–because he was. Sporting a shoulder-holstered .45 automatic pistol and a scowl, he paced silently before them, then stopped and spoke:

"You're the drunks I picked up last night. Looks like my luck is running bad. Well–I'm stuck with you, but I'll tolerate no nonsense!"

They felt their hard luck had been confirmed and aggravated by the advent of a "smart-ass, bloody Yank." Besides, he was too old for combat. En masse requests for transfer were denied. Before alternatives could be considered, Dawley checked out in the Lancaster in record time and they were posted to 12 Squadron, 1 Group Bomber Command at Wickenby.

Lt. Dawley had been rejected by the USAAF, whereupon he went to Canada and became a bomber pilot in the RCAAF. The USAAF accepted his transfer; then, because of his experience in English aircraft, he was loaned to the RAF. He was 28 years of age–far past the average for pilots.

Although Dawley had gotten the charges against Allen and Stephens dropped, they were all skeptical, and when they boarded Halifax bomber DBB 258 on Jan. 26, 1944, for their first flight together, the F/Sgts. were silently contemptuous and were determined to yield no more than they "damned well had to." The flight was recalled after only thirty minutes.

Dawley's skill gained their interest as he alternated with Pilot Officers Berry and Smitheringale during the next ten days. On February 7, Dawley and crew flew Lancaster P2 ED 585, the first Lanc in which they flew together. The machine's easy handling characteristics and Dawley's extraordinary skill enabled him to put the craft through maneuvers meant only for fighter planes. After a several sharp banks, he leveled the plane, then suddenly yanked the nose up, attempting a loop. With throttles "through the gate," the 5,000 horsepower plus Rolls Royces clamored for grip as the sixty-nine foot monster stood on its tail and shuddered. The F/Sgts.'s heretofore grudging respect erupted into cheers, competing with the roar of Merlins. The Lanc fell forward in a controlled dive and popped several rivets along its 103-foot wingspan. Again, the flight was recalled after thirty minutes, but this time it was a jovial, talkative crew that disembarked from the "bloody Yank's" Lanc.

Dawley's rebel trait had marked him as one of them.

Dawley was entitled to American rations of candy and cigarettes, for which he was permitted to fly to either Wratting Common or Shipdham. Before landing, he performed stunts to demonstrate the Lancaster's superiority for the Americans who flew the clumsy Liberators and B-17s. The rations were shared with a grateful crew, cementing their friendship.

At last, the cohesive crew was ready for combat. Each member was to make an orientation flight with an experienced crew. Allen failed to check in and missed one of the first 1,000 bomber raids on Berlin.

For their first mission they were assigned an old, doubtful Lancaster designated O-JB 709. Traditionally, it was named after the letter on the fuselage. At 2355 hours, February 20, 1944, old Oboe thundered down the runway, straining under its load of 15,000 pounds of bombs. It moaned and vibrated, but Lancaster dependability persevered and the "Hard Luck Crew" lifted off for Stuttgart. After climbing to a given altitude over the base, they sat course for the first leg. As they crossed the coastline, they checked equipment again, test fired the guns and passed the "can." Three thousand tons of explosives were dropped within an hour despite heavy anti-aircraft fire and fighter opposition. Oboe and crew returned without mishap after seven hours and twenty minutes flying time. Bomb aimer Allen described their second and third missions in a letter to his parents on February 27, 1944:

"At the moment life seems a very topsy turvy sort of existence, when day and night don't mean a thing, and dates and times are non-existent. For until today life hs been very hectic since about four days ago, and one begins to learn the value of a quiet evening in the billet. But to start at the beginning, about the morning of the 24, that would be Thursday.

"We learnt that operations were on and that meant work. Cleaning guns, fitting them in the aircraft and thoroughly testing all equipment in the aircraft, and by the time we had done all that it was time for dinner. After dinner, briefing and preparing the maps, for the raid was to be on Schweinfurt. Early flying meal and then out to 'O' for 'Oboe' which has been our plane so far. Through (sic) recheck, time for a smoke and a talk to the ground crew.

"Airborne and flying in a southerly direction. Our first bit of trouble was getting mixed up in a German raid on this country–through that and out over the sea. For the next few hours the gunners are tensed-up, straining their eyes for fighters. Higher and higher we get until we reach the ceiling above 20,000 feet if the plane is a good one.

"Getting near the target, I go down into the nose and get everything ready. I can already see the target about sixty miles ahead, and as we get nearer the flak opens up, and searchlights finger the sky, searching–ever searching. Over the target bomb doors open and I have to count ten out loud while letting the bombs go at their appropriate time. On reaching 'Five' someone says, 'Let the . . . things go!' But we've traveled many hundreds of miles just for these few seconds, so you don't "bombs away." Down goes the nose and at full speed we head out into the quieter darkness. In the broad daylight caused by the fires, you see many other aircraft pushing their way into the stream–the unluckier ones far below you, clouds of smoke cover the town, but even through it, you can see the fires, and again one wonders how anything can survive destruction in that few miles of inferno.

"Now we are headed back home, back across those hundreds of miles, back to base, feeling tired, but nevertheless still wide awake. Back over the base, other aircraft circling as we descend; then–undercarriage jammed–the lights showing that it has come down fail to come on. After vain efforts to get it down, we decide to risk it and go in. Lower and lower until that final few seconds when the aircraft stalls and you feel yourself dropping onto the runway, and you think, 'Will it hold?' Bump-bounce-bump, it holds and you breathe easier.

"Debriefing, a swig of rum, breakfast, then at seven o'clock into bed.

"At twelve o'clock, five hours later, the loud-speaker summons down to flight line again. Operations on again, this time everything is rushed, so there is very little time for thoroughness. Target this time is Augsberg. Into the sky this time at dusk, and on climbing above the clouds, we are greeted by a marvelous sunset, all colours of the rainbow, while round about us I can count more than twenty other aircraft and at zero hour they will run on course as though timed by some synchrinised mechanism.

"The rest of the story is very much the same, this time more searchlights and heavier defences. We flew close over Lake Constance, and could see the unblacked out towns on the other side in Switzerland. Through the target area and out the other side untouched. One fellow I saw caught in searchlights over Munich, and getting anti-aircraft pumped too close for comfort, but he managed to get through. Some fires and but for the heavier defences it might have been Stuttgart or Schweinfurt.

"In returning to base, all our electrical equipment went wrong.That meant that we had no lights on our wingtips to warn other aircraft of our presence–among other things. There were several other planes circling the field waiting to land, and as we had no communication with the ground, we could not even warn them of our presence. We had to dodge their lights, finally we flew down over the watchtower and let go a red flare. Apparently this was ignored for as we came around to land, another plane was closing right down upon us unaware of our presence and trying to land. At the last moment, when a crash seemed inevitable, we fired off another flare and he saw us just in time and roared up over our heads as we went in and landed. So ended my third trip. And last night we had free. Today it is snowing hard so there is nothing doing again.

"In our free nights we usually make our own suppers. Jack and Joe lay rabbit snares, and so far have caught two upon which Jock performed the necessary cleaning operations, and after they had ben boiled and fried, tasted very nice indeed. Jock had some fish sent from home–sole, skate, and place, and they also tasted very good. His father is the skipper of a fishing vessel, so he got them fresh from the sea." (End of letter.)

A few days after raiding the ball bearing works in Augsberg and impeding the production of Messerschmitt aircraft and diesel engines for submarines and tanks, they raided Stuttgart for their second time on March ½. Lancaster S-jb 462 made the trip in eight hours and ten minutes–fifty minutes longer than their first mission.

On March 3, Dawley's crew initiated a new plane, Lancaster V-ME 645, on a cross-country training flight. "Victor" soon became their regular ship. They made a mascot doll from pipe cleaners and named it Vickie. Vickie made its maiden mission on March 15, when they raided Stuttgart again. In eight hours flat, they were back at Wickenby. Allen's mother sold Vickie and a letter from the crew at a war auction. The buyer left Vickie with Mrs. Allen and she returned it to the crew.

Although the Lancaster was the best four-engine plane in the world and could lift off easier with up to 18,000 ponds, accidents were not uncommon. On the night of March 28, Victor lined up with a number of Lancs headed for Frankfort. One after another the death-laden machines lifted off without mishap; then the plane in front of Victor veered to port, characteristic of Merlin-powered Lancasters. Struggling for altitude, it clipped the hedgerow, bounced, and crashed, exploding. Racing in its wake, Victor followed the same pattern. The shaken pilot opened the Merlins and yanked the plane clear and over the burning wreckage. They returned safely in six hours and twenty minutes.

So far they had been fortunate. No fighters had directly attacked Victor, and the flak had missed, but tragedy struck on the home front. Jock's father and brothers were killed when their fishing boat hit a mine. The gloom lifted a bit when Dawley's wife in Michigan gave birth to a daughter, Mary Jacqueline, and indirectly an additional name for Victor.

On the port side of the cockpit they happily painted a pink stork holding a diaper-suspended bomb, and over it MARIJAC.

On March 30, Air Chief Marshal Sir Arthur T. "Bomber" Harris announced Operation Grayling, in which nearly 800 bombers were to attack the heavily industrialized city of Nuremberg. At 2145 hours the Marijac-Victor roared away to participate in the ill-fated mission. Adverse weather and radar-equipped night fighters proved disastrous for more than 100 bombers. Redshaw's navigational skill kept them well within the stream and safe from the fate of stragglers. For the first time ever, Redshaw raised from his navigator's niche and looked out. Cloud cover coupled with radar-jamming tin foil dropped by the attackers rendered the anti-aircraft fire largely ineffective, but all about, Lancsters and Halifaxes were breaking up under attack from twin-engine JU 88s and ME 110s. Redshaw never again looked out. Low on fuel, they landed at Facklingworth after eight and one-half hours flying time.

Flights of more than eight hours consumed the bulk of the Lancaster's full-up capacity of 2,154 gallons, and one mission to Danzig Bay almost proved disastrous. On April 9/10, they sowed mines (gardening) in the Bay and bucked strong headwind on the return leg. After logging eight hours and twenty-five minutes, they landed at Wickenby with enough fuel for ten minutes.

Reasons for a planes failure to return from a mission were seldom known. A high percentage were lost through mid-air collisions in the darkness; such might have been the fate of Oboe, their first combat craft, for it simply vanished during the mining mission.

The raid on Kartsruhe, April 24/25, was their 13th. With the loss of another seasoned crew they now became by default the most experienced crew in the squadron, and they had seventeen missions left to complete their tour.

Ground crewmen prided themselves on their uncanny ability to predict survivors, based on discipline and morale. The Marijac-Victor group, always their top pick, justified their faith. The "Hard Luck Crew" had become the "Magnificent Seven." Though fractured by personality clashes on the ground, they were a highly-disciplined team in the air, and their cameras proved their bombing accuracy. But the worst lay ahead.

The Mailly-Le-Camp raid on May 3/4 destroyed more than three-quarters of the Panzer training base, but the RAF suffered one of its heaviest loss ratios of the war. Some of Hitler's finest production fighters–ME 110s and single-engine FW 190s–tore into the invaders with vengeance. The Messerschmitts were equipped with Naxos radar that could pick up H2s transmissions at thirty miles, and a few hosted a formidabletwin 30 MM upward-firing cannon. The Focke-Wulf, built to compete with the Spitfire, was an excellent plane; their four wing-mounted 20 MM cannons (two Mausers and two Oerlikons) could fire 610 pounds per minute. British bombers were rapidly ripped from the moonlit sky as they circled flares in a holding position, awaiting instructions from their master bomber. "Firepump two, this is Firepump one. Take over, I've been hit and am going down,"came a calm, clear English voice relinquishing control to his backup.

As the Marijac-Victor began the target run, F/Sgt. Percival, the cool-headed rear gunner, reported a F-W bearing down on the rear starboard. In spite of the Lanc's maneuverability and Dawley's evasive tactics, the German blew holes through the fuselage and right wing. But percival's four Browning .303 machine guns ad Stephens' two, unraveled the fighter; its engine flamed. Their elation was short-lived, for the stricken craft flew alongside as though its pilot might be considering ramming. Within a few seconds, however, the plane veered away and exploded. The pilot died with his plane. The fighter was one of at least eight downed that night. An incendiary cannon shell had gone through the starboard fuel tank a few inches from the fuselage, but failed to explode.

Interrupted on the run to the target, bomb aimer Allen ignored pleas to drop the "bloody bombs" and proclaimed a "dummy run." The pilot swung out and around for another run. Allen released the 11,500 pounds of bombs (one 4,000 pound "blockbuster" and fifteen 500 pounders) and the Lanc abruptly lifted. Their cameras proved perfect hits on the barracks.

With fuel rapidly flowing from the holed tank, they tensed for the two and one-half hour trip home. They landed n a south coast field as the last of the fuel ran out. The dud incendiary had stopped a few inches from a fuel line in the near engine nacelle. Dawley kept the shell for a souvenir. Of the 346 Mailly bombers, forty-two were lost–four of which were from 12 Squadron. The Marijac-Victor crew was indeed a "Good Luck Crew."

Aircraft were rarely seen over Halifax, Yorkshire, and long-time residents especially remember being visited by a low-flying Lancaster on a sunny afternoon in May, 1944. Soon after the Mailly-Le-Camp raid, the Marijac-Victor crew were on one of their frequent cross-country training flights when Lt. Dawley decided they should visit Allen's hometown and pay their respects to his mother. The giant plane swept down over the Pennines and through Halifax at zero altitude, a hazardous maneuver for the most agile of aircraft. The bomber that had carried terror to the Germans now momentarily frightened the citizens of Halifax. Golfers on the Ogden Reservoir dropped face down as the plane approached the 18th Fairway as though about to land. Circling again, they flew so low over Illingworth that the mid-upper gunner raised his eyes to see the time on the church steeple clock: it was ten to three. The rector, who was hosting a ladies's tea, ran into the garden and shook his fists skyward.

Major Youngman of the Homeguard, wearing a fresh dress uniform, was sitting down for tea in his Ovenden home when the slipstream cleaned his chimney, covering him and his living room with an avalanche of soot.

A startled window cleaner fell from his ladder and through a newly-cleaned window. Allen's mother was in the bath and was clearly seen waving a towel from the second-story window, more in dismay than joy. The aircraft spotter on duty knew the identity of the culprits but, being a friend of Allen's father, did not report the incident.

The next big operation came on May 21/22, when 700 Lancasters dropped 2,000 tons on Duisberg. Thirty bombers were lost. The Marijac-Victor survived and continued short-range raids during which time Redshaw became a commissioned flying officer. They participated in the first strong British daylight raid since 1942, when on June 14,1944, 234 Lancasters escorted by Spitfires of 11 Group bombed naval vessels at Le Havre, France.

Warriors hardly need an excuse to relax and seek diversion, but Mike's approaching twenty-first birthday gave impetus for a celebration. Allen, Stephens and Dawley wedged into Allen's open-topped Fiat with a jug of whiskey and headed for Allen's home in Halifax. They got drunk on the way and Dawley emptied his ever-present .45 through the roof. Upon reaching Mike's home, they staggered inside and, after being introduced, Dawley collapsed onto the floor. In spite of his "raid" on their fair city only
a month before, he was received as a native son.

The 30th and last mission for the Marijac-Victor's crew was on the night of June 17/18. They completed the Aunoye raid and arrived over Wickenby at dawn. Dawley made a victory dive over the tower and brought the plane to rest. They ate and went to bed. Dawley left for the United States while they slept. He had slipped away as quietly as he had come. The "Unruly Six"–least likely to survive, had been welded into a disciplined, fighting team by a Yank in the RAF. from Detroit, Michigan.

First Lt. Lail K. Dawley, Flying Officer Stan Redshaw, and soon-to-be Flying Officer Mike Allen received the DFC. The rest of the crew, excepting Joe Pickering, received the DFW. It was never understood why Pickering didn't get the award. A monetary consideration accompanied the distinction and, according to tradition, the officers donated theirs to the RAF. benevolent fund.

Everyone got leave before being reassigned. All of them went innto the training Command except for Ted Percival, who drew another gunner's tour. He baled out over Holland and was shot by the SS upon landing. Mike Allen said, "The good die young. Ted was the cool-nerved quiet one, the gentleman of the crew. Jock and I were the hell-raisers."

Of the eleven aircraft flown by the "Hard Luck Crew," only Marijac

Victor V-ME 645 survived the war; it was scrapped in August, 1946. 12 Squadron lost 115 bombers during the course of the conflict; that's an astounding loss rate, considering that 14 bombers comprise a squadron.

After the war, Allen immigrated to the US and, after knocking around a bit, married. He was a computer programmer for more than 20 years in Houston. He and wife Mary Frances now live in Nacogodches.

Percival's widow married. Pickering and his family settled on England's East Coast, near Cambridge. Contact with the other crew members–except for Lail Dawley—was lost. He and Michael Allen corresponded and visited. Upon returning to the States, Dawley received his DFC from Lord Halifax at a public investiture. He also received several American awards. Slipping unobtrusively into civilian life, he became an appliance salesman for a large chain of stores in Detroit.

In 1973, former bomb aimer Michael Allen recorded a visit to his homeland and the airfield at Wickenby:

"After thirty years abroad the English landscape was basically unchanged. In the clean, stiff air of a summer afternoon, I carefully mounted the rusty stairs leading to the roof of the derelict control tower at Wickenby. Off to the west the spires of Lincoln Cathedral were clearly visibly solid and unchanged through the centuries. Scattered across the immediate area were fragments of the runway and tin huts to show that once there had been a single cell of a vast war machine.

"Except for the creaking of a battered windsock, I stood alone as a silent sentinel to those few hundred who had formed the nucleus of 12 Sqdn. Group 1 RAF. Bomber Command. I started my tape recorder to recall those events from the spring and summer of 1944 when the 'Hard Luck Crew' of Lancaster V-'Victor' ME 645 arrived to start their tour of operations. I vividly recalled the sight of bomb carriers loaded with incendiaries and that one 4,000 lb. 'cookie' snaking toward the sleeping Lancs at dispersal. As though on cue, the silence was shattered by the roar of bombers. A flight of bat-winged jets swept directly overhead and seemed to dip their wings in salute to a bygone era."

In Mike's home a dam-buster model Lancaster sits on a bookcase near his log book, a "Victor" scrapbook of photos, and a copy of *Lancaster–The Story of a Famous Bomber*. The mascot was eventually lost in a road accident. "We weren't heroes," Mike said. "We were too young to be afraid and grasped the opportunity to sow our 'wild oats' in the glamor of the RAF."

All members of the RAF were heroes to their countrymen. The Nettletons, Swales, and lesser known but no less courageous members of the RAF Bomber Command had wrought a niche alongside fighter pilots Farquhar, McKellar, and brother legions while keeping England free.

21
Adlai T. Mast, Jr., a Yank in the RAF

Adlai T. Mast, Jr. is from an old and prominent family in Nacogdoches, Texas. Mr. Mast has a unique WW II story that is presented in his own words. Hear Mr. Mast:

"I was cadet section marcher in the Santa Ana, CA, pilot school. While marching 50 GI foot soldiers (who were from the Pacific War Zone–hoping to become pilots and get out of the infantry), I dismissed them while passing the PX. This being wrong–I was caught and given 1 demerit for each GI. This meant 'wash out' so I had to do something fast: Remembering a notice that the Royal Air Force wanted men with flying time, I contacted the Wing Commander and told him I was his next ace waiting to join him! Naturally, the CO got wind of this, and called me on the carpet. He was from Texas and knew my family (his wife was from Nacogdoches). He tried to talk me out of my venture–saying my parents would kill him–but I held my ground.

"I learned to fly with the English–learning, too, their language for operations, mechanics–and way of life. My first flying was in Australia. Back in the states "they" thought a hot fighter pilot would make a wonderful 4-engine pilot. The pilot would fly VIPs–from Washington to anywhere in the world. From the excitement of being a free spirit on my own to pushing a C54 to all around the globe. My single engine mistakes had been all mine, and only I would suffer the consequences. No more! 'They' thought pushing four engines would be soothing to my nerves after flying with the RAF?

"One day I was told to pick up a plane and crew at the Kodak factory in Reading, PA. It was a customized B-24 with a single fin and large engines. In order to conserve weight and increase speed, armament had been removed. We had never seen a plane like this–all plexiglass and crammed with cameras. We just saw all this as we headed for the cockpit. It was customized by Kodak for the purpose of taking pictures of the deployment of the atomic bomb from a plane. We received secret order to open when in flight. First 'leg' was to refuel in Billings, Montana. Even repeated warnings from a ground engineer who told us the runway would be a little short, and we would need to take off at full throttle to get up didn't prepare us for the type of aircraft we had. True to the ground engineers' admonitions, take-off was tricky due to weight. My co-pilot asked, 'Where the hell are we going?' because we were pulling up as hard as we could and barely cleared some Reading buildings. Toward Billings about seventy miles out the facilities chart showed two runways. Only one was concrete, and I requested landing on that–saying I would take all responsibility for cross wind landing. The 'Tower' said negatory!

"As soon as I let my nose wheel down the asphalt gave way and off the nose wheel came to a grinding halt. The four props and plexiglass disintegrated. We were told that only two of these planes were made, and the fuss that came out of Washington and Great Falls, Montana, was special, too! The crew was laughing and shouting because they knew they weren't going back to South Pacific. The crew sensed their destination even though orders gave few details. These men were war weary and apprehensive about leaving the states again.

"Orders told me a certain general to call, and he said, 'Mast, I hope you're drunk!' I closed the field, posted guards and was exonerated by the control tower tapes with my requesting the concrete runway. Based on this tape and my military record, the general then commended me, thank goodness, for landing skill against natural and man-made adversity. Whew!

"The one trip that really sticks in my mind, after all the excitement in single engines is a sharp memory. I picked up six of the finest looking young men I'd ever seen in Preswick, Scotland. They were on board as I went to the cockpit. They were dressed all in white, guns were white, and they had white sleds and mean white dogs. They held their dogs so I could pass. I dropped them behind Russian lines and high tailed it out of there. No running lights, restrictions on my exhaust, radio silence, and those boys had no idea of ever coming home. That is what heroes are 'made of.'

"How lucky can you be, after destroying much of Uncle Sam's equipment (in the air and on the ground), I came home without a scratch."

Note: The late Adlai T. Mast, Sr. was a pilot during WWI. Dr. Bobby H. Johnson of the History Deptartment, Stephen F. Austin State University, Nacogdoches, recorded an oral interview with him.

22

Tom Henry, record-holding fighter pilot and San Antonio celebrity

Tom is a product of West Virginia, son of an industrialist. He became a bricklayer, graduated from university and went to war as a fighter pilot. His buddy from his home country went with him. First, of course, was training at the Army Air Corps ultimate base at San Antonio. Inadvertently, they received a lesson in human relations and civil law, the latter courtesy of an unattended milk wagon and its one-horse power plant–considerably less than trainers.

The pair ventured into town and bent their elbows too many times in too many bars. Inebriated, they sauntered about, searching for excitement. The deliveryman left his horse-drawn milkwagon to tote a bottle to a door. That was all the time the airmen needed to take command. They leaped aboard. Tom grabbed the reins and lashed them against the animal's back. And they were off, the wagon racing through the streets and careening around corners as though Santa Anna's army was after them.

It was San Antonio's finest that were after them; the culprits were soon yanked from the milkwagon and slammed into a paddy wagon. But they weren't parked in jail for long. The mayor–perhaps from patriotism, or a sense of the future–thought a banquet honoring the duo more appropriate than jail. After all, the young men were preparing to fight for America and freedom everywhere. Besides, no real harm had been done. The horse–except for being winded and needing extra oats–and the wagon survived in serviceable condition. The mayor, however, could have had no inkling that the pair would almost immediately be the sole survivors of their squadron–in one fell swoop.

No war is without irony. While based on a Pacific island, new Republic P-47s (Thunderbolts) were delivered to the unit. Republic sent a representative along to demonstrate how to pilot the planes. The runway ended on a bluff. The factory man revved the engine and released the brakes. The heavy craft, called a flying tank, roared down the runway, zoomed off the bluff, then promptly plunged into the drink!

At last, the 465 Squadron, 507 Fighter Group, was ready for combat. They landed on an island recently taken, but not secured. There were no quarters, not even tents; therefore the pilots slept beneath their planes. Tom and his buddy went into the jungle to heed nature's call.

While they were gone, they heard firing. Tom and friend hadn't as much as sidearms. They returned to find all the pilots dead. Japanese had come down from the mountains, killed, and quickly fled. It was a massacre. Tom instantly became leader of a non-existent squadron. Friend, of course, became his wing man, and they maintained those positions throughout the war.

Green pilots filled the ranks of the squadron. They were assigned to support marines assaulting Japanese on a mountain. Tom ordered his men to not fire until he did, for marines were on the lower slope. The new and impatient airmen disobeyed orders and killed marines. The squadron had but short respite before marines with blood in their eyes poured into their ranks and "beat the hell out of us, me included," Tom said.

During a fierce sea battle involving American ships, Tom, in the heat of battle, forgot the admonishment to not follow enemy planes too closely in such situations. Tom was in hot pursuit, even as a battleship was firing at the same plane. The ship's guns blew Tom out of the sky. His plane began sinking. In another forgetful moment, he forgot to release his seat harness before inflating his life vest. Air rushed into the vest, wedging him tight against the harness. And the water was rising in the cockpit. To drown after being shot down by one's own countrymen would be an inglorious end! Brute strength and determination set him free. He was taken aboard and fed fried chicken. Being without a plane, he figured–hoped–to get a little rest.

Smoke had scarcely lifted from the battle until he found himself in a new P-38 Lightning. He was standing onshore when he saw a torpedo sink a tanker. Ah! There would be no fuel, and he would finally get a little leisure time! Nope! Fuel was available, putting him back into action.

Tom flew them all, including Thunderbolts, Lightnings, multi-engines, and his favorite, the Mustang. Though Tom was slender, the Mustang's seat was too narrow for comfort. While flying long escort routes, he shifted from one cheek to the other. He described the huge Thunderbolt as having a 500 gallon main tank and two underwing tanks of 150 gallons each. Cruising on a lean mixture, the fuel lasted about eight hours. Upon engaging in combat, the wing tanks were jettisoned. The 500 gallons lasted approximately 45 minutes of combat.

Near the war's end, Tom flew over the prisoner of war camp in Japan that held Gregory "Pappy" Boyington, the Flying Tiger and Marine ace, who was shot down near Rabaul. Another prisoner happened to be a bricklayer from Beaumont, Texas. After the war, Tom was working in Beaumont, when a bricklayer said he was very happy to see American planes fly over his prison. Tom asked if he could identify the lead plane. He described it perfectly by green cowling and number. "That was me,"

Tom said. The fellow was beside himself with excitement, giving his hero a hug. And he insisted that Tom teach him to fly.

Tom stayed in the reserves and learned to fly jets. He was supervising work in Austin, Texas, when the war in Korea began. He was called to active duty. The F-86 Sabre Jet was America's ultimate fighter. The enemy's equivalent was the Mig 15. Some Mustangs were flown, even shooting down several of the superior Migs. Tom became fond of his Sabre Jet, as he had his old Mustang; even after graduating to more sophisticated aircraft, he considered the F-86 the ultimate.

Ellington Field became Tom's base of operations while in the reserves. His home was now Houston. He eventually resigned, but eventually went back in. Back trouble hounded him, though. Upon landing at Ellington, he had to be lifted out. Consequently, he was redlined from flying. He remained in the reserves for a long time. At age 75, the doctor who gave him a physical examination pronounced him to be in better shape than Chuck Yeager. Tom jokingly said he was okay except for a minor case of dandruff!

Combat footage shot by his planes' cameras was shown to Boy Scouts and various other groups. Then it was stolen from his locker at Ellington Field; as if that weren't unfortunate enough, a burglar stole his medals and other awards from his home.

Tom continued the masonry trade to retirement age. He was one of the most popular foremen in Houston. Laborers were afforded dignity. Other tradesmen enjoyed his cooperation and respect.

Tom suddenly lost his wife several years ago. With the approval of his offspring, he had her cremated, rented a plane and scattered her ashes over the Kemah and Seabrook areas, their favorite weekend places.

The former fighter pilot, now 83 years of age, travels considerably by commercial air. He attends reunions of his 465 Squadron. Old Friend and Tom once hosted a reunion in Houston. Tom visited Friend in West Virginia. They went through training and the entire war together, and they still share the air. Friend took him up in his plane, treated him to a tour of moonshine stills in the mountains. I asked whether they compared products from the various kettles, but got no definite reply. Oh, well . . .
.

Daughter Peggy lives nearby and regularly looks in on Dad. Tom recently attended a grandson's graduation and proudly announced that the lad has an appointment to the Air Force Academy. It is hoped that the young man will never be in a position to equal his grandfather's record of the most combat hours for a fighter pilot in the Pacific Theater.

23
Harvey's Barber Shop, San Antonio

Harvey's barber shop at 11817 West Avenue in San Antonio is the counterpart of Milford's in Nacogdoches:

John Tucker, 80, is an independent businessman, but is often in Harvey's. John is a story, himself, having joined the Navy when he was under-aged. Two of Tucker's friends are former Tuskegee Airmen; another, Robert A. Dawson, was killed while training. A graduate of Phyllis Wheatley High School, Dawson was San Antonio's first licensed African American pilot. His memory is honored by the Robert A. Dawson Park and Community Center at 2500 East Commerce. His likeness in flight gear is portrayed on an exterior wall. Tucker was friends with the famous silent movie star, Francis X. Bushman.

Things were tough everywhere during the 1930s; the neighborhood of John's youth was one of the toughest. But a bacon poultice doing double duty? John, his brother and friends often played marbles. Friend Jake stepped on a nail. His mother bandaged the wound with a bacon poultice. One evening, his mother called him to eat. John noticed that the poultice was missing and asked, "Jake, where's your poultice?"

"Mama fried it for supper."

John and other young boys worked the kitchen at the St. Anthony Hotel. Certain affluent people dined there every Saturday night. Steaks with only a few bites taken were destined for the garbage. The waste was an affront to the labor force that saw one of their own eat a bacon poultice.

The Tucker brothers were allowed to attend a show once per week, with strict orders to come home after seeing it through once. Knowing they would get their behinds busted, they stayed until the lights came on!

John was always fascinated with trains. His brother always wanted to be a soldier. John retired from the railroad. Brother Riebe retired from the Army. John lived in California for years. He drove a new Cadillac home to San Antonio in 1961. Eventually, he suffered a stroke. His doctor advised him to stay active, and he is. He is a favorite at Harvey's, has been for 15 years. John has many experiences to relate. He is a font of knowledge and wisdom and an all-around fine gentleman. I have listened, learned, laughed and left happier and wiser; you can, too. He won't mind if you tell him a few stories. And, as at Milfords', you can get a good haircut.

* * *

Carl T. Simons, Jr., was cutting hair and watching television in Harvey's when the airliners crashed into the World Trade Center and the Pentagon on September 11, 2001. The author entered the shop shortly after the attack, Carl said that as soon as the first plane hit, his mind flashed back almost sixty years and he said, "That's Pearl Harbor again." He should know, for he was there.

Carl was born in Army Tripler Hospital in Honolulu, September 1, 1934. On December 7, 1941, they lived in quarters on Jarod Boulevard, which runs from the officers' club to the fence separating Hickam Field from the ship channel. On that fateful date, seven-year-old Carl was in his front yard entertaining himself with a baseball, bat and glove when he saw the Japanese airplanes come in from the north; fascinated, he dashed inside and practically dragged his mother out to see them.

The late Thermon J. Hassell of Nacogdoches was a 24-year-old coxswain on the battleship *California*. T. J. finished breakfast and came on deck to look upon Ford Island. Like young Carl Simons, he saw the first Zeros approach; the first three attacked seaplanes. Bombs blew mud and water hundreds of feet into the balmy air. General orders sounded. Torpedo planes attacked to perfection, he remembers, and the *Oklahoma* was hit. He didn't think it was in immediate danger of sinking. Then torpedoes hit the *California*, knocking out its power. Hassell saw the *Arizona* explode and lift out of the water. Smoke so obscured the harbor that no explicit attack plan was discernible; he described the attack as similar to "freeway traffic," but the smoke afforded a small bit of protection. Only minutes later, however, he was in the water "looking at its (*Oklahoma*'s) keel." He described two sailors in a round rubber raft, paddling furiously. The raft simply spun returning to the hull. About two hours after the attack, Hassell was one of 30 who returned to the scene.

Mrs. Simons immediately realized the danger, dragged Carl inside and hunkered with him and his sister behind the couch. Immediately, the house was strafed, knocking out the large plate glass window in the living room.

Carl's father, a 2nd lieutenant, was just finishing his duty as officer of the day in the provost marshal's office. He and a driver dove into an Army sedan and drove to the Simons' quarters. They picked up the family and raced parallel to the flight line toward the main gate. The main barracks was a three-story concrete structure that billeted single enlisted personnel. Out front was a baseball field. As the sedan passed, Carl watched Army Air Corps troops dash onto the field and fire at the planes with rifles, pistols and probably Thompson submachine guns. Lieutenant Simons tried to keep Carl's head pressed down, a difficult task: the boy was determined to watch the excitement. And watch it he did–saw two soldiers cleaved in half by a Zero's machine gun fire. Then the sedan was out the gate and racing away to a small measure of safety afforded by a large banyan tree.

Lt. Simons and the driver left on foot. Simons returned after an hour or so with a jeep and drove the family to Carl's aunt's home at 1777 St. Louis Drive on St. Louis Heights. The officer left and returned after a couple of days. Fearing invasion, the government commandeered all available ships to evacuate civilians. On Dec. 10, the Simons family sailed on the *USS Lurline* from Aloha Tower. Under submarine escort, they reached Fort Mason at San Francisco. Lt. Simons reported to Fort Lewis, Washington, before shipping for the South Pacific and the war. Carl, his mother and sister settled on their farm at Kerman, California.

(Ironically, five years before the Simons family fled to San Francisco, Polly Adler—one of America's most famous madams—fleeing stress, sailed on the *USS Lurline* from San Francisco to seek peace in Hawaii. In 1936, New York Gov. Herbert Lehman appointed Special Prosecutor Thomas E. Dewey to crack down on organized prostitution. Dewey disavowed interest in Adler because she was an independent operator. Skeptical, Adler closed her house and went to Hollywood; acquaintances there ignored and isolated her; so she went to Hawaii.)

Carl Thomas Simons was born August 7, 1900. He enlisted in the Army at age 14 and served during W. W. 1. With a long career already served, he would be separated from his family for the duration of the war. He served in Australia, Guadalcanal, the Philippine Islands, Bougainville and Saipan. He retired with the permanent rank of captain almost immediately after the war, and died of a stroke in 1956.

The former baseball field in front of the main enlisted men's barracks is now a parking lot for the Pacific Air Force, but what Carl saw there hasn't changed—the scene haunted him for decades. His aunt's former home on St. Louis Heights remains as do the memories.

Particularly disturbing is the fact that—as Carl put it and others of that era know—fewer than 1,000 Japanese marines could have swarmed over Oahu and effectively controlled Hawaii in its entirety. Fortunately, the Japanese intelligence network was faulty. Unfortunately, the United States failed to believe its own intelligence, beginning with General Billy Mitchell's report on Japan and Germany in 1924 and through ignoring radar picking up aircraft approaching Oahu from the north on Sunday, December 7, 1941. Mitchell had even predicted in uncanny detail that Japan would attack from carriers and without declaring war! Decades of arrogance, stupidity, personal vendettas and neglected truth were laid bare on that infamous Sunday in 1941, vindicating Colonel Billy Mitchell, who had died nearly six years previously.

24
Max Lucado, San Antonio minister/author

Football is said to be a religion in Texas. As a youth, West Texas native Max Lucado's ambition was to minister to that religion. Of course, coaching that sport doesn't preclude coaching people in God's word. Famous UT football coach Darrell Royal also taught Sunday school. But people throughout the world are grateful that Max is a full-time minister and writer.

The Lucados—Jack, an oil field mechanic, and Thelma, a nurse— were members of the Church of Christ in Andrews, Texas. Max became a Christian at an early age; however, his teenage years put a pack of beer in one hand and a bucket of wild oats in the other. The result was a failed crop along his path; that path terminated in a pickup truck in a Piggly-Wiggly parking lot. He turned to his buddy and reckoned aloud that surely life offered more than sitting in a pickup in a grocery store parking lot with a case of beer that furnished no buzz. Max made a spiritual u-turn out of that lot, but he knew God held the steering wheel. Max had graduated from Andrews High School, and he was destined to attend a school of a higher calling—Abilene Christian University. A gifted Biblical studies professor made the subject interesting. Winsome Denalyn Preston also proved interesting. Max eventually rededicated his life to the Lord.

For two summers during his university years, Max sold books door-to-door in Georgia. Many who answered his knock were obviously hurting and fearful. Despair bent their shoulders, pain and loneliness etched their faces. The truth that visited him in that grocery parking lot in Andrews returned with a vengeance: Surely life offered more than this! Something had to be done.

Max went to Brazil to help missionaries plant congregations. But to become admitted to the country as a full-fledged missionary, one was required to have a degree in theology and two years experience with a church. He earned a master's degree and obtained a position with a small congregation in Miami, Florida. Having studied journalism and always fond of English and writing, he wrote brief articles for the weekly bulletin. Denalyn came to Miami to teach. Within much less than a year, the former schoolmates married.

Max and Denalyn went to Brazil. At the suggestion of a friend, Max reworked and compiled his bulletin contributions into a book and submitted it to fifteen publishers. Only Tyndale Press was interested.

They published it as *On the Anvil* in 1985. Multnomah Press published *No Wonder They Call Him the Savior* the following year.

Before Jack Lucado died of Lou Gehrig's disease in 1986, he requested that Max return from Brazil to be near his mother. After five years in Brazil, Max and Denalyn and their daughters, Jenna and Andrea, returned. Max became the pulpit minister for the Oak Hills Church of Christ on Fredericksburg Road in San Antonio in 1988. Daughter Sara was born the following year.

While planning a series of sermons titled "The Seven Sayings From the Cross," Max browsed a bookstore for a book to complement the lessons. He left disappointed. No book addressed itself to the common reader. His desire to read such a book prompted him attempt to write one.

Max's books are upbeat, written in conversational style. All are taken from his sermons. He doesn't believe that people attend church in order to feel rotten; that's self-flagellation! He stresses God's love, tenderness and grace. A Christian's countenance shouldn't resemble that of a mule–no long faces, please! The picture in his office is of a laughing Jesus.

My parents, Henry and Margie Fish, and sisters, Edna and Jane, were Christians. I was the prodigal son, but attended worship. My parents invited my buddy to go with us. He declined, saying that going to church made him "feel bad."

Well, ol' buddy, it made me feel bad, too! I envied my friend's freedom to fish or indulge in another worthy endeavor. I reluctantly entered church, parked my bucket of wild oats beneath the pew and sat beside my godly family. And who wouldn't feel bad, given our preacher! For all the world, it seemed that he parked a wagon load of smoking brimstone–enough for everybody, and a double share for me–in front of the pulpit. With the hammer of guilt in one fist and the scythe of damnation in the other, he warned that attending worship on Sunday morning and a movie that afternoon were diametrically opposed–a mix that angered God and led directly to hell. I avoided looking out the windows for fear of seeing smoke. Surely fire and brimstone surrounded the building and perdition poised at the exit to pounce on everyone who spurned the invitation. I sweated the sermon and the invitation–especially the invitation. The "amen" had scarcely rolled off of lips when I grabbed my bucket of oats and fled that sulphuric atmosphere. I could scarcely wait to enjoy wild oats and clean air with my buddy. Something is surely wrong if one must flee worship to breathe freely. Without neglecting the consequences of sin, Max Lucado accents the positive.

If one shudders during one of Max's sermons, it was probably caused by either fever or a quiver of exhilaration–most likely the latter. He has reminded you that God is not angry at you, doesn't want you to panic. We are God's children; why shouldn't He be happy to communicate with us? And shouldn't we be happy that Jesus is never out of touch with God, speaking for us? Knowing that, how can one leave worship feeling having been beaten flat by a sermon? Be quiet and hear the Master. Remain calm and know peace. Practice compassion and grow in love.

We have all heard about individuals who were certain a sermon was aimed directly at them. Max's sermons aim to be inclusive. He assumes there are several types needing what he has to say; they are harried businessmen, poor elderly widows, busy mothers with families and single mothers. He believes every pew hosts at least one fractured heart.

Louie White, former minister of the Broadway Church of Christ in Pearland, Texas, delivered a sermon on guilt. He said guilt is black rocks that the devil puts in our pockets. Louie issued the invitation. There was neither sulphur nor smoke in the air. I responded.

The Oak Hills congregation rapidly grew from less than 600 to more than 1,000 by the mid 1990s. Three services per Sunday were soon necessary. One Sunday in February, 1997, 264 people became members. After moving to the large, new plant on 1-10 West in 1999, the congregation continued to grow at a phenomenal rate, having about 3,000 attending each Sunday. Almost half attendants were not regular church goers. They come with hearts bursting with all the problems that plague the human race. No brimstone and fire rains down to compound their guilt and fear. Many find balm and come back.

Max is one of the best selling authors of Christian books. More than 28,000,000 copies have sold. A young mother bent on suicide bought *Tell Me the Story* to leave to her children. She began reading it and decided to live. She wrote to him, saying that his words made her feel like she was holding onto Jesus. His daughters, Jenna, Andrea and Sara helped to write *The Crippled Lamb*, which became a best seller. He published more books in his first ten years than did Billy Graham in twenty years.

Graham is one of Max's favorite people. You will find no animosity between Max and other ministers. He addressed the first Promise Keepers conventions for clergy in Atlanta in 1996. The former minister of Trinity Baptist Church, Buckner Fanning, and Max occasionally exchanged pulpits–both proving immensely popular.

His awards are many:

ECPA/CBA Christian Book of the Year 1995, 1996, 1998.

Gold Medallion Award (6), Gold Medallion Finalist (6).

Teenage Christian Magazine Writer of the Year, 1983.

One of seven admired Christian authors, *Christianity Today*, 1993.

Outstanding Young Man in America, 1983.

Alumnus of the Year, Abilene Christian University Communications Department, 1987.

Young Alumnus Award, Abilene Christian University, 1991.

Christian Reader Reader's Choice Award, 1991.

Churchman of the Year, San Antonio Community of Churches, 1991.

Campus Life Award, 1994.

By December 25, 2001, he had published 46 books, 33 booklets, 17 children's books, 14 gift books, two fiction, 17 inspirational publications by the fall of 2002, and numerous magazine articles.

Max was selected to be the keynote speaker at the National Prayer Breakfast in Washington, D. C. on February 4, 1999. President Bill Clinton and Vice President Al Gore were present.

After the tragedies of the attacks on the World Trade Towers and the Pentagon, President George W. Bush quietly summoned fourteen ministers to Washington to pray for God's guidance. Max was among them. Upon learning that Max was from Andrews, the President, who grew up in Midland, said, "Ah, the Andrews Mustangs! " Max played center for the Mustangs football team.

There's much to evidence his character: He takes no salary from the church. He founded a non-profit organization to aid single mothers. He credits many with helping him with ideas and editing, not the least of whom is his secretary, Karen Hill. Downplaying his work, he said that God chose him. He declines to speak at writers' conferences because, "I don't have a clue." Success is relative, he believes. Do the best with your God-given talent and God will get you there. Do your utmost and the Master will take up the slack–that's grace. He speaks and writes much about grace.

An example of his unusual insight is the example cited in *He Still Moves Stones*. It eventually occurred to him that Jesus didn't move the stone from his tomb to get out; he was already out! He moved it so that the Marys could see in! A Savior who emerged through the wall to appear to his apostles could do that.

The Oak Hills Church of Christ is low key and uncluttered with ostentatious hierarchy. No one wears a robe or crown. Max often leaves his tie at home. He doesn't rush away through a private passage after a sermon to a waiting limousine and chauffeur. He considers himself a minister first, a writer second–both being his life's passions. Perhaps he is best described by his favorite Bible verse, Hebrews 6:10:

"For God is not unrighteous to forget your work and labour of love, which ye have showed toward his name, in that ye have ministered to the saints, and do minister."

25
Julia Mercedes Castilla: Hispanic Writer of the Year

Julia and the author met during the spring of 1974 at a meeting of the Houston Writers CraftShop in the publisher's antique shop. We were both at the beginning of our careers. Julia worked valiantly to learn English. My handicap was pure ignorance of my native langue.

Texas won independence through people of highly diverse backgrounds. Julia survived revolution in her native Colombia. Although from a privileged background, when she came as a bride to the States with her husband, she had to learn to boil water. Nothing in her upbringing had prepared her for the life of a poor doctoral student in a foreign land. But she learned well, and she continues to contribute to priceless culture. Thanks, Julia, for your persistence and enriching our lives and future generations. Here's her story:

Julia Mercedes Castilla writes for children, young adults and adults. Her books, short stories and articles have been published in Latin America, the United States, Africa and India. She writes in English and in Spanish. She was born in Bogotá, Colombia, South America where she graduated from high school. She did her university studies in English Literature in the United States. She is married to Alberto Gómez-Rivas and has three children. She has lived in Houston with her family for a number of years.

Among her works are: *Aventuras de un Niño de la Calle*, Editorial Norma, 1991. This title has over 23 printings. *Pirinolo the Street Master*, Zimbabwe Publishing House, 1997. *Emilio*, Editorial Norma, 1997, with over 8 printings. *Emilio*, Arte Público Press, 1999. *Pirinolo the Street Master*, Cambridge India, 1999. *Luisa Viaja en Tren*, Panamericana Editorial, 2001. This title appeared in the School Library Journal in 2003. *El Tesoro de la Prodiosera*, Editorial Norma, 2002. *Varios Cuentos Cortos*, Millenium Press, 2004. Her newest book as of this writing is *Nadie Se LLama Perucho Corchuelo,* published by Panamericana Editorial in late 2004.

Most of her books deal with social themes. She is frequently invited to speak at conferences, schools, libraries and other functions. Several articles and reviews have been written about her work, along with interviews in newspapers and magazines. *The Review of Texas Books* chose *Emilio*, English version, as "Editor's Choice". The Department of Education has this title on its list of books. *Pirinolo the Street Master* was chosen as the best book by several schools in Zimbabwe, Africa. She was chosen as Hispanic Writer of 2004.

Sources

1. Belle Starr was no bandit queen:

Aikman, Duncan. *Calamity Jane and the Lady Wildcats*. New York: Henry Holt and Company, 1927.

Breihan, Carl W. *Younger Brothers*. San Antonio, TX: The Naylor Book Company, 1961.

_____, with Charles A. Rosamond. *The Bandit Belle*. Seattle, WA:

Hangman Press as presented by: Superior Publishing Company, 1970.

Elman, Robert. *Badmen of the West*. New York:Ridge Press/Pound Books,,1974.

Harman, S. W. *Hell on the Border*. Fort Smith, AK: Phoenix Publishing Co., 1898, 1920.

McLoughlin, Denis. *Wild and Woolly*. Garden City, NY: Doubleday & Company, Inc., 1975.

Nash, Jay Robert. *Bloodletters And Badmen*. New York: M. Evans and Co., Inc., 1973.

Shirley, Glenn. *Belle Starr And Her Times: The Literature, The Facts, and The Legends*. Norman, OK: University of Oklahoma Press, 1982.

_____. *Henry Starr: Last of the Real Badmen*. New York: David McKay Company, Inc.,   1965.

Starr, Henry. *Thrilling Events, Life of Henry Starr; by Himself*. College Station, TX: Creative Publishing Co., 1982.

Ulyatt, Kenneth. *Outlaws.*Harmondsworth: Kestral/Penguin, 1976.

Wellman, Paul. *A Dynasty of Western Outlaws*. Garden City, NY: Doubleday and Co., 1961.

Younger, Cole. *The Story of Cole Younger by HIMSELF*. St. Paul, MN: Minnesota Historical Society Press, new material © 2000, Minnesota Historical Society. Original edition: Chicago: Henneberry Co., 1903.

2. Henry was a Starr:

McLoughlin, *op. cit.*

Shirley, *op. cit., Henry.*

Starr, *op.cit.*

3. Robert Potter, first secretary of the Texas Navy, and Mrs. Page:

Dahmer, Fred. *Caddo Was . . . A Short History of Caddo Lake*. Austin:

University of Texas Press, 1995, © 1989 by Fred Dahmer.

Fischer, Ernest G. Fischer. *Robert Potter, First Secretary of the*

Texas Navy. Gretna, LA: Pelican Publishing Company, 1976.

Hacker, Margaret Schmidt. *Cynthia Ann Parker, The Life and the Legend.* El Paso, TX,: Texas Western Press, 1990.

Handbook of Texas Online: Texas Navy. Vol. 5, p. 679. Texas State Historical Association, 1996.

James, Marquis. *The Raven.* New York, NY: MacMillan Publishing Co., 1929.

Kirkland, Elithe Hamilton Kirkland. *Love is a Wild Assault.* Fredericksburg, TX: Shearer Publishing,. 1984. First edition: New York: Doubleday and Company, Inc., 1959.

The Redland Herald, A supplement to *The Sunday Sentinel*– Nacogdoches County, Texas, February 15, 1981-December 5, 1982, by Lucille Fain.

Updyke, Rosemary Kissinger. *Quanah Parker Comanche Chief.* Gretna, LA: Pelican Publishing Company, 1999.

4. Adah Isaacs Menken: naked on a horse:

Amarillo Globe-News: Books: "Floozie fables" 03/11/01

Butts, J. Lee. *Texas Bad Girls: Hussies, Harlots, and Horse Thieves.* Republic of Texas Press.

The Handbook of Texas Online: Ochiltree, ThomasPeck. Updated July 23, 2001. Joint project of the General Libraries at The University of Texas at Auston ad the Texas State Historucal Association.

sfmuseum.org/bio/adah.html

James. *op.cit.*

Jewish Heroes and Heroines in America from Colonial Times to 1900, a Judaica Collection Exhibit. "Adah Isaacs Menken: Noted Actress and Poet" by Seymour "Sy" Brody. Florida Atlantic University Libraries.

Liberty Gazette, Liberty, Texas, October 8, 1855. Municipal Library, Liberty Texas.

Louisiana Division of Archives, Records Management, and History blackhistory.eb.com/micro/736/73

Murphy Memorial Library, Livingston, Texas.

The Redland Herald, supplement to *The Sunday Sentinel*, Nacogdoches,Texas, Feb. 15, 1981-Dec. 5, 1982, by Lucille Fain.

Sentilles, Renee M. *Performing Menken: Adah Isaacs Menken and the Birth of Celebrity.* Cambridge, UK: Cambridge University Press, 2003.

Steffan, Truman Guy. *Lord Byron's Cain.* Austin, TX: The University of Texas Press, 1968.

Trammell, Camilla Davis. *Seven Pines Its Occupants and Their Letters, 1825-1872.* Dallas: Southern Methodist University Press, n.d.

Polk County Enterprise, Livingston, Texas.

Linda Nicklas and Pamela Lynn Palmer, Director of Special Collections, and Assistant, respectively, of the Ralph Steen Library, Stephen F. Austin State University, Nacogdoches, Texas.

Darlene Mott, Librarian/Reading Room Supervisor, Sam Houston Regional Library and Research Center, Liberty, Texas.

Wanda Bolinger, Polk County Museum, Livingston, Texas.

historychannel.com/tdih/lit.html

kirjasto.sci.fi/byron.htm.

englishhistory.net/byron/chronol.html.

encyclopedia.com/printablenew/08252.html.

kodak.com/US/en/newsletters/inCamera/July 2001/mazeppa.shtml.

"American West–History--Women of the West–Adah Isaacs Menken," by Narcisse Whitman.

"Women in American History" from the editors of *Britannica Online*.

5. Cullen Montgomery Baker, "Swamp Fox of the Sulphur":

Crouch, Barry A. and Donaly E. Brice. *Cullen Montgomery Baker, Reconstruction Desperado*. Baton Rouge, LA: Louisiana State University Press, 1997.

Dahmer. *op.cit.*

Gibson, Elizabeth. "Cullen Baker, Texas Outlaw" The Old West July 11, 2000.

The Handbook of Texas Online.

James. *op. cit.*

6. Gail Borden Jr.'s Terraqueous Machine:

Dunlop, Richard. *Wheels West, 1590-1900*. New York, NY: Rand McNally & Company, 1977.

Frantz, Joe B. *Gail Borden, Dairyman to a Nation*. Norman, OK: The University of Oklahoma Press, 1951.

The Handbook of Texas Online: Borden, Gail, Jr. Texas State Historical Association, 1997-2001. Last updated July 23, 2001.

James. *op.cit.*

7. Annie:

Historical marker in Grandview, Texas, and local legend.

8. Another Annie "Diamond Bessie"

Chatham, Jimmie F. "William Jefferson Fergusson, Marion County Lawman (1860s-1885)" Dateline: Jefferson, Texas: The Trial of the Century. texaslegacy.homestead.com/AbeRothschild~ns4.

Pilcher, Walter F. *Diamond Bessie. The Handbook of Texas Online*: Texas State Historical Association, 1997-2001. Updated July 23, 2001.

The Texas Travel Magazine. TexasEscapes.com.

"The Diamond Bessie" play staged annually in Jefferson, Texas.

9. Alabama-Coushatta:
Alabama-Coushatta tribe of Texas: www.alabama-coushatta.com/history-main. No date.

Fox, Vivian. *The Winding Trail*. Austin, TX: Eakin Press, 1983.

10. Famous Oaks of Texas:
Texas Historic Trees. TexasEscapes.com. 1998-2003.

Haislet, John A., comp. *Famous Trees of Texas*. College Station, TX: Texas A & M Press, 1971.

11. Cynthia Ann and Quanah Parker:
Drannan, Will (associate of Kit Carson). *Thirty Years on the Plains and in the Mountains.*

Erickson, John R., Bill Ellzey (Photographer). *Through Time and the Valley.* Austin: Shoal Creek Press, 1978,

Hacker. *op. cit.*

James. *op. cit.*

Neeley, Bill. *The Last Comanche Chief: The Life and Times of Quanah Parker.*

Updyke. *op. cit.*

The Genealogy Forum: Native American Resource Center. goodies.freeservers.com/quanah. n.d.

The Handbook of Texas Online
Comanche Lodge-Quanah Parker, *The History of the Great Comanche War Chief Quanah Parker.*

"Quanah Speaks: The American Forefathers." Presented in association with Amazon.com.

"The Patriot" Vol. 10 No. 44, Nov. 9, 2001, published by *The Altus Times.*

Roy L. Fish interview with Curtis Davis, great grandson of Quanah Parker, July 7, 2001.

12. Yellowstone Streaker: John Colter's run for life:
The Lewis and Clark Journals
Encyclopedia Americana, 1963

"This Day in Old West History," (August 20, 1804), (February 11, 1805), (Sept. 20, 1806). historychannel.com/tdih/oldwest.A&E Networks, 2001, 2002.

Sheldon, Addison Erwin. *History and Stories of Nebraska* .

"PBS Online–Lewis and Clark inside the Corps."

"Re John Colter With Lewis and Clark Expedition," posted Feb. 15, 1977, by Michael Coulter.

Bradbury, John. *Travels in the Interior of America,*. London: Sherwood, Neely, and Jones, 1819. Reprinted in Chittenden, H. M. "The American Fur Trade in the Far West."

Thomas, James. *Three Years Among the Indians and Mexicans,*New York, NY: John Wylie & Sons, 1846.

"Burial sites of the Corps of Discovery Members." www.nps/gov/jeff/Lewis/Clark2/CorpsofDiscovery/theOthers/burialsites.htm#John Colter.

"The Life and Times of John Coulter." "The John Colter Legend" on www.edjohnston.com/edsci/colter1.htm.

"This Day In Old West History," history channel.com., A&E Television Networks, 2001.

13. Joe R. Lansdale's Funny House:
Personal interview.

14. Clarence E. Sasser, Medal of Honor Recipient:
"The Houston Post," 1969; Aug. 20,1979 (by Post reporter, Doug Freelander); and March 20, 1986.

Veterans Voice, Vol. 3, No. 2, by the Texas Veterans Land Board of the Texas General Land Office.

Touchstone, Literary Quarterly, Vol. 1, No. 2, 1976. Interview by Roy L. Fish, contributing editor.

15. Nacogdoches history:
The Handbook of Texas Online
The Rio Grande Valley.Org
lsjunction.com/people/long
Texas State Library & Archives Commission
The Sunday Sentinel, Nacogdoches, TX, Oct. 6, 1985; Jan. 11 and 18, 1987.

Old Nacogdoches University Virtual Tour, The Center for East Texas Studies, Stephen F. Austin State University, Nacogdoches, Texas.
James. *op. cit.*
Fischer. *op.cit.*
Kirkland. *op. cit.*

16. Nacogdoches authors and other personages:
Karle Wilson Baker: written by Charlotte Baker Montgomery
Charlotte Baker Montgomery: written by Charlotte Baker Montgomery.

Ardath Mayhar: Written account by Ardath Mayhar, "View From Orbit." *Nacogdoches Daily Sentinel,* June 28, 1981 and July, 5, 1981.

Joe R. Lansdale:
The Nacogdoches Daily Sentinel, Oct. 29, 1987 and Oct. 22, 1995.
San Antonio Express-News, Sept. 17, 1995.
Houston Chronicle, Oct. 8, 1995.
Interview by Roy L. Fish.
L. K. Feaster: interview by Roy L. Fish.

Carol J. Scamman: interview by Roy L. Fish.

Alfred S. Shivers: written account by Alfred S. Shivers.

Garland Roark:

The Nacogdoches Daily Sentinel July 22, 1979, Oct. 3, 1985 and Nov. 8, 1985.

Correspondence between Garland Roark and Roy L. Fish, Oct. 11, 1979, Oct. 16, 1979 and Oct. 28, 1980.

Roark, Garland. *Wake of the Red Witch.* Garden City, NY: Doubleday, 1946.

Interviews with Sharon Roark Zilmer.

Wayne Davis:

The Roundup Magazine (article by Richard C. House) Sept.-Oct., 1993.

Interview with Roy L. Fish.

Dr. Archie P. McDonald: condensed from resume.

Joe E, Ericson: from notes prepared By Carolyn R. Ericson.

Tim James, attorney:

The Britannica Precise–James, Harry (Haag); davidmulliss.com/au/ HarryJames/index, Harry James and his Big Band

Interview by Roy L. Fish.

Bob Murphey: Attorney/Humorist: East Texas Historical Association–Best of East Texas.

The Pine Log (SFASU) Oct. 12, 2000.

Interview by Roy L. Fish.

Gene and James Milford's Barber Shop: personal observation by Roy L. Fish.

Wilford "Crazy Ray" Jones:

The First Lone Star State Fair (1852) lsjunction.com/facts/fair. Inside Cowboys.com, Nov. 29, 1996 and Feb. 11, 1997.

Interview with Ella Mae Sleet Sheffield, by Roy L. Fish.

Interview with Gene Milford, by Roy L. Fish.

17. The Ezekiel Airship:

"The Ezekiel Airship," Camp County Historical Committee, 1976.

"Texas Highways," Article by Randy Mallory. Jan., 1990.

Time-Life Books, 1980.

Conversation with various citizens of Pittsburg, Texas.

18. Wiley Post:

The Daily Oklahoman, Nov. 23, 2001. Article by Mary Ann King.

The Handbook of Texas Online.

acepilots.com/post; firstflight.org/shrine/wiley_post; Smithsonian National Air and Space Museum.

Mohler, Stanley R., Bobby H. Johnson. *Wiley Post, His Winnie Mae, and the World's First Pressure Suit.* Washington, D.C.:Smithsonian Institution Press, 1971.

Post, Wylie. *Around the World in Eight Days* Garden City, NY: garden City Publishers, 1931.

Sterling, Bryan B., Frances N. Sterling.*Forgotten Eagle: Wiley Post, America's Heroic Aviation Pioneer.* New York: Carroll & Graff, 2001.

Interview with Margie Cheek.

Interview with Samantha Robb, librarian of the Elliot-Lasater (Maysville, Oklahoma) Public Library.

The Maysville News Commemorative Edition, June 13, 2002.

19. David Lee "Tex" Hill, Flying Tiger Legend, San Antonio:

Flying Tiger Exhibit, Institute of Texan Cultures, San Antonio, May 8, 2002; Smithsonian National Air and Space Museum and The National Air and Space Society;

San Antonio Express-News articles by Sig Christenson;

Toland, John. *The Flying Tigers.* New York, NY: Dell Publishing Co. Inc., 1963.

The American Volunteer Group "The Original Flying Tigers," by Ed Rector, 2nd Sqdn, Vice Squadron Leader; *Flying Tiger to Air Commando,* by Chuck Baisdon; *Zeros over China, 1941-1942,* by Daniel Ford;

Greenlaw, Olga. *The Lady and the Tigers.* New York, NY: Books, Inc. Distributed by E. P. Dutton & Co., Inc., 1943.

About, Inc., copyright 2002;

Davis, Burke. *The Billy Mitchell Affair,.* New York, NY: Random House, 1967.

Lord, Walter. *Day of Infamy.* New York, NY: Bantam Books, 1957.

20. Michael Allen, R. A. F., and the "too old" Yankee pilot:

Michael Allen's war-time diary.

Interview by Roy L. Fish.

21. Adlai T. Mast, Jr., R. A. F.:

Written account by Adlai T. Mast, Jr.

22. Tom Henry, record-holding fighter pilot (and San Antonio celebrity) Interviews by Roy Fish.

23. John Tucker:

Interview by Roy L. Fish

City of San Antonio Parks & Recreation Department: Dawson Park.

Cary Clack column, *San Antonio Express-News*, July 10, 2002.

Interview with Cary Clack by Roy L. Fish, July 16, 2002.

Carl T. Simons:

Interview of Carl T. Simons by Roy L. Fish (July 22, 2002).

Interview of Thermon J. Hassell, former coxswain on the battleship *California* on December 7, 1941. Hassell was featured on the cover of *Parade Magazine* commemorating the 50th anniversary of the attack on Pearl Harbor.

The Houston Post, December 1, 1991. Thermon Hassell and nine other survivors are featured on the front page in "They Remember Pearl."

Adler, Polly. *A House is not a Home*. New York, NY: Popular Library, 1953, 1959. Published by arrangement with Rinehart Books, Inc.

24. Max Lucado, San Antonio minister/author:

Wichita Eagle, July 4, 1992.

Leadership/92.

Dallas Morning News, June 20, 1992, by Daniel Cattau; April 13, 1996, by Anne Belli Gesalman; March 21, 1998; December 24, 2000, by Berta Delgado.

Servant, January, 1994.

Christian Advocate, January, 1994, by Sherrie Eldridge.

The Christian Communicator, March, 1994, by Sherrie Eldridge.

San Antonio Express-News, April 9, 1995, by J. Michael Parker; September 17, 1996, by J. Michael Parker; March 30, 1997, by Jasmina Wellingnoff.

Deseret News, Salt Lake City, Utah, June 12, 1999, by Jerry Johnston.

Christian Retailing, February 3, 1999; July 7, 1999, by G. Sean Fowlds.

The Blade, Toledo, Ohio, September 26, 1998, by Blade Religion Editor.

The Holland Sentinel, Holland, Michigan, Oct. 24, 1998, by Steve Rabey.

Christianity Today, February 8, 1999.

Publishers Weekly, May 31, 1999.

New Man, May/June, 1999.

USA Today, 1999, by Nancy Hellmich.

The Southeast Outlook, August 17, 2000, by Ninie O'Hara.

Comment by Mike Haynes, teacher of journalism at Amarillo College, July 5, 2001.

Max's sermons.

Index

Owen, Indian agent, 20
Owen, U. S. Senator Robert, 35
Oxford, NC, 40

P:

Pacific, 121, 122
Page, Harriet, 43-69 *passim*, 135
Page, John D., 66
Page, Joe, 44, 49, 50, 51, 55, 56, 57, 61, 62, 64
Page, Solomon, 43-70 *passim*, 139
Page, Virginia, 44, 49, 50, 55, 56
Page Oak, Clarksville, TX, 106
Palmer, Pamela Lynn, 79
Palo Duro Canyon, 117
Pan-American Motion Picture Co., 39
"Panda Bear, The", 181, 183
Panhandle, 117
Panola Co., TX, 66, 91
Panther Creek Press, 172
Paris, France, 78, 82, 174
Paris, TX, 13, 92, 93, 121
Parker, Benjamin, 108, 109, 116
Parker, Billy, 176
Parker, Cynthia, 59, 108-120 *passim*
Parker, Daniel, 108, 109
Parker, Isaac, 108, 110, 111, 116
Parker, Judge Isaac, 20, 22, 29, 32, 33, 34, 37
Parker, James, 111, 112
Parker, James Pratt, 108, 110, 111, 116
Parker, John, 108, 109, 110, 111, 112, 116
Parker, Juanita, 112
Parker, Mary, 116
Parker, Pecos, 112, 114
Parker, Chief Quanah, 59, 108, 112, 114, 116, 118, 119, 120
Parker, Sally, 108, 109-110
Parker, Silas, 108, 109, 116
Parker, Topsannah "Prairie Flower", 112, 114, 115, 116, 119, 120
Parsons, Kansas, 16
Paschal, Ridge, 10
Pearl Harbor, 205
Pearland, TX, 209
Pease, Gov. E. M., 90
Pease River, 113
Pennsylvania, 134
Pennsylvania Avenue, 133
Pentagon, 205
People's National Bank, Harrison, Arkansas, 39
Percival, Ted, 189, 196, 197
Pere La Chaise, 82, 83
Perry Co., Arkansas, 85
Perryman, Moses, 19, 20, 22
Petty Ferry, 87
Petty, Hubbard, 85
Petty, Mary Jane, 85, *also see Baker, Mary Jane*
Philippine Islands, 180, 206
Phillips, Frank, 175
Phillips Petroleum Company, 115
Phyllis Wheatley High School, San Antonio, TX, 204
Piedras, Col. Jose, 45, 133
Pickering, Joe, 189, 197
Piggly-Wiggly, 207
Pilar de Nacogdoches, Nuestra Senor Church, 129
Pilar St., Nacogdoches, TX, 79, 134
Pin Indians (Federal troops, Civil War), 27
Pine, TX, 166
Pittsburg, TX, 166, 168, 170, 172
Pittsburg Foundry & Machine Shop, 166, 167, 170
Plummer, Sheriff Henry, 23
Plummer, James, 110, 111